STUDENT TEXTBOOK - B

THE FIGHT
FOR FREEDOM

True Stories of America's
War for Independence

★ ★ ★

RICK & MARILYN BOYER

First printing: November 2015

Master Books®, P.O. Box 726, Green Forest, AR 72638
Master Books® is a division of the New Leaf Publishing Group, Inc.

ISBN: 978-0-89051-909-7
ISBN: 978-1-61458-457-5 (ebook)
Library of Congress Catalog Number: 2015947570

Cover design by Diana Bogardus.
Interior design by Terry White.

Scripture quotations taken from the King James Version of the Bible.

Please consider requesting that a copy of this volume be purchased by your local library system.

Printed in the United States of America

Please visit our website for other great titles:
www.masterbooks.com

For information regarding author interviews,
please contact the publicity department at (870) 438-5288.

Blessed is the nation whose God is the Lord (Psalm 33:19).

Master Books®
A Division of New Leaf Publishing Group
www.masterbooks.com

Contents

HOW TO USE THIS BOOK:

There are 34 chapters in all, one for each week of the school year. Each chapter is divided into three sections, and there are at least two ways you can use this text, depending on what best fits your schedule. You may chose to adapt the material in whatever way best suits your specific needs.

SUGGESTED PLAN: FIVE DAYS PER WEEK

Student will read selections (outlined in detail in the available Teacher Guide) on Monday, Tuesday, and Wednesday. Projects suggested in the Teacher Guide will be done on Thursday. On Friday, students may listen to the free audio selection supplied on UncleRickAudios.com, which serves as a fun way to review what they've learned, and then complete the test questions provided in the Teacher Guide.

ALTERNATIVE PLAN: FOUR DAYS PER WEEK

Students will read selections on any three days of the week you choose. They will then answer 1/3 of the questions supplied in the Teacher Guide each day when they finish reading. On the fourth day, they may listen to the free audio selection provided, and do the projects from the Teacher Guide.

HOW TO ACCESS THE AUDIO SELECTIONS:

Each chapter has an audio selection. You can access the download at http://UncleRickAudios.com/fightforfreedom and save to your computer, put on a mobile device, or make into a CD, whichever you prefer. Use code FREEDOM for free access to the audio files. Publisher's Note: Since the audio selections do concern a time of war, we recommend that all audios be previewed by an adult to determine the age-appropriateness of the material.

The Grand Union flag (left) is considered the first American flag, prior to the Stars and Stripes (right).

WHO IS UNCLE RICK?

Hi! I'm Uncle Rick, the family storyteller. I love to tell boys and girls exciting true stories about America's history. I also like to record wonderful old books about America. God's hand is so plain in the history of our country!

In this book, you'll often see me dressed in my founding era outfit. That's because, whatever period of American history I'm teaching about, I always want to call our attention back to the godly principles of America's founding.

I hope you love America as much as I do. God has blessed our nation with freedom, prosperity, and peace. He has made America the leading nation of the world. Millions of people have come here from other countries seeking a better life. Millions more hope to come someday.

The people who built America gave us a nation founded on the principles of Scripture. It is that wonderful heritage that gave us liberty in the beginning and has kept us free for over two hundred years. I hope you will enjoy learning about our country's history with me. The freedom and justice that we enjoy today are God's gift to us. Let us treasure and protect that gift so we can pass it on to future generations.

(You can listen to my audiobooks at UncleRickAudios.com.)

George Washington as a farmer

CHAPTER I

GEORGE WASHINGTON

Growing in Greatness

A PROMISING START

When we think of the beginning of America, we often think of George Washington. After all, he led the American army to win our independence from England. Then he led the Constitutional Convention — the meeting that formed the government of the new United States of America. And when the new country elected its first president, people chose George Washington to lead them once again.

George was born on a big farm in Virginia on February 22, 1732. His father was a wealthy man who owned several farms. He also owned part of a business that made and sold iron. George's father died when the boy was only 11, so young George was raised by his mother and his older brother, Lawrence.

George only went to school for a few years, but he had a very good education. He learned about the business of farming by helping his mother run the family farms. He was an excellent horseman. He loved to gallop around the fields and chase foxes through the woods. He also loved his dogs, who hunted the foxes with him.[1] George grew up strong and healthy.

At school, George was already becoming a leader. He could run, jump, and wrestle better than the other boys. He could throw farther than any of them.[2] The story is told that he once threw a stone across the Rappahannock River. Another time, it is said, he threw a rock from the ground below to the top of Natural

The initials G. W. carved in the stone at the bottom of Natural Bridge. Some people say that George Washington carved them there. It is believed that as a young man, Washington surveyed the area including Natural Bridge. Before the Revolution Thomas Jefferson bought the huge bridge from King George for just 20 shillings—only a few dollars today.

Bridge, a distance of 200 feet.[3] That's a long way to throw a rock straight up! All the boys expected to be soldiers one day. When they played soldiers in the schoolyard, George was always chosen to be a leader.

The Young Surveyor

George loved the outdoors. With only a dog and his gun, he would often take long trips into the wild Virginia woods. He learned how to shoot and trap animals for food, cross rivers, cook over an open fire, and make his bed upon the ground. This experience was good training for the soldier's life that George would one day live.

George admired his mother very much. She taught him to be strong, responsible, and hardworking. She loved her son, and he loved and respected her. All through his life, George told other people what a wonderful mother he had been raised by. When he was 14 years old and wanted to become a sailor, his mother did not like the idea. She thought he was too young to leave his family. George obeyed his mother and stayed home to help on the farm.

He went back to school for a while and learned how to measure large pieces of land. This is called surveying. Because North America was still being explored, there was a great need for surveyors. George became an expert at marking off boundaries and laying out roads.

Nothing can be more hurtful to the service than the neglect of discipline; for that discipline, more than numbers, gives one army the superiority over another.[4]

George Washington

George Washington Birthplace National Monument, Westmoreland County, Virginia., photo by James G. Howes, 2007.

George had a friend named Lord Fairfax. Lord Fairfax was an old man, but he liked George very much. He liked George's adult-like qualities, though George was only 16 years of age. Lord Fairfax asked George to go with a team of surveyors to measure some of his land in the western part of Virginia. So, one spring day George and his companions started over the mountains with their tools.

It was a rough and dangerous trip. There were no roads or bridges to make travel easier. There were no houses to

Mary Ball Washington

George Washington and Christopher Gist cross the Allegheny on a raft (a painting by Daniel Huntington)

sleep in at night. Deep rivers, wild animals, and enemies were all around. Some nights they slept beside the dying campfire. When the weather was bad, they slept in tents or built huts. One night they saw some Indians doing a war dance! George and his friends quietly slipped away.

In about a month, George returned with maps and figures showing the lands of Lord Fairfax. Few men could have done a better job. Lord Fairfax gave him the job of head surveyor of Culpepper County. He was only 17 years old!

George and Lord Fairfax became great friends. George spent three years in the wilderness marking out land boundaries. He often visited Lord Fairfax, reading the many books in the Fairfax home library and having long conversations with the older man. He found that he learned much by spending time at the Fairfax plantation.[6]

When he was 20, George lost his older brother, Lawrence, to a sickness called tuberculosis.

—— " ——

My mother was the most beautiful woman I ever saw. All that I am I owe to my mother. I attribute all my success in life to the moral, intellectual, and physical education I received from her.[5]

George Washington

—— " ——

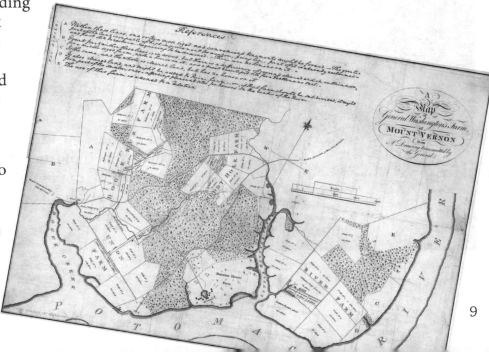

A map of General Washington's farm of Mount Vernon from a drawing transmitted by the general. Surveyed and drawn by George Washington, and printed in 1801.

The earliest authenticated portrait of George Washington shows him wearing his colonel's uniform of the Virginia Regiment.

Lawrence had inherited the beautiful plantation Mount Vernon when his father died. Now he left Mount Vernon to George, and the young man found himself running two large plantations with many hired workers and slaves. It was a big job, but young Washington was up to the task. Then, his whole life changed. War broke out between England and France.

THE FRENCH AND INDIAN WAR

You remember that at this time Virginia was one of 13 English colonies in America. There was no United States yet. So George Washington was an Englishman. That meant he would fight for the English in the war with France.

France had colonies in America, too. Most of them were in what is now Canada, but some were further south. Some of these were in lands claimed by England, also. Governor Dinwiddie of Virginia sent messengers to the French army in this area to leave and go back to Canada. But none of the messengers were successful in getting to where the French soldiers were.

Governor Dinwiddie needed a strong man to lead another group of messengers. The man needed to be someone who knew the wilderness and was strong enough to make the long, hard journey. He had to be a man who was not afraid of French officers. He chose George Washington, though he was only 21 years old. Perhaps Lord Fairfax told the governor what a good man Washington was.

The little group fought its way through woods, across rivers, and over rough mountains. When they finally came to the French fort, the French commander received them politely. But when Washington delivered the message from Governor Dinwiddie, the French commander did not like the answer he got.[7]

"Mr. Washington, I am afraid I cannot oblige you," said the man in his bright uniform. "We need forts in this Ohio River country so that we can more easily reach our trading posts on the Mississippi. I have orders to hold this region, and I must obey them."[8]

Virginia colonial governor Robert Dinwiddie, by unknown artist.

Reconstructed Fort Necessity, southern Pennsylvania (CC0 1.0).

The French officer treated the men kindly and asked them to stay with him for many days. But once Washington saw that he could not change the commander's mind, he hurried back toward eastern Virginia with his answer for the governor.

Washington's party traveled through rain and snow, fighting through dense forests where enemies waited to attack. Once an Indian shot at Washington, but he missed. The horses got too tired to travel. Rather than waiting for them to rest up, Washington and his woodsman friend, Christopher Gist, plunged into the forest alone and on foot. No time could be lost! At last, they reached Williamsburg.[9]

Now it seemed that war was certain. The governor had another job for his young messenger.

"Mr. Washington, I need you to take 150 men and cut a road out to Fort Duquesne. We must send an army out there and defeat the French."[10]

But the French were also ready to fight the English. Just after Washington crossed the mountains, he ran into a group of French scouts. In the fight that followed,

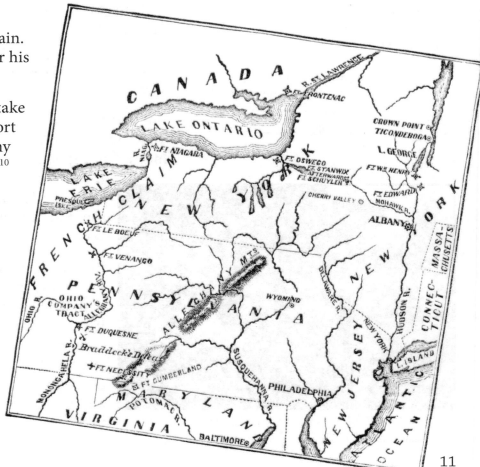

Map of the "scene of operations" of the French and Indian War. *Harper's Encyclopedia of United States History*, Harper & Brothers, 1905 (PD-US).

Hand-drawn map by George Washington, accompanying a printing of the journal he kept of his 1753 expedition into the Ohio Country, 1753 (PD-US).

Nothing is a greater stranger to my breast, or a sin that my soul more abhors, than that black and detestable one, ingratitude.[15]

George Washington,
in a letter to Governor Dinwiddie,
May 29, 1754

the French commander was killed, and his men were all captured. It was Washington's first real battle.

More men came to help Washington. He knew the French would send more soldiers to the region, also. So he built Fort Necessity so he could fight better. But the French force that arrived had four times as many men as Washington! His men fought bravely in the knee-deep mud and water, firing at the enemies hidden in the woods around them. Finally, they ran out of bullets and had to give up their fort and leave.

THE FALL OF A PROUD GENERAL

The English king sent a general named Braddock to fight the French. General Braddock was a brave man, but he did not know how to fight in the woods. He was used to fighting on open battlefields with one army lined up neatly facing the other. He thought his men were too brave to hide behind rocks and trees as the Americans and Indians did.

General Braddock liked young Washington and gave him a job as a staff officer. That meant that George worked close to the general and carried messages for him. Washington tried to explain that the French would fight like their Indian friends, shooting from hiding places where they were hard to see. Benjamin Franklin said the same thing.[11]

But General Braddock had confidence in his soldiers. These Indians "may be dangerous to your raw Virginia militia," he replied to Franklin. "But it is impossible that they should make any impression on the King's troops."[12] He said the same thing to Washington. But he would soon learn how wrong he was.

Braddock and his army set out to take Fort Duquesne from the French. It was a large army with 2,000 men, many wagons, and cannons. It could not move very fast along the wilderness road, so it stretched out for many miles. Washington nervously looked at the woods around them. He was afraid that the French and Indians would attack their line and cut it to pieces.

George Washington on horse, soldiers fighting during the battle of the Monongahela, 1854 (PD-US).

12

Finally, it happened. The leading soldiers of Braddock's force saw an Indian ahead on the path. The man disappeared into the woods, and Braddock's men ran back to the main force to tell the general that there were enemies ahead. But it was too late. The French and Indian fighters ran through the woods and lined up on both sides of the British column. Hundreds of rifles boomed from the bushes, but the British soldiers could not see their enemies to fire back.

Washington's men knew how to fight in the woods. At the first shots, they broke from their lines or columns and scattered, hiding behind bushes and waiting to see a puff of smoke from an enemy rifle so they had a target to shoot at. But the English troops formed up in a neat line on the road, just as they had been trained to do in Europe. They were cut down like cornstalks.

Washington begged Braddock to order his men to take cover. But the general thought he knew more about fighting that a young colonel in the Virginia militia. He kept his men in formation until more than half of them were killed or wounded. Then Braddock himself was shot down, and the army fell apart.[13]

An engraving of General Edward Braddock.

Though Washington had no real authority over the British soldiers, he managed to organize a retreat. The panicked British soldiers were willing to listen to anyone who could lead them out of this awful battle. Washington got the army turned around and moving. Then, with his 100 militiamen, he kept the French and Indians back so the army could escape. They left behind so many supplies that the Indians were willing to let them go while they searched through the abandoned wagons for things to steal. From that day on, George Washington was known as the hero who saved Braddock's army from being wiped out.[14]

Pride goeth before destruction, and an haughty spirit before a fall.

Proverbs 16:18

THE MAN BULLETS COULDN'T KILL

Most historians believe that without George Washington, there would have been no United States of America.

After all, he was commander of the American army in the Revolutionary War. He was our first president. Perhaps even more important, he was president of the Constitutional Convention. So Washington led us to victory in the War for Independence, led us in creating the government of the new nation, and led us as president in our first few years as a nation.

And we almost didn't have him.

Well, humanly speaking, anyway. You see, when George was 23 years old and we were still English subjects, he was a colonel in the militia that helped the British Army during the French and Indian War. And he was part of the fighting in a major battle of that war, one in which every other officer was shot off his horse. But not George.

Washington went with British General Braddock on a march to take Fort Duquesne (near present-day Pittsburgh, Pennsylvania) from the French. The British and colonial forces far outnumbered the French and their Indian allies. It should have been easy. But when the two armies ran into each other a few miles from the fort, Braddock's men in their bright red coats formed up in neat lines to fight as they had on open European battlefields. The French and Indians dove for cover in the bushes. The British were shot down, standing in even ranks like sitting ducks.

Officer after officer was killed or wounded. Soon only Braddock remained to shout orders and only

The Tragedy of Braddocks Defeat.

Washington to carry them to the various units scattered through the woods. Then a bullet caught Braddock in the chest, and he hit the ground.

Washington, with the help of his Virginia woodsmen, knew how to fight in the woods. He organized his men for a rear guard action and covered the retreat of the redcoats, which was by now a frantic race to the rear. It was his first major action with a large force.

As he put distance between his shattered force and the enemy, Washington finally found a moment to examine himself for wounds. He had been shot at. He found four bullet holes in his coat and bullet fragments in his hair, but he was unhurt — the only officer alive and still mounted. A few days later, he wrote to his family:

> By the all-powerful dispensations of Providence, I have been protected beyond all human probability or expectation; for I had four bullets through my coat, and two horses shot under me yet escaped unhurt, although death was leveling my companions on every side of me.[16]

However, the story doesn't end there. Years afterward, in 1770, George Washington and his friend Dr. James Craik returned to the neighborhood of the battle. Washington got word that an old Indian chief wished to see him. The two sat down beside a council fire, and the chief informed Washington that he had been one of the warriors helping the French in that battle 15 years before.

The chief said he had instructed his braves to single out the men on horseback, knowing that they were the leaders of the British. As fewer and fewer remained mounted, he personally turned his attention to Washington. He told Washington that he had fired his own rifle at him 17 times but could not hit him.

He decided that Washington was under special care of the Great Spirit. He stopped shooting at him and ordered his braves to cease trying as well. Then he said:

> I have traveled a long and weary path that I might see the young warrior of the great battle … I am come to pay homage to the man who is the particular favorite of Heaven, and who can never die in battle.[17]

This true story is just one of many times when God acted mightily to preserve Washington and make him successful in battle. You'll hear this much and more in the audio book, *Uncle Rick Reads The True Story of George Washington* by the famous historian, Elbridge Brooks.

Wedding of George Washin
and Martha Dandridge Cu
on January 6, 1759,
at her estate in Virginia

GEORGE WASHINGTON

God's Man for America

GOOD NEWS AND BAD NEWS

One day, George was given some war letters to take to the government at Williamsburg. Riding along the road, he decided to stop at a friend's house for dinner. At that home, he met a young lady about his age. She was Martha Custis, a young widow. After dinner, Washington found Mrs. Custis so charming that he chatted on and on with her, even after his horse had been taken from the stable and saddled for him to go. When Washington returned from Williamsburg, he stopped at the Custis plantation to see Martha. When he left the plantation, Washington carried with him Martha's promise to marry him.

More battles followed, but the French and Indian War finally ended, and young Washington rode home to claim his bride. They lived at Mount Vernon, and they were very happy together.

Washington was elected to Virginia's colonial government, the House of Burgesses. He took his bride to Williamsburg, where the couple was admired by the country planters and legislators who came to town for the governor's reception. George was the hero of the war, and pretty Martha was the belle of the ball. When the legislature, or government meeting, opened for business, Washington was immediately embarrassed, as the speaker praised him in front of all the people.

WAS WASHINGTON A GODLY MAN? Before the Revolutionary War started, King George ordered Boston Harbor to be blockaded, meaning no ships were to go in or out on business. This was punishment for the Boston Tea Party. The king wanted to make it hard for Boston to get food and other things the people needed. The blockade was to begin on June 1, 1774. Washington wrote in his diary that day, "Went to church and fasted all day."[1] Washington didn't even live in Boston! But still he spent a day in fasting to pray for the people of the city.

The Destruction of Tea at Boston Harbor, depicting the 1773 Boston Tea Party, by Nathan Currier, 1846 (PD-Art).

So long and great was the praise heaped upon him that when Washington politely stood to reply, no words came to him. He was brave as a lion when facing French soldiers and bullets in the wilderness, but he was such a humble man that praise was hard to handle.[3] The speaker relieved his embarrassment: "Sit down, Mr. Washington," he said. "Your modesty is equal to your valor, and that surpasses any language that I possess."[4] Washington was happy to sit down.

There were other powerful speakers in the House of Burgesses. A young lawyer named Patrick Henry brought bold claims against the king. His speech was so beautiful and powerful that people were amazed. Some accused him of treason, or betrayal, against the king. Others loudly clapped and shouted his praises. Henry said that the Stamp Act was not legal. He said that it was an unfair burden on the colonies. Washington agreed. When the king put a tax on tea, Henry again spoke against the move, and Washington was among those who promised not to buy tea again until the tax was taken off.

Soon Washington and Henry, with a few other Virginians, were sent to the first Continental Congress at Philadelphia, Pennsylvania. Washington listened carefully, but he did not make speeches. Many people were surprised that he was so young. They could hardly believe he had been only in his twenties when he saved Braddock's army.

The other members of the Congress knew that Washington was a man to be respected. One of them said, "If you speak of

I am… determined to be cheerful and happy, in whatever situation I may be; for I have also learned from experience that the greater part of our happiness or misery depends upon our dispositions, and not upon our circumstances.[2]

Martha Washington

The Boston Tea Party Museum on the Congress Street Bridge in Boston, Massachusetts (CC BY-SA 3.0).

solid information, and of sound judgment, Colonel Washington is unquestionably the greatest man on the floor."[5]

At this time, the king was angry at the people of Boston, Massachusetts, for dumping tea at the Boston Tea Party. He had closed Boston Harbor so no ships could bring goods into the town. He said the harbor would stay closed until the people of Boston paid for the tea they had dumped. Congress decided that it would help Boston. Soon wagonloads of food and other needed things were on their way to Boston from the other colonies. Washington went home and began again to drill his militiamen. It looked as if there would be another war.

> ❝
> *The Hand of Providence has been so conspicuous in all this, that he must be worse than an infidel that lacks faith, and more than wicked, that has not gratitude enough to acknowledge his obligations.*
>
> George Washington
> in a letter to Thomas Nelson Jr. on August 20, 1778
> (www.georgewashingtonsociety.org/)
> ❞

CHOSEN TO LEAD

The next year, 1775, a second Continental Congress met. There had been a battle at Lexington and Concord in Massachusetts between British soldiers and colonists who lived there. The British had tried to steal guns and powder that the people had been saving up in case of war. The colonists had driven the British back to their post in Boston, but it seemed that more battles would soon take place. The Americans had the British locked inside Boston, and the new army wanted to drive them completely out of the city. The army needed a leader. Washington was the only man for the job.

He was still humble. He said, "I am not worthy of this honor."[7] But the Congress voted on the question, and Washington got every single vote. He took command of the army.

He wrote a letter to his wife to tell her of his new job. He also told her that he did not feel that he was a good enough soldier for the task. But he had been called by his country to lead the army, and he had to be loyal to the call. He mounted his horse and headed for Boston.

Along the way, Washington the war hero and commander of the army was cheered by excited crowds. Everyone turned out to see him when they heard that he was coming along the road. The students at Yale gave him a real college welcome. They met him with a band and a parade.

Infantry: Continental Army, 1779-1783, by Henry Alexander Ogden, c.1897 (PD-US).

George Washington taking command of the Continental Army, July 3, 1775.

On July 3, 1775, Washington sat on his horse under the famous Harvard Elm on Cambridge Common. He drew his sword and took command of the continental army. The task before him was huge. He had thousands of men to train. He had to find rifles and cannons for the army. But with all this upon him, he managed to keep the British in Boston. He looked forward to the day when he could drive them out of the city.

It took months. One night in March 1776, Washington secretly sent some of his best troops to build earthen fortifications on a hill called Dorchester Heights. From the hilltop, the Americans could fire their cannons right down into the city. The next morning, British General Howe was stunned to see a fort on top of the hill. He said that his army could not have done as much work in six months as the Americans had done in one night. He knew he didn't have a chance with the black cannon muzzles pointed down into the town. He put his men on ships and sailed away. Boston was free![8]

Now Washington led his army to New York. He knew the British would try to take the city. He built a fort on Long Island to protect New York. Soon, General Howe arrived with 30,000 soldiers and many ships to attack him. In this great battle, part of Washington's army got separated from the rest and was defeated by Howe. Howe thought he had Washington trapped on the island. But through the brilliance of Washington and a heaven-sent cloud of fog, the American army was able to escape across the river without the loss of a single man.[9]

> *No man has a more perfect reliance on the all wise and powerful dispensations of the Supreme Being than I have, nor thinks His aid more necessary.*
>
> General Washington
> in a letter to Rev. William Gordon
> May 13, 1776.

Bronze statue of a Minuteman in Concord, MA. It was sculpted by Daniel Chester French from melted down Civil War cannons.

Here is another amazing demonstration of God's Providence in behalf of the Americans. First, General Howe waited two days without following up on his victory and capturing the rest of Washington's army. Then, a stormy wind kept British ships from coming up the river to attack Washington's trapped men. Washington collected all the boats he could find. The boats carried his men across the river to safety. But what would happen when morning light came? Would the British destroy the remaining men with their cannons? Just as the sun was coming up, God sent a fog so thick that the British army could not see the Americans run away. The entire army escaped across the river!

The Story of Isaac Potts

You might have seen the famous painting of Washington praying in the snow while his horse waits nearby. The painting is based on an incident when Mr. Potts, a Quaker who lived near Valley Forge, happened to see and hear the General praying. The story is told in the diary of Rev. Nathaniel Randolph Snowden, a friend of Potts:

I knew personally the celebrated Quaker Potts who saw General Washington alone in the woods at prayer. I got it from himself, myself. I was riding with him (Mr. Potts) in Montgomery County, Pennsylvania near to the Valley Forge, where the army lay during the war of the Revolution. Mr. Potts was a Senator in our State & a Whig. I told him I was agreeably surprised to find him a friend to his country as the Quakers were mostly Tories. He said, 'It was so and I was a rank Tory once, for I never believed that America could proceed against Great Britain whose fleets and armies covered the land and ocean, but something very extraordinary converted me to the Good Faith!' 'What was that,' I inquired? 'Do you see that woods, & that plain. It was about a quarter of a mile off from the place we were riding, as it happened.' 'There,' said he, 'laid the army of Washington. It was a most distressing time of ye war, and all were for giving up the Ship but that great and good man. In that woods pointing to a close in view, I heard a plaintive sound as, of a man at prayer. I tied my horse to a sapling & went quietly into the woods & to my astonishment I saw the great George Washington on his knees alone, with his sword on one side and his cocked hat on the other. He was at Prayer to the God of the Armies, beseeching to interpose with his Divine aid, as it was ye Crisis, & the cause of the country, of humanity & of the world. Such a prayer I never heard from the lips of man. I left him alone praying.'

'I went home & told my wife. I saw a sight and heard today what I never saw or heard before, and just related to her what I had seen & heard & observed. We never thought a man could be a soldier & a Christian, but if there is one in the world, it is Washington. She also was astonished. We thought it was the cause of God, & America could prevail.' He then to me put out his right hand & said 'I turned right about and became a Whig.'[10]

The Prayer at Valley Forge, painted by H. Brueckner, c.1866 (LOC).

Bronze statue of Nathan Hale at the Wadsworth Atheneum, 1889 (CC BY-SA 3.0).

A Brave Man

After escaping from Long Island, the Americans fought several more battles in the area. Washington wanted to know more about the British army in New York. He asked for a volunteer to sneak into the British camp and find out how many men they had and where their cannons were placed. Young Captain Nathan Hale stepped forward and offered himself.

Dressed as a country schoolmaster, Hale slipped past the British guards. He walked around the city and made notes about the defenses. But when he tried to return to General Washington, he was caught by the British and hanged. His last words were, "I only regret that I have but one life to lose for my country."[11] What a brave, patriotic man!

A Christmas Surprise

General Howe, the leader of the British troops, led his army toward Philadelphia. It seemed he was going to try to capture the men in Congress. This would have ruined the Patriot cause. So Washington moved his army between Howe and Philadelphia. There was a battle, and Washington had to retreat before the larger British army could overtake them.

To get away, Washington crossed the Delaware River. He collected all the boats he could find for many miles up and down the river. The British had no way to follow him. They decided to wait until the river froze over so they could cross on the ice. Many of the British officers thought the war was almost over. They went back to New York to spend the Christmas holiday having parties and feasts. But Washington had a Christmas surprise in store for them.[13]

Washington Crossing the Delaware, painted by Emanuel Leutze, c.1851 (PD-Art).

Christmas Day came. Several hundred Hessian soldiers camped at Trenton, New Jersey, nine miles from Washington's camp. Hessians were German soldiers King George had hired to help fight against the Patriots. He found it hard to hire enough English soldiers for the war because many Englishmen did not want to fight their colonist brothers in America. Washington had a plan to attack the Hessians on Christmas night. He would surprise them and win a great victory. If he won, the starving American soldiers would be encouraged to keep on fighting. The other Patriots would gain courage too.

Washington and Lafayette at Valley Forge, painted by John Ward Dunsmore, c.1907 (PD-US).

Washington gathered his boats. He had large rafts for his horses and cannons. It was so cold that large chunks of ice floated in the river. His men pushed them out of the way with poles and paddles. Then they reached the other shore and marched through a terrible winter storm to surprise the Hessians.

The Hessians had been celebrating Christmas. There had been much eating and drinking. When the Americans charged through Trenton, most of them were asleep. They never suspected that the American army would try to move across the icy river and march through falling ice and snow. Their leader was killed, and over 1,000 Hessian soldiers were captured. Washington had won again.

A Hard Winter

Howe did not try to capture Philadelphia again until spring came. Then there was a great battle in which both armies lost about 1,000 men. The British army was much larger, so the Americans slowly backed off. Summer and fall passed, and the army made a winter camp at Valley Forge in Pennsylvania. It would be a winter of awful suffering.[14]

The men built log huts. They were small, drafty, and smoky. There was not enough food, and their clothes were ragged. Some had no shoes and left bloody footprints in the snow. Washington wrote to Congress that nearly 3,000 of his men were "barefoot or otherwise naked."[15] Sometimes there

Baron von Steuben Drilling Troops at Valley Forge, by E. A. Abbey, c.1904 (PD-US).

General George Washington, painted & engraved by E. Savage (1790).

was no food at all. Most of the time there was very little. Many of the men had only piles of straw for a bed. What a horrible time!

While the British army in Philadelphia had parties and banquets, the Patriots suffered cold, hunger, and sickness. Many of the soldiers died. But though Washington was sad over the suffering of his soldiers, he never gave up. He encouraged them by keeping them busy. A German soldier named von Steuben came to help train them. Day after day, he taught them more about fighting. They drilled and drilled. Slowly they became confident even though they were hungry.

In the spring, the British moved back to New York. Washington's men, braver because of their rough winter training, fought and beat the British in the Battle of Monmouth in New Jersey. For the next three years, the British held New York, but they did not dare to come out and fight Washington.

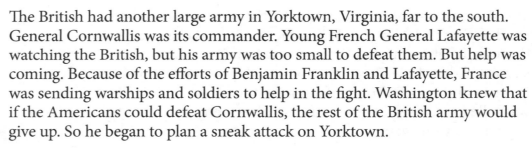

THE LAST BIG BATTLE

The British had another large army in Yorktown, Virginia, far to the south. General Cornwallis was its commander. Young French General Lafayette was watching the British, but his army was too small to defeat them. But help was coming. Because of the efforts of Benjamin Franklin and Lafayette, France was sending warships and soldiers to help in the fight. Washington knew that if the Americans could defeat Cornwallis, the rest of the British army would give up. So he began to plan a sneak attack on Yorktown.

With 2,000 ragged Patriots and 4,000 French soldiers in their neat uniforms, Washington headed south. He was nearly to Philadelphia before the British figured out what he was doing. Then it was too late to send help to Cornwallis. Soon, Yorktown was surrounded by thousands of American and French soldiers. In the nearby harbor, many French ships fired their cannons at the British lines. Finally, Cornwallis had to surrender. Soon, the war was over.

Americans celebrated with bonfires and cannon shots. Washington and his men were heroes. Washington met with his officers in Fraunces' Tavern in New York to say good-bye. It was a sad parting from his brave men. Washington embraced each one as they said farewell. Then he traveled to Annapolis, Maryland, where Congress was now meeting. There he resigned as commander-in-chief of the army. He had served through the war without accepting any pay. All he wanted was to make his country free and then go home to Mount Vernon.

It was General Washington who said, "It is impossible to rightly govern a nation without God and the Bible." No wonder Washington bent over and kissed the Bible when he was sworn in as president![16]

After a time at home, he was again called to serve his country. The colonies were free from England, but they needed to decide what kind of government they would have now. Some wanted Washington to be their king. But he said that a king would be a very bad thing for America. They wanted to become one country instead of 13 independent states. They needed to write a plan. It was called the Constitution. They knew George Washington was the man to lead the meeting.

When the Constitution was done, it said that a president must be elected. Once again, America called George Washington. He took an oath that said he would rule as the Constitution said he should. Now he was president.

When his time in office was done, the people elected him to another term. They wanted him to serve a third term after that, but he refused. He said it was time to let another man take the job. John Adams was elected as the second president of the United States of America.

At last, George Washington could go home to Mount Vernon to stay. He spent his last years farming, fox hunting, and enjoying his friends and family. He died in 1799. The whole country was sad. They felt as if their father had died. Indeed, Washington is still called "The Father of His Country."[16]

Give the last word to Washington's great enemy, King George III. The king asked his American painter, Benjamin West, what Washington would do after winning independence. West replied, "They say he will return to his farm."

"If he does that," the incredulous monarch said, "he will be the greatest man in the world."[18]

Washington's Farewell to His Officers, by Alonzo Chappel, 1866 (PD-US).

George Washington on his death-bed.

25

Franklin's experiment

CHAPTER 3

BENJAMIN FRANKLIN

The Making of the Man

BOYHOOD IN BOSTON

Young Deborah Read of Philadelphia, Pennsylvania, was standing in the doorway of her father's home in Philadelphia when she saw a young man go walking along the street. She couldn't help smiling as he went by. He looked so funny! She didn't know that she was looking at her future husband, Benjamin Franklin.[1]

Benjamin Franklin had been traveling, and he was tired, dirty, and hungry. His clothes were wrinkled. He had his coat pockets stuffed with extra shirts, socks, and other things he needed. He had walked many miles, slept wherever he could, and eaten very little. He had just arrived in town and bought three big rolls from a baker. As he passed Deborah Read's house, he was eating one roll and had the other two tucked under his arms. What a strange sight he was! I think I might have smiled myself if I had seen him. Wouldn't you?

Benjamin Franklin became one of the most important men in early America. He was known in many countries for his wisdom and the great things he had done. He was a printer by trade. He was also an author and an inventor. He did many different jobs in his life. He learned a lot by doing many different types of things.

Ben was born in 1706. That was less than 100 years after the first English settlers came to America. He was born in a very large family, and he had 16 brothers and sisters. His father wanted him to go to college and be a minister, but he only went to school for two years. Ben's father was a hard worker but a poor man. He didn't have enough money to send Ben to college. So Ben went

Deborah Read Franklin, by Benjamin Wilson, 1758 (PD-Art).

Do you know what a statesman is? It is a wise, respected, and experienced leader. That is how early Americans thought of Benjamin Franklin. He was one of the oldest and wisest of our Founding Fathers.

Franklin's first visit to Philadelphia.

to work in his father's business, helping to make soap and candles.

Ben wanted to be a sailor. Growing up in Boston, he often saw ships and sailors. He loved the water and liked to spend time swimming and boating with his friends. He became so good at handling a boat that the other boys wanted Ben at the tiller to help steer the boat whenever the waves and wind became rough. He loved the stories the sailors would tell when they walked around town. But Ben's father did not want him to be a sailor, so he took Ben to visit different places where people were working. He hoped Ben would see a kind of work that he liked better than being a sailor.[2]

Ben did not like working in his father's shop. What should the Franklins do with their little boy? Mr. and Mrs. Franklin knew that Benjamin loved books. He seemed to always have a book in his hand any time he wasn't working. Perhaps Benjamin should be a printer.[3]

In those days, there were no public libraries. People couldn't just check out books and read them. They had to buy books from printers. Ben did this whenever he had a little money. When he finished reading a book, he would trade with a friend, and they would each have a new book to read.[4]

YOUNG BEN

Even as a boy, Ben was becoming a leader. There was a fishing hole near Ben's home where he and his friends liked to fish. But the land at the edge was marshy, and the boys had trampled it into a nasty mud hole. Ben told the other boys that they needed to build a stone wharf to fish from. But where would they get the stones? Ben had the answer. A pile of stones nearby was going to be used to build a house. After the workers had left the job one day, Ben led his friends to the pile. They carried the stones away one by one. Some of them were so big that two or three boys had to work together on one stone! The next morning, the workers found that their stones were gone, and there was a new wharf at the edge of the water. When they found out who had taken their stones, the boys' fathers punished them. Ben tried to explain to his father that the wharf was a useful project, but the excuse was not accepted. Ben's father taught him that anything that was not honest was not useful.[5]

Learning a Trade

Benjamin's older brother James was a printer. Their father thought it would be good for Ben to work for James as an apprentice. An apprentice is a person who works for someone else just to learn a trade. Ben signed a paper that said he had to work for James and that James had to pay for Ben's food and lodging. Ben would only be paid in money for the last year of his apprenticeship. Apprentices had to work hard, but Ben knew he would learn the trade well by working in the shop.

So Ben began to work in his brother's printing shop. He worked hard and spent many hours in the shop. Here he got to read books and other papers as they were being printed. He would read several hours at night after working hard all day. It seemed as though he could never get all the books he wanted. Because he wasn't being paid, he had very little money. Then he had an idea.

Tell me and I forget, teach me and I may remember, involve me and I learn.

Benjamin Franklin

Ben lived in a boarding house. James lived there, also, and so did his other apprentices. The boys worked for free, but James had to pay the landlady for their rooms and meals. One day, Ben went to James with an offer to buy his own meals, if he just got half the money that had been paid to the landlady, so he could save the rest. James was happy to agree. Now Ben's food would only cost him half as much.[6]

Now Ben could buy more books. He also had more time to read. When James and the other young men would go to the boarding house each day for lunch, Ben would run out and buy a pastry or some fruit to eat. He would spend the noon hour in the print shop alone. After he finished his small meal, he could read until the shop opened up for the afternoon.[7]

He kept on reading and learning. No one could have guessed it, but Benjamin Franklin would one day be given degrees by several great universities. He only went to school for two years in his whole life, yet he insisted, "The

Benjamin Franklin at work on a printing press, by Charles E. Mills, c. 1914 (PD-US).

door to learning is never closed." He became a very educated and wise man.

When Benjamin Franklin was 20, he wrote a plan for how he would live his life. He made a list of qualities that he thought he needed to learn to show in his life. He would work on one character quality each week. He kept track of his progress with a chart.

Here are some of the values he wrote about in 1741:

☆ **Temperance**. Don't eat or drink too much so that you're drowsy much of the time.

☆ **Silence**. Speak only words that are useful and good. Don't talk about nonsense.

☆ **Order**. Have a place to put all your things. Have a time to do each thing you need to do.

☆ **Resolution**. Resolve (or decide) to do what is right. Then do what you have resolved.

☆ **Frugality**. Don't spend money except when it will do good for yourself or others. Do not waste anything.

☆ **Industry**. Never waste time. Always be doing something useful.

☆ **Sincerity**. Don't be a deceiver. Speak only what you really think.

☆ **Justice**. Don't harm anyone by doing wrong to them. Don't fail to help when you can.

☆ **Moderation**. Avoid extremes. Don't get angry quickly.

☆ **Cleanliness**. Keep your body, clothes, and house clean.

☆ **Tranquility**. Don't get upset at little things or things that can't be helped.

☆ **Humility**. Be humble, listen to advice, and don't think you are always right.[9]

Franklin wrote many years later that learning character qualities had been useful to him. He said diligence and frugality had made him wealthy. He said his hard study had make him a useful citizen and won the respect of educated people. He said

Sometimes we have to sacrifice to get things we want. Ben was wise to spend his money on books instead of silly things that many other boys like. He also showed self-control by eating a small lunch in order to have more money for books. Have you ever given up something you wanted in order to get something better?

sincerity and justice had caused his country to trust him. He said even though he knew he was not perfect in these qualities, they had made him a better man and caused other people to like being with him.[10]

Benjamin Franklin, by Benjamin Wilson, 1759 (PD-Art).

BECOMING A MAN

Benjamin also read a newspaper called the *New England Courant*, which belonged to James. When he started it, it was only the second newspaper published in America. Ben wanted to write articles for the newspaper. But James thought Ben was too young to write articles. He thought his younger brother was not smart enough.

So Ben wrote articles and slipped them under his brother's door at night. They were signed by Silence Do-good. This was a name Ben had made up so James would not know the articles came from his little brother.[11]

James liked the articles, so he printed them in his paper. Many people read the articles and liked them. Everyone knew that Silence Do-good was not the author's real name, so they guessed who he or she might really be. Most people thought the writer was probably some well-known person in Boston. That made Ben feel really good! No one guessed the writer was just a boy.[13]

When James finally found out that the articles came from his little brother, he was angry. He did not like all the attention and praise that Ben got from people who read the newspaper. He was unkind to Ben and made his job very hard. Finally, Ben ran away.

And that is why he appeared on Market Street in Philadelphia on that autumn day when Deborah Reed spotted him. He had tried to find work as a printer in New York, but no one needed a hand. He heard that there might be a job for him in a print shop in Philadelphia, so he paid for a ticket and boarded a boat to New Jersey. Sailing, rowing, and walking, he finally arrived at his destination.

> 66
>
> *If you would not be forgotten*
> *As soon as you are dead and rotten,*
>
> *Either write things worthy reading,*
> *Or do things worth the writing.*[12]
>
> Benjamin Franklin
>
> 99

I remain, Sir, Your Humble Servant, SILENCE DOGOOD[14]

Ben was finally hired by Samuel Keimer to help in his print shop. Ben showed Keimer how well he could do the work. He worked hard and kept on learning his trade. Ben saved

An 18th-century map of Philadelphia, 1752 (PD-US).

his money and bought books. He loved to learn, so he spent much time reading. He found friends who liked to read, also, and he formed a club to talk about the books they read and important ideas they learned. Together, Ben and his friends helped each other to get a good education without going to school.[15]

One day, a man came into the printing office and talked to Ben. He was finely dressed and appeared to be rich. He introduced himself as Sir William Keith, the governor of the province, and wished to spend some time with young Mr. Franklin in the tavern.[16]

Mr. Keimer couldn't refuse to let Ben off work for a little while when the governor wanted to see him. So off went the amazed young printer for a chat with the governor.

Governor Keith told Ben that neither Keimer nor the other printer in town, a man named Bradford, did very good printing work. He had heard that Ben was a skilled printer. He thought Ben should start his own print shop. Surely his father would help him by lending him some money.[17]

So Ben went home to Boston for a visit. His family was so happy to see him again! Except for his brother James. Ben was dressed in a fine suit and had money in his pockets from working hard and saving carefully. It was clear that he was living better than he had as James' apprentice. James seemed a little angry that Ben was doing so well.

Ben gave his father a letter from Governor Keith. The governor said young Ben was a bright young man and a good printer. He said he thought Mr. Franklin should give Ben the money to buy his own printing press and set up his own shop.

Mr. Franklin was proud of Ben, but he thought Benjamin was too young to start his own business. He would not give him the money. He said Ben should wait a few years and then try his idea.

When he returned to Philadelphia, Ben went to see Governor Keith. He read the letter Mr. Franklin had written. Mr. Franklin said that he thanked the governor for his kind words about Ben, but thought he was too young to have his own print shop.

Governor Keith assured him that he would help him get started. He told Ben to board a ship to England and find good printing equipment. He said he would buy the equipment for Ben, and Ben could pay him back after he got started in business. He would send letters aboard the ship for Ben to take to England. The letters would introduce him to the people there. They would promise payment from the governor for anything Ben needed to buy.

So off went Ben to England. You can imagine how shocked and hurt he was to find out that Governor Keith had sent no letters for him! Years later, Ben found out that the governor was known for making promises he could not keep. He was not rich at all.[18]

But Ben Franklin knew his trade. He was a good worker and a hard worker. He got a job for an English printer and started saving his money to go back to America and start his career over again.

Well done is better than well said.[19]

Benjamin Franklin

Portrait of Benjamin Franklin, by Joseph-Siffrein Duplessisl, c.1785 (PD-Art).

Ben was in trouble! He was thousands of miles from home with little money and no friends. But he had something very important — a trade. He had worked hard to learn printing, and he was good at it. He was also a hard worker. He was able to find a job and save money to travel back home. Every young person should know at least one way to make a living. That is why Ben used to say, "He that hath a trade hath an estate, and he that hath a calling hath a place of profit and honor."[20] What do you think might have happened if Ben had not known how to work?

Benjamin Franklin
in his study

CHAPTER 4

BENJAMIN FRANKLIN

The Great Statesman

BACK IN PHILADEPHIA

Once he got back to Philadelphia, Ben worked in a store for a while and then started his own print shop. He married Deborah Read, and they worked hard to make their business succeed. Together, they published a newspaper, the *Philadelphia Gazette*. Ben also wrote an almanac called *Poor Richard's Almanack*, which included practical tips, weather forecasts, word puzzles, and more. The almanac gave advice on planting crops, keeping house, and many other useful things. It also contained many of Ben's favorite sayings: "A penny saved is a penny earned." "Early to bed, early to rise, makes a man healthy, wealthy, and wise." "A good wife and health is a man's best wealth." The almanac was very popular with the people.

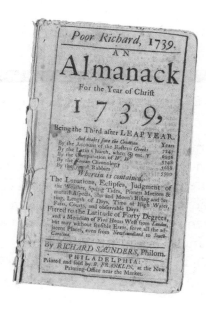

By working hard and being thrifty, Ben and Deborah grew wealthy. But they didn't keep their money for themselves. They helped other people start businesses. They gave to charity. Ben was a friend of the famous evangelist George Whitefield. He gave Whitefield money to care for the children in his Georgia orphanage.[1]

Ben did much to make his city a better place. He led the city in paving the muddy streets with large, flat stones. He got some men together and formed a volunteer fire department. He helped start the first library in America where people could check out books. He helped to build a hospital. He started a school, which one day would become the famous University of Pennsylvania. Ben also invented the Franklin stove, which heated houses better than other stoves and used up less firewood.

God brought Whitefield from England to preach the gospel in the American colonies. He traveled thousands of miles and preached from Georgia in the south to Maine in the north. He traveled mostly on horseback and carried a folding pulpit to stand on when preaching. He sometimes preached as many as five sermons in a day. It is estimated that he preached over 2,000 sermons from his folding pulpit. Whitefield was the most famous preacher of the Great Awakening, a mighty revival in which thousands were saved. God used the Great Awakening to prepare the American colonies for the separation from England and independence. The preachers were not afraid to preach against the wrong and illegal actions of King George. Sometimes they led the men of their church into the American army during the War of Independence. The English called them The Black Robe Regiment. King George called the war the Presbyterian Parsons' Rebellion.[2]

Glass Harmonica

Franklin Stove

In fact, Ben was quite an inventor. He discovered that lightning was electricity, and he invented the lightning rod so houses would not burn down when lightning struck.

He invented bifocal glasses (Uncle Rick wears those) to help people to see better. He also made swim fins and a musical instrument called a glass harmonica.

Some people said Ben should get a patent for his Franklin stove. A patent was a paper from the king that said no one but the inventor of a machine could make and sell the machine. This was so the person who invested the time and money to invent something could be paid for it without other people stealing his idea. But Ben said no.[3] He wanted other people to benefit from his inventions as he did from theirs.[4]

FRANKLIN PROVES LIGHTNING IS A FORM OF ELECTRICITY

Franklin believed that lightning was a form of electricity. To find out for sure, he made up an experiment. He would fly a kite in a rainstorm and see if electricity would come down the wet string. But the rain would ruin the paper kite! Clever Ben made a kite of silk so water would not hurt it. He tied a metal key at the end of the string where he would hold it. Then, on a rainy June day in 1752, he and his son sent the kite into the cloudy sky. They stepped into a nearby barn to stay dry. Ben held onto a dry silk string tied to the key on the kite string. He thought the dry string would not carry an electrical shock to him. He was right. As lightning flashed through the dark clouds, electrical charges were carried down the wet kite string, but they did not shock Ben. When he held his other hand a few inches from the key, a spark jumped from the key to his hand. Now he knew lightning was electrical! Later, other men would try his kite experiment for themselves. Some of them were killed by the electricity. Franklin invented the lightning rod, a metal rod placed on the roof of a house to carry the electricity to the ground without harming the house. Years afterward, Franklin's own house was struck by lightning, but it was not burned because he had a lightning rod.

1752

Storytime with Uncle Rick

Fight for Freedom

OFF TO ENGLAND

The people of Pennsylvania loved Ben more and more as years went by. They knew he wanted to help others. So they elected him to be the clerk of the Assembly of Pennsylvania and later to be a lawmaker in the assembly. Every year for ten years they elected him to help make laws for the colony, even though he never asked anybody to vote for him. The people trusted Ben Franklin.

In 1754, the colony sent Ben with some other men to make a treaty with the Iroquois Indians. They were also to make a plan for a union of the 13 colonies. This was while Patrick Henry was still a boy and George Washington was still a surveyor! The wisdom of Franklin was already at work planning how to unite the colonies. It was a clear look ahead to a time when America would become a nation.

Then England and the colonies in America began to fight. The king kept doing things that he did not have a right to do. He wanted to get money from the colonies. He wanted them to pay taxes. He did not want them to trade with other countries — just England. He sent soldiers to make the Americans do what he wanted them to do. The Americans sent Benjamin Franklin to England to talk to the leaders. He was a wise man who would know what to do and say.

The king passed a law called the Stamp Act. It was a kind of tax. He said the people in the colonies must buy his stamped paper to do business. This made the colonists angry! Ben went to work to have the Stamp Act repealed.

He wrote articles to the English newspapers telling how the Stamp Act was hurting the colonies. He wrote many letters to great men in England trying to make them see the truth. He went to speak to Parliament (where English laws are made). He answered over 200 questions they asked him about the act. Finally, the act was repealed. There was great rejoicing, and Ben sent his wife a fine London gown to celebrate.

Franklin stayed in England for eight more years. He was trying to get the king to treat his people in the colonies fairly. He spent much time talking with William Pitt, a great English statesman who was friendly to America. Pitt introduced a bill in Parliament to help England and the American colonies get along better. But Parliament did not pass his bill. It looked as if there was no way to avoid war between the mother country and her colonies across the Atlantic.[6]

What good is science that does not apply to some use?[5]

Benjamin Franklin

William Pitt, 1st Earl of Chatham, after Richard Brompton, 1772 (PD-Art).

37

A Long and Useful Life

Franklin sailed back home and arrived just after the Battle of Lexington and Concord in 1775. Pennsylvania sent him to the Continental Congress. Congress made George Washington general of the new Continental army. Ben was chosen to be one of five men who were asked to write a document saying that the colonies weren't colonies of England any more. From now on, they were free states. This document became very famous. It is called the Declaration of Independence.

If I were an American, as I am an Englishman, while a foreign troop was landed in my country, I never would lay down my arms—never, never, never![7]

William Pitt

It wasn't long before Ben had to leave home again. This time he was asked to sail to France to get help for the colonies. Everyone knew England had a strong army and navy. The Americans were just getting started. They needed a strong friend to fight with them if they were going to have a chance to beat England and be free.

Declaration of Independence by John Trumbull, 1819 (PD-Art).

France and England were enemies. They had fought several wars before. One of those was the French and Indian War. In that war, the colonies had fought with England against the French. Now, the king of England had turned against his colonies and treated them like enemies. The king of France wanted to help the colonies because he hated England.

At first, the king of France did not want to take sides. But he did give money to Ben for the colonial army. Many of his army officers went to America to fight with the colonists. Later, he took a stand publicly and sent soldiers and ships to help. He hated the English, and he had a great respect for Benjamin Franklin. With the help of France and many acts of God on behalf of the colonies, America defeated England and became a free country.

(PD-Art)

Years later in 1787, Benjamin Franklin was a part of the Constitutional Convention. The Constitutional Convention was a meeting of American leaders who wrote a plan for the 13 colonies to come together and become the United States of America. The men were having a hard time agreeing on how to build the new country. Finally, Ben suggested that the convention pray each day and ask God to help them decide the right things to do. He said, "I have lived, Sir, a long time, and the longer I live, the more convincing proofs I see of this truth, that God Governs in the affairs of men. And if a sparrow cannot fall to the ground without his notice, is it probable that an empire can rise without his aid?"[9]

The Body of B. Franklin, Printer; like the Cover of an old Book, Its Contents torn out, And stript of its Lettering and Gilding, Lies here, Food for Worms. But the Work shall not be wholly lost; For it will, as he believ'd, appear once more, In a new & more perfect Edition, Corrected and amended By the Author.[11]

Ben Franklin
(Eulogy that he wrote for himself.)

Benjamin Franklin died at the age of 84 on April 17, 1790. In his last hours, he looked at a painting of Jesus on his bedroom wall and said, "He is the one who came to teach us to love one another."[10]

Franklin's Return To Philadelphia in 1785, by Jean Leon Gerome Ferris, date unknown (PD-Art).

General
Anthony Wayne

CHAPTER 5

MAD ANTHONY WAYNE

The Storming of Stony Point

A CLEVER GENERAL

The War of Independence is sometimes called the American Revolution or the Revolutionary War. It is the most important war in our country's history. That is because it was the war that won our freedom. If we had lost that war, the 13 English colonies in America would not have become independent states. Then they could not have joined together and become the United States of America.

The Revolutionary War is also an exciting war to read about because it was such a hard war to win. The American patriots were fighting against England, the most powerful nation in the world. England had a big army and a big navy. America had only a small army and no navy at all when the war started.

George Washington had a difficult job. He had to recruit new men to be soldiers. Then he had to train them to fight together. He had to find the money to buy them guns, cannons, wagons, uniforms, food, and horses. Many people in the colonies did not want to break away from England. They were still loyal to King George. Some of these people fought with the British. Some of them spied on the American army and told the English what they learned. General Washington had to be very wise in order to beat the British when he had so many problems. But God gave General Washington wisdom. Washington made plans to use tricks to beat the British armies, even when they had more men than he did.

Variety of Continental Army soldiers, by Charles M. Lefferts, c.1910 (PD-Art).

In the early days of the war, much of the fighting was done by minutemen. These were patriots who were willing to leave their farms or jobs at a minute's notice to fight. The minutemen defeated the British at the Battle of Lexington and Concord. Most of them had never been in an army, but they were good shots. They had grown up hunting for meat in the forests of New England. Sometimes the people would go to worship at the village church on Sunday, and the minutemen would train together after church was over. Sometimes the pastor of the church would lead his men into battle.[1]

General Washington needed a lot of money to buy guns and to pay his soldiers. Congress had a hard time getting money for him. Robert Morris, one of the men who signed the Declaration of Independence, was a very rich man. He gave more than $2 million to the American army to fight the war. Because America was very poor in her early days as a country, the government was never able to pay Morris back. But Robert Morris never complained about it. He was more concerned about the patriots gaining their freedom.[2]

You have also heard how Washington's ragged soldiers, some of them leaving bloody footprints in the snow from bare and injured feet, marched to Trenton on Christmas night in 1776 to attack the Hessians early the next morning. That was a holiday surprise!

THE BATTLE OF DORCHESTER HEIGHTS

Storytime with Uncle Rick

Fight for Freedom

Let me tell you about an instance of the marvelous hand of God in behalf of the colonists. It happened at Dorchester Heights. At this time, the British had captured Boston. Washington knew he needed to strengthen Dorchester Heights (which was a big hill) to try to drive the British away. During the night, the soldiers carried bales of hay and drove wagons with supplies up the hill. It was a hazy night, down at the foot of the hill, that is. Once the men got to the top, it was crystal clear, and they could see to build their fortifications.

In the morning, when the British general awoke, he was surprised to see that the colonial army captured the hill! He was reported to have said, "The American army got more done in one night than my men would have gotten done in six months!"[3]

Still, he prepared his cannons on his ships to take the hill. That night, a natural disaster occurred in favor of the American troops. A terrible storm blew up, such as no one had ever seen. It blew the British ships around and broke their masts. In the morning, the general saw his ships wrecked and knew by the time he got things repaired, the Americans would have an advantage.

Reverend William Gordon, a local preacher, later said, "When I heard in the night how amazingly strong the wind blew, I pleased myself with the reflection that the Lord might be working delivery for us and thus prevent the diffusion of human blood. It proved to be so."[4]

Without shedding a drop of blood, the British quickly withdrew their 10,000 soldiers from the city of Boston on March 17, 1776. The victory at Dorchester Heights gave great confidence to the Americans!

View of the city of Boston from Dorchester Heights, by Robt. Havell, 1841 (PD-US).

MAD ANTHONY WAYNE

In 1779, Washington needed to give the British another surprise. The British army had captured an American fort at Stony Point in New York. From this fort, they could keep the American army from taking troops and supplies across the Hudson River at King's Ferry. This was a big problem because the patriots needed those things badly and there were not many places where the river could be crossed. Washington needed to get Stony Point back from the British.

Some patriot spies told General Washington that the nearby British army under General Clinton was about to move. But they did not know where Clinton was going. Was he going to move up the Hudson River and capture other crossing places? That would make things even harder for the American army.

But Clinton did not move up the river. Soon the patriots heard he was moving inland and raiding in several different places. He was being very cruel, burning homes and even churches. The British hated the American churches because many of the preachers were preaching against the evil things the king of England had done. Now British officers led 2,600 men into Connecticut. They killed many people, even women and children.[5]

General Clinton hoped to make General Washington so angry that he would send part of his army to fight the British in Connecticut. If Washington divided his forces, the British could attack smaller armies and destroy them. But Washington was not fooled. Even though he felt bad because he could not drive the British out of Connecticut, he knew he had to keep his army together. He had to protect the rest of his forts on the Hudson River to win the war.

Washington also needed a victory. Because his army was small and did not have many things it needed, he had not been fighting many battles to drive the British out of the areas they held. He had mostly been fighting battles just to keep his own army from being destroyed. They had lost some battles, and they felt badly

Passage of the Delaware, by Thomas Sully, 1819 (PD-Art).

The British blamed the pastors for being rebel-rousers. They called preachers by the name of the Black-Robed regiment as most preachers in those days wore black robes when they preached. If a preacher was caught by the British, he was treated extra shamefully.

about that. They seldom had the food, clothes, and money they needed. Many of them had given up and gone home. They were ragged and hungry. He needed to give them a victory in battle so they would have the courage to fight on.

Congress and the people of the colonies were discouraged, too. General Washington needed to win a battle and take some territory away from the British to show his people that they could win.

Washington decided to take back Stony Point.

That would not be easy. The British had moved many men and guns into the fort there. It was built on a huge rocky bluff near the river. It was 200 feet above the valley floor. It was protected from the rear by marshy ground that was hard to cross. The enemy had protected its top with six different sets of cannons. Below they had built a fence of logs. But the logs did not stand straight up. They leaned outward from the fort, and their ends were sharpened so they would be hard for men to climb over. There were 600 soldiers inside.

Washington talked with his generals and made a plan, knowing that the fort was too strong to be taken by direct assault. It would need to be attacked at night when the British were not expecting them. They wondered who would be the best man to lead this attack.[7]

It wasn't long before they had their answer. Someone suggested General Anthony Wayne.

Wayne was such a bold fighter that his men called him Mad Anthony Wayne. He was one of the toughest fighters of the entire Revolutionary War. He had a love for battle. He was brave but careful. He

General Anthony Wayne at the Battle of Stony Point, 1779, by Joseph Brightly, c.1818 (PD-US).

was always on the alert and solid as a rock. When his commander told him what he wanted, Mad Anthony excitedly volunteered. Washington would plan the battle, Anthony would do the fighting.

Anthony Wayne, American general, by Trumbull and Forest, 18th century (PD-US).

THE MIDNIGHT ATTACK

The plans were made with great care. Washington rode down and spent an entire day looking over the situation. Trusty men who knew the area well guarded all the roads and every trail so spies and deserters, soldiers who tried to leave the army, couldn't pass.

Washington told Wayne the attack would have to remain secret until the very moment it started. If the British had any warning of what was about to happen, all their soldiers would be awakened and ready. Washington believed that a ten-minute notice to the enemy would blast all their hopes.[8]

The attack would begin at midnight. Washington hoped the night would be dark and rainy. Most of the soldiers would not even load their rifles. They would attack with their bayonets so that no early shot would warn the enemy of the attack.

But there were two companies who did load their guns. These men would attack one side of the fort, firing and shouting to make as much noise as possible. The British would rush to that side of the fort while Anthony's main force attacked quietly from the other side with their bayonets. If things went well, it would be a total surprise.

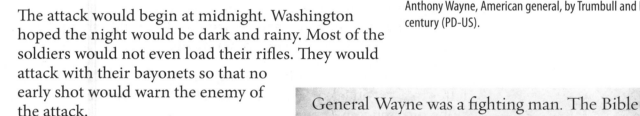

General Wayne was a fighting man. The Bible says a lot about fighting. We have enemies in our lives, too. We need to be always ready to fight against Satan for the Kingdom of God!

PREPARING FOR BATTLE

About 1,300 men of the famous light infantry were chosen for the job. They were some of the best fighters on the Continental Army. They were well-skilled with the bayonet and could fight well against the strongest soldiers the British could send against them.

In the middle of the day on July 15, the men assembled for inspection. After inspection, they marched down the road toward the southwest. The march to Stony Point had begun. That hot afternoon, the men picked their way along rough and narrow roads, up steep hillsides, and through swamps and woods. Sometimes the woods were so thick that the men had to walk single file. No soldier was allowed to leave the ranks without special permission.

At 8 p.m., the army came to a halt at a farmhouse 13 miles from camp. They were now about a mile from Stony Point. No one was allowed to speak. The tired men dropped on the ground and ate their supper of bread and cold meat in silence.

A little later, the order of battle was read. For the first time, the men knew what was ahead of them. No doubt many brave men felt their knees shake when they heard what a hard battle this might be. Many of them might be dead before sunrise.

Until 11:30 p.m., they rested. Then each man pinned a piece of white paper to his hat so his fellow soldiers would not attack him by mistake in the dark. No man was to speak until they received the final order to attack. Then they were all to shout the watchword. That was, "The fort is our own!"

Wayne felt he might not live through the battle. He wrote a letter to a friend, asking him to look after the Wayne children if he did not come home. He ate his supper wondering if he would have breakfast as a victor inside the enemy's lines or if he would be heaven.

A slave named Pompey was their guide. Pompey had sold cherries and strawberries to the fort's defenders and knew the fort's password. For his service in this battle, Pompey's master set him free and gave him a saddle horse, one bred for riding, as a reward.

Wayne divided his army into three groups. A few of the men were to start the attack and get the enemy fighting. While they did this, other men would chop away the sharp logs that surrounded the fort. Then, the main body of the troops would rush through the gaps.

The patriots had to wade through water up to their waists in some places. Soon the British heard noise and began shooting. The patriots heard drums inside the fort calling the soldiers to wake up and fight. They had to hurry and swarm into the fort.

The riflemen rushed to the front. The British met them with fierce anger. Behind them, the axe men chopped away at the logs so many soldiers could rush through at once. Bullets fell like hail through the darkness. Two columns rushed the main fort, while a third fired their rifles directly in front to make it seem as if the main attack was there. The redcoats were fooled, rushing down to meet them while the main body of the patriots scrambled into the fort from behind.

Mad Anthony was struck in the head by a bullet, and he thought he was dying.

"Carry me into the fort!" he called to his aides. "Let me die at the head of the column!"[9]

It was only a scalp wound, and soon he was able to fight again.

"The fort's our own![10]

"The fort's our own! The fort's our own!" came the shout from all sides of the fort. The patriots drove the British at the points of their bayonets to all corners of the fort. Soon they were surrendering, begging not to be killed. Only one man, a captain, escaped from the fort. He jumped into the river and swam a mile to a British ship. He told the ship's captain what had happened. General Clinton heard the news at breakfast.

The news spread like wildfire. Wayne and his light infantry were the heroes of the hour. Two days later, Washington and his top officers rode down to Stony Point and heard the whole story. Because of his head wound, General Wayne was not able to go with Washington on his tour of the battlefield, but several of his officers did so.

The patriots had only 15 men killed and 83 wounded. The British had 566 men killed, wounded, or captured. It had been an overwhelming victory, thanks to God's blessing and the cleverness and courage of Mad Anthony Wayne and his men.[13]

> "Dear General, the fort and garrison with Colonel Johnson are ours. Our officers and men behaved like men who are determined to be free."[11]
>
> General Wayne
> to George Washington

General Wayne with the Legion of the United States, 1794, by H. Charles McBarron, Jr., date unknown (PD-USGOV).

Major William Hull, who had fought in the battle, said the commander in chief shook hands with the men, and, "with joy that glowed in his countenance, here offered thanks to Almighty God, that He had been our shield and protector amidst the dangers we had been called to encounter."[12]

Connecticut countryside in 1787

CHAPTER 6

CAESAR RODNEY

The Midnight Ride

ANOTHER RIDER FOR FREEDOM

On the evening of April 18, 1775, silversmith Paul Revere mounted a borrowed horse and galloped for the towns of Lexington and Concord in Massachusetts. He had been to Concord just two days before. He had warned the patriots that they needed to move the cannons and war supplies stored there. American spies had heard that the British would soon march to Concord to steal the supplies.

Paul Revere received word that the march would come the next day. He left for Concord once again. He gave the alarm at patriot homes along the way. Men turned out with their muskets and hurried to their militia meeting places. Other men mounted horses and rushed north and south to spread the word. At Lexington, Revere stopped at the house of Reverend Jonas Clark to warn John Hancock and Samuel Adams. After talking with them, he rushed on toward Concord.

But Revere did not get to Concord that night. He was captured by a British patrol a few miles west of Lexington. Concord was warned by Dr. Prescott, who had joined Revere on the road and escaped the king's patrol by jumping his horse over a stone wall.

But now we begin the story of another midnight ride, a ride that was completed. It was a very important ride, like that of Paul Revere. But it was important in a different way. The rider was Caesar Rodney.

> 66
>
> *No one was either Tory or Whig; it was either dependence or independence.*[1]
>
> Caesar Rodney
>
> 99

Caesar was the eldest of eight children. At 17, when his father died, he assumed the responsibility of caring for his mother and siblings and managing the Byfield plantation. No wonder he was prepared to be a leader of other men!

Rodney was an important man in the little state of Delaware. He had been elected as a sheriff, a judge, and several other government jobs in Delaware. He had served in the French and Indian War. He was well liked and greatly respected. People knew him as an honest man and a good leader.

But Caesar Rodney had a problem. He had cancer. It had grown in his face and caused an ugly sore. He often covered most of his face with a scarf. He didn't want others to see his cancer. He took treatments from doctors for his disease, but there was only so much they could do. There was better treatment in England, but Rodney would not go to England.[2]

> **"**
>
> *Territory is but the body of a nation. The people who inhabit its hills and valleys are its soul, its spirit, its life.*[3]
>
> James Garfield
>
> **"**

Why not? Because Caesar Rodney was a patriot. He had been elected to represent Delaware in the Continental Congress. The Continental Congress was discussing what to do about the king's bad actions. They were talking about breaking away from England and making the colonies into a new country. They needed all their members together to work out the problems. Caesar Rodney was also a brigadier-general in the Delaware militia. He was needed to help control the Tories of the state, who were always causing trouble. No, he would do the best he could with the doctors in America. He was needed too badly to go away to England for months.[4]

Because he was an officer in the Delaware militia, Caesar Rodney had to divide his time between Congress and Delaware. While he was away from Congress working to raise money and volunteers in Delaware, some Tories started a riot. Caesar Rodney had to gather his men and stop the violence. He got his militiamen together, and they went to fight the Tories. When he got back to his home on the evening of July 1, 1776, he was tired and sick. He needed to rest and sleep.

But then a messenger came with a letter from Thomas McKean. McKean and George Read were the other representatives from Delaware to the Continental Congress. McKean's letter begged Rodney to return to Philadelphia at once.

Map of Delaware 1804 (PD-US).

50

There was going to be a vote the next day. Some of the colonies were going to vote to break away from England and the king. Others were going to vote to remain English colonies. Delaware's vote might be needed to tip the balance in favor of independence. Rodney's vote was needed.[5]

Thomas McKean believed the colonies should be free from England. George Read, another good man, thought they should remain colonies of England. If Caesar Rodney could get back to Philadelphia in time for the vote, he would break the tie between Delaware's representatives. His state would then vote for independence.

George Washington said, "Human happiness and moral duty are inseparably connected."[6] Sometimes it is very hard to do our moral duty. It is good that we have men like Caesar Rodney as our examples.

A Ride That Had to Be Taken

Tired, sick, and troubled, Caesar Rodney knew what he had to do. He called for a carriage, threw his carpetbag in, and climbed up to the seat. With a clatter of hoofs and a scattering of gravel, he was on his way to Philadelphia, 80 miles to the north.

It was not a ride he wanted to take. Besides his cancer, he struggled with asthma. It sometimes made it hard for him to breathe. At other times, he could not stop coughing. He pulled his scarf over his mouth to keep out the flying cloud of dust stirred up by the horse's galloping feet.

These were dark days for the American colonies. The king and Parliament had been making laws for the Americans that they had no right to pass. English soldiers had been living in some colonists' houses without paying rent. The king had broken up the lawmaking assemblies in some of the colonies. He had closed Boston Harbor so the people of Boston could not buy the things they needed that came only by ship. There had been fighting at Lexington and Concord. There had been the battle of Bunker Hill. Surely there would be more fighting and killing.

The patriots had shown that they were strong and brave. After retreating from Bunker Hill when the gunpowder ran out, the minutemen welcomed General George Washington as their new commander. Under his leadership, they had driven the British out of Boston. Now Washington and his men were in New

Caesar Rodney of Delaware, artist unknown, 1888 (PD-US).

York, and a British battle fleet was on its way with thousands of soldiers to attack him.

The stakes were high. Rodney knew that if the colonies voted to fight, it would mean a long, hard war with much suffering. But if they did not fight, the king would keep making unfair laws. His voice had to be heard in Philadelphia. He had to be there in time.

Tiny Delaware had once been a part of the great Pennsylvania colony, but it had separated to form its own state. Now it had sent three men to the Continental Congress. Rodney, McKean, and Read were all good friends. But Read was against American independence. If Rodney could not get to Congress in time to vote, McKean would vote yes, but his vote would be canceled out by Read's "no" vote. There would be a tie among Delaware's representatives, and that would make it harder for the cause of independence to win.

The country shall be independent, and we will be satisfied with nothing short of it.

John Adams

Terribly tired and coughing from the dust, Caesar Rodney rode on. He had been a young man when the cancer appeared. It had spread from beneath his eye and down his nose. Perhaps it was because of this that there was never a painting made of him. John Adams of Massachusetts said Rodney was "...the oddest looking man in the world; he is tall, thin, and slender as a reed, pale; his face is not bigger than a large apple, yet there is a sense and fire, spirit, wit and humor in his countenance."[7] However, it was Rodney's character that stood out.

Battle of Bunker Hill, by Howard Pyle, c.1897 (PD-Art).

Now a thunderstorm darkened the sky, and rain came pounding down. Rodney was soon soaked to the skin, but it gave some relief from the July heat. At least, he thought, it turned the dust into mud that would not make him cough. He wished he had been able to go to England. Doctors there could have helped him with his cancer. Instead, he was driving as fast as he could to sign his own death warrant.

Death would be the result if the colonies fought England and lost. All the men who had led the colonies to defy the king would be tried and possibly hanged as traitors. The danger stopped some representatives from supporting American independence.

One of these was John Dickinson of Pennsylvania. Dickinson was a true patriot. He had written a pamphlet titled *Letters from a Farmer in Pennsylvania*. It had been an attack on the Townshend Acts, which placed taxes on tea, lead, paint, and other products. Dickinson believed the king was wrong, but he also believed declaring independence would bring disaster to the colonies. The British would invade by the thousands, and there would be blood, suffering, and death everywhere. Dickinson believed the colonies were not strong enough to fight mighty England.

Portrait of John Dickinson, by Charles Willson Peale, 1780 (PD-US).

Dickinson reminded his fellow colonists of things they already knew. America had no navy and only a ragtag militia for an army. They did not have enough guns, cannons, or gunpowder. They were not trained to fight together. They had no money for supplies.

Wherefore seeing we also are compassed about with so great a cloud of witnesses, let us lay aside every weight, and the sin which doth so easily beset us, and let us run with patience the race that is set before us …

Hebrews 12:1

America would not just be fighting England. The king would hire the fierce Hessian soldiers from Germany. He would pay the Indians to attack American settlements. He had a great army and the most powerful navy on earth. The patriots would have to fight their own neighbors as well, for many colonists were Tories.

Finally, Dickinson sat down. Men looked at each other, wondering who could answer Dickinson's arguments. He had been a convincing speaker. Several representatives looked toward John Adams. Would he speak?[8]

Hessian troops in British pay in the US war of independence, by C. Ziegler After Conrad Gessner, 1799 (PD-Art).

John Adams

WHAT JOHN ADAMS SAID

Adams stood. He was not a tall man like Washington. He did not have Washington's commanding ways. But he was brilliant, and he was a great speaker. He had been the lawyer defending the British soldiers after the Boston Massacre. Even though most of his neighbors thought the redcoats had done wrong, Adams had convinced the jury that the soldiers had been attacked by a mob throwing rocks, snowballs, and chunks of ice. Greatly outnumbered, Adams argued, the redcoats probably had no way to defend themselves but with their muskets. Adams won the case.

Now he stood in front of the Continental Congress and used all his wisdom for the cause of independence. As the storm battering Caesar Rodney shoved its dark clouds into Philadelphia, Adams reminded his neighbors of the king's abuses. He told them that the patriot militiamen had passed the trial of fire in the French and Indian War. He said they would fight to defend their homes and families. Perhaps he said to the whole Congress what he had told his friend, Benjamin Rush: that they would win their freedom if they trusted in God and confessed their sins.[9]

Thomas Jefferson later wrote that Adams "came out with a power of thought and expression that moved us from our seats."[10]

Someone suggested a trial vote to see where the delegates stood at present. Starting with New Hampshire, each colony's representatives gave their votes. When Georgia submitted the last vote, nine colonies had voted for independence. Pennsylvania and South Carolina still held out. New York's delegates did not vote because they did not know the wishes of their assembly. Delaware could not vote because its two delegates disagreed. If only Rodney would come, their tie could be broken.

Adams, Franklin, and others talked to the delegates from Pennsylvania and South Carolina, desperately hoping to persuade them to change their votes. They hoped that every one of the colonies would vote for independence. It would take unity among all of them to survive a war with England.

Meanwhile, Rodney had traded his buggy for a horse during the night. Riding quickly through the rough roads, he had felt his legs whipped and slashed by unseen branches and briars. His horse had slipped and slid at one moment and struggled through deep mud the next. Tired, sick, and soaked to the skin, the patriot drove on. He had to arrive in time to vote for freedom.

Thomas Jefferson

The sunrise was hidden by the storm clouds, but finally the sky grew light. On galloped Rodney, so weary he could barely stay in the saddle. The morning passed and afternoon came. Had they already voted? Was his ride for nothing? Finally, the roofs of Philadelphia came into sight through the rain and mist.

The speech by Adams had convinced the delegates from South Carolina. They changed their vote to yes. The Pennsylvania delegates listened to Franklin and Payne. Dickinson and fellow Pennsylvanian Robert Morris were not in favor of voting yes, but they saw that nearly all the other men disagreed. They decided to be absent for the final vote so there would be unity.

Now Delaware had to make up its mind.[11]

Hoofs clattered on the cobblestones in front of the state house. Thomas McKean looked out. Rodney had come! He hurried to meet him, and the two walked into the meeting room together. Rodney was worn out and spattered with mud. He took his seat, and the assembly got ready for a final vote. When Delaware was called for, Read voted no, and McKean voted yes.

When his name was called, Caesar Rodney wearily rose to his feet.[12]

The tie was broken. Delaware had made up her mind.

Though it would be a week before New York's government would allow its delegates to cast a vote for independence, every man in the room knew that America would fight for freedom. It was July 2, 1776. Two days later, on July 4, the Continental Congress officially adopted the Declaration of Independence. It was to be America's official birthday.

Caesar Rodney had done what seemed impossible for a weary, sick man. He had reached Philadelphia by an all-night ride to cast his vote for freedom. His illness continued, and he died in 1784. He lived long enough to see his country win the war for independence. The United States of America was born.[15]

Endurance: It wasn't enough for Mr. Rodney to start out on his 80-mile race to Philadelphia. If he had stopped before he reached Congress, his efforts would have been wasted. God gave him enough endurance to finish his very hard job.

Robert Morris

"I arrived in Congress (tho detained by thunder and rain) time enough to give my voice in the matter of independence . . . We have now got through the whole of the declaration and ordered it to be printed so that you will soon have the pleasure of seeing it."[13]

Caesar Rodney
in a letter to his brother Thomas

In Washington, DC, near the Washington Monument, there is a memorial park and lagoon honoring the signers of the Declaration of Independence. One of the 56 granite blocks there bears the name of Caesar Rodney. In 1934, a statue of Rodney was placed in Statuary Hall in the United States Capitol building. A large horseback statue of Caesar Rodney, picturing his famous ride, looms over Rodney Square in downtown Wilmington, Delaware. An image of him on horseback appears on the U.S. Delaware state silver quarter.

———— " ————

I arrived in Congress (tho detained by thunder and rain) time enough to give my voice in the matter of independence … We have now got through the whole of the declaration and ordered it to be printed so that you will soon have the pleasure of seeing it.

Caesar Rodney
(Rodney's own account of his dramatic ride and the Declaration of Independence is contained in a letter he wrote to his brother Thomas.)

———— " ————

SYBIL LUDINGTON

Another famous rider of the Revolutionary War was a 16-year-old girl named Sybil Ludington. This Connecticut girl was the oldest of 12 children. Her father was an officer in the militia. On April 25, 1777, the British general Tryon attacked Danbury, Connecticut, with 2,000 soldiers. He marked the homes of Tories with chalk so they would not be harmed. He was after military supplies that the patriots had stored in Danbury.

When the redcoats found the supplies, they found barrels of rum. Instead of destroying it, they decided to drink it. Soon drunken soldiers were all over town, robbing and burning homes.

Storytime with Uncle Rick
Fight for Freedom

Statue of Sybil Ludington on Gleneida Avenue in Carmel, New York by Anna Hyatt Huntington.

Mr. Ludington was called to gather the militia. He sent riders out to tell the men to assemble. His daughter Sybil volunteered to be one of the riders. She mounted her horse, Star, and set off in the twilight on a ride that would take her on a 40 mile route. She rode twice as far as Paul Revere!

Sybil carried a stick as she rode. She used it to beat on doors to wake up militiamen who were sound asleep in bed. At one point, she was stopped by a robber. Sybil hit him with her stick, and he soon let her go. It was morning before Sybil got home.

The militiamen assembled as quickly as they could. They were not in time to save Danbury, but they attacked the British as they left the town and punished them for their drunken vandalism.[16]

CAESAR RODNEY'S RIDE[17]

In that soft mid-land where the breezes bear
The North and South on the genial air,
Through the county of Kent on affairs of State,
Rode Caesar Rodney, the delegate.

Burley and big, and bold and bluff,
In his three-cornered hat and coat of snuff,
A foe to King George and the English State,
Was Caesar Rodney, the delegate.

Into Dover village he rode apace,
And his kinsfolk knew from his anxious face,
It was matter grave that brought him there,
To the counties three upon the Delaware.

"Money and men we must have," he said,
"Or the Congress fails and our cause is dead,
Give us both and the King shall not work his will,
We are men, since the battle of Bunker Hill."

Comes a rider swift on a panting bay;
"Ho, Rodney, ho! you must save the day,
For the Congress halts at a deed so great,
And your voice alone may decide its fate."

Answered Rodney then; "I will ride with speed;
It is Liberty's stress; it is Freedom's need."
"When stands it?" "To-night." "not a moment to spare,
But ride like the wind from Delaware."

"Ho, saddle the black! I've but half a day,
And the Congress sits eighty miles away —
But I'll be in time, if God grants me grace,
To shake my fist in King George's face."

He is up; he is off! and the black horse flies
On the northward road ere the "God-speed" dies,

It is gallop and spur, as the leagues they clear,
And the Clustering mile-stones move a-rear.

It is two of the clock; and the fleet hoofs fling
The Fieldsboro dust with a clang and a cling,
It is three; and he gallops with slack rein where
The road winds down to the Delaware.

Four; and he spurs into New Castle town,
From his panting steed he gets him down
"A fresh one quick! and not a moment's wait!"
And off speeds Rodney, the delegate.

It is five; and the beams of the western sun
Tinge the spires of Wilmington, gold and dun;
Six; and the dust of Chester street
Flies back in a cloud from his courser's feet.

It is seven; the horse-boat, broad of beam,
At the Schuylkill ferry crawls over the stream
And at seven fifteen by the Rittenhouse clock,
He flings his rein to the tavern jock.

The Congress is met; the debate's begun,
And Liberty lags for the vote of one
When into the hall, not a moment late,
Walks Caesar Rodney, the delegate.

Not a moment late! and that half day's ride
Forwards the world with a mighty stride;
For the act was passed; ere the midnight stroke
O'er the Quaker City its echoes woke.

At Tyranny's feet was the gauntlet flung;
"We are free!" all the bells through the colonies rung,
And the sons of the free may recall with pride,
The day of Delegate Rodney's ride.

Benjamin Rush

CHAPTER 7

BENJAMIN RUSH

The Good Doctor

LEARNING TO BE A DOCTOR

Benjamin Rush was a Christmas Eve baby, born on December 24, 1745. His father was a farmer in Pennsylvania. His father died when Benjamin was only six years old.

What was his mother to do now? She had several growing children in her home and no husband. But Mrs. Rush was not a person to give up. She moved her family to Philadelphia and started a grocery store.

Mrs. Rush intended not only to feed her children, but also for her sons to get a good education. When Benjamin turned nine years old, she sent him to live with her brother, the Reverend Dr. Findlay. Dr. Findlay was the principal of an academy in Nottingham, Maryland.[2]

Benjamin learned and grew in Dr. Findlay's home and school. Very early in his life he learned to fear and love God. He was also taught the importance of hard work and good habits. He learned to take care of his responsibilities. This early training made him a good and steady man all through his life.

Dr. Findlay loved Benjamin, and he was a good teacher. He was a dedicated Christian. He believed in training boys for this world and for heaven. In everything he taught them, he reminded them of their duty to God.

We profess to be republicans, and yet we neglect the only means of establishing and perpetuating our republican forms of government, that is, the universal education of our youth in the principles of Christianity, by means of the Bible; for this divine book, above all others favors that equality among mankind, that respect for just laws.[1]

Benjamin Rush

Benjamin returned to Philadelphia in 1769. He set up an office as a doctor. He treated many poor people. Many of them could not afford to pay a doctor, so he treated them for free. Later, he started a special medical clinic just for poor people. He also helped with the beginning of medical care for animals. Today, animal doctors are called veterinarians.

Portrait of Benjamin Rush, Charles Willson Peale, 1783 (PD-Art).

Benjamin was a good student. He went to college while he was still a boy and graduated when he was only 15. After college, he wanted to be a doctor. He found a respected doctor in Philadelphia and studied under him for six years. Then, in 1766, he went to England for more medical training.

While in England, the young doctor had an unusual mission. The College of New Jersey was looking for a new president. They asked Benjamin Rush for help. They wanted to hire John Witherspoon for the job. Witherspoon was a Presbyterian minister in Scotland. They needed someone to talk to him and his wife. The leaders of the college asked him to visit John Witherspoon and ask him if he would come to New Jersey.

Dr. Witherspoon was interested in going to the college, but there was a problem. His wife had heard terrible stories of Indian attacks in America. She was afraid to go there. Benjamin explained how things really were in New Jersey, and finally Mrs. Witherspoon said she was willing to go. Dr. Witherspoon became famous as a preacher and teacher. He taught many of the Founding Fathers in the college. The school's name was later changed to Princeton University.

A Wedding and a War

Benjamin Rush married a young lady named Julia Stockton. Her father, Richard Stockton, was a famous lawyer and judge. He would one day be a member of the Continental Congress. He would sign the Declaration of Independence, just as Benjamin Rush would.

Julia was only 16 years old when she married Rush, but the two were happy together. They had 13 children.[4]

Benjamin Rush knew a man named Thomas Paine. Paine would be a very important man in the War of Independence because of papers that he wrote. Benjamin encouraged him to write a piece called *Common Sense*. That paper encouraged people to be brave in resisting the British king. Millions of copies of *Common Sense* were printed and sold. Many people decided to fight for freedom after reading it.

Rush was one of nine men who represented Pennsylvania in the Continental Congress. He was also a good friend of John Adams of Massachusetts. He signed the Declaration of Independence on August 2, 1776.

During the War of Independence, Dr. Rush was a surgeon in the continental army. He was nearly captured by the British while treating some wounded soldiers. He later wrote important papers about hospitals, army diseases, and the effects of the war on the army and the citizens.

He took care of wounded soldiers after the battles of Brandywine and Princeton. The British allowed him to cross their lines to treat wounded men in British territory.

In 1787, after the war was over, Rush worked hard to get people in Pennsylvania to vote for the U.S. Constitution. He believed it was a great document. He said the federal government it created was a "masterpiece of human wisdom."[6]

Julia Stockton (Mrs. Benjamin Rush), by Charles Willson Peale, 1776 (PD-Art).

THE DISEASE AND THE FAITHFUL DOCTOR

In August of 1793, a dark cloud of danger came over Philadelphia. A terrible disease called yellow fever spread through the city. Dr. Rush identified the first case. The other doctors of the city asked Rush to make a plan to fight the disease. He wrote a list of rules to help people keep from getting sick and to treat the disease. The rules were published in the newspaper so everyone could read them and know what to do.

One of the rules he wrote said that people should not visit a person who was sick with yellow fever. When people read that rule, they decided they should get as far from the sick people as possible. They started leaving town. Soon, hundreds of wagons loaded with children and household goods were passing through the streets. Everyone was afraid. They knew that many people who got yellow fever died. It was hard to cure.

Rush wrote to his wife. He said, "I have advised all my families to leave the city if they can. The only way to keep from getting the disease is to flee from it."[7]

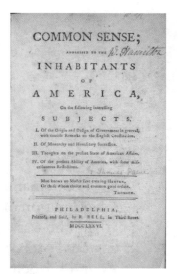

Cover of Common Sense, the pamphlet, by Thomas Paine, 1776 (PD-US).

Benjamin Rush, by Charles Willson Peale, date unknown (PD-Art).

Walking through the town, it was hard to find a smiling face. All through the streets were signs of the disease. A person could walk for hundreds of yards without meeting anyone except for looking for a doctor or someone to bury a dead family member. There were wagons and carts carrying dead bodies to graves.

Dr. Rush would not leave the sick people. Even though his life was at risk, he stayed in Philadelphia and fought for a cure. He studied medical books looking for anything that might help. He found a book written more than 50 years earlier that had an idea for a cure. Dr. Rush took the idea and began to mix a medicine.

He gave the medicine to five sick people. Four of them got well. At last, he had found a medicine that would help. He told other people about the medicine, and others began to mix it up and give it to the sick. Still, there was no way to keep people from getting yellow fever in the first place. Thousands still had the disease, and many more were about to get it.

Dr. Rush had some medical students who helped him treat the sick. He also had a beloved preacher, Rev. Richard Allen. All of them worked very hard. In one week, Dr. Rush visited over 100 patients every day. For many weeks, he seldom had time to sit down for a meal. Sometimes he kept on treating patients while he ate. He was so busy in his office that one day 47 people were turned away before 11 a.m.

Many doctors had left the city because they were afraid of getting yellow fever from their patients. There were not enough doctors to care for all the sick people. At one time, there were only three doctors left in town to care for 6,000 people.[8]

Some of Benjamin Rush's friends tried to get him to leave the city. They reminded him that he could help no one if he was dead. But he replied that God had placed him in that city for that time. He said he would not abandon the post that God had given him. He was willing to give up his pleasures and his rest. He was even willing to give up his life for his patients.[9]

> Dr. Benjamin Rush had signed the Declaration of Independence knowing that if he was captured by the British, he would probably be hanged. He stayed in Philadelphia to treat sick people, even though he knew he could catch the disease and die. Yet he would not leave the job God had given him to do. What a great example to you and me!

In those days, people did not know that yellow fever is carried by mosquitoes. When a mosquito bites someone who has the disease, it can carry it to the next person it bites. When the frost killed most of the mosquitoes, the yellow fever died out as well.

Benjamin Rush was a hero in Philadelphia. His fame spread across American and even across the sea. He received gifts from foreign kings. But he still remained humble. He still looked for ways to serve others. And what did Benjamin Rush think of the Bible?

He said: "The Bible contains more knowledge necessary to man in his present state than any other book in the world."[10]

Rush was a leader in the fight to end slavery. He helped start two colleges. He served as treasurer of the U.S. Mint. He also taught medicine at the University of Pennsylvania. He taught over 3,000 students in his lifetime.

At the age of 67, Benjamin Rush died after being sick for only a few days. He was mourned by the entire country.[11]

> *Let nothing be done through strife or vainglory; but in lowliness of mind let each esteem other better than themselves.*
>
> Phillipians 2:3

YELLOW FEVER

Finally, Rush did catch the yellow fever. He got very sick. He had a dream one night while he was ill. He dreamed that a crowd of people had gathered in front of his house. They were begging him to come and help their families and friends. He started to turn away, but a woman rushed up to him. She cried out, "Oh, Doctor! Don't turn away from the poor! You were doomed to die of the yellow fever; but the prayers of the poor were heard by heaven. Our prayers have saved your life!" He got well again and went right back to treating every sick person, rich or poor.

(CC BY 4.0)

The yellow fever swept on through town in September and October. Over 1,000 people died in the first 12 days of October. Then, a heavy frost came and the disease miraculously stopped spreading.[12]

Storytime with Uncle Rick

Fight for Freedom

James Armistead

CHAPTER 8

BLACK PATRIOTS

Forging the Way for Freedom

WENTWORTH CHESWELL AND ANOTHER FAMOUS RIDE

Most Americans know about Paul Revere's famous ride. Many of them know that William Dawes also rode for Concord that night in hopes that at least one of the men would reach Jonas Clark's house. There they would warn John Hancock and Sam Adams that the British were coming to arrest them for treason.

But not many people know that another rider headed out in a different direction that night. He was Wentworth Cheswell, an African American patriot of New Hampshire.

Wentworth Cheswell was the grandson of a slave named Richard Cheswell. Richard had gained his freedom in 1717. He became the first African American to own property in the colony of New Hampshire.

Richard married and had a son whom he named Hopestill. Hopestill grew up and became a house builder. He worked hard and had a successful business. Because he did good work, many wealthy people called him to build homes for them. He built a house for John Paul Jones and another for the Reverend Samuel Langdon, a patriot pastor and the president of Harvard University.

When Hopestill's son was born, he was named Wentworth after colonial governor Benning Wentworth.

Wentworth was the first African American elected to public office. In 1768, Wentworth was elected town constable — the first of many offices he held throughout his life. Two years later in 1770, he was elected town selectman (the selectmen were considered the "town fathers" of a community). Other town offices in which he served included seven years as auditor, six years as assessor, two years as coroner, seven years as town moderator (presiding over town meetings), and 12 years as justice of the peace. For half a century — including every year from 1768 until 1817 — Wentworth held some position in local government.

At the age of 21, Wentworth had already become an established and educated property owner and a strong member in his local church, even holding a church pew.

Benning Wentworth, by Joseph Blackburn, 1760 (PD-Art).

Because Wentworth's father was able to pay for a good education, Wentworth went to the academy at Byfield, Massachusetts. The school was 30 miles from his home, but young Wentworth liked learning. He studied many subjects in books. He also learned to swim and to ride horses well.

Wentworth later became a teacher. He married Mary Davis and had 13 children. By the time he was 21 years old, he was an important man in the community. He was educated, owned property, and was a leader in his church.

Wentworth was also a patriot leader. The town elected him to the Committee of Safety. His job was to carry important messages between leaders and towns. It was at this time that he took his midnight ride.[1]

In April of 1776, Wentworth signed an important paper along with 162 other Newmarket men. This was the Association Test. By signing, Wentworth promised to fight against the British if the colonies declared independence. In 1777, he joined the American army in the Light Horse Volunteers.

Cheswell's company marched 250 miles to Saratoga, New York. There they joined General Horatio Gates. They fought hard against British General Burgoyne and won the first American victory in a major battle.

Proverbs 20:6 tells us: "Most men will proclaim every one his own goodness: but a faithful man who can find?" Wentworth Cheswell was a faithful man. His neighbors knew that they could depend on him to do his job and to do it honestly. That is why they kept giving him more and more authority as a community leader. They knew they could trust him.

Later, Wentworth was elected to help write the first state constitution of New Hampshire. He also helped to start the town library. He was the town's unofficial historian as well. He recorded stories of Newmarket's early days and wrote articles about things that were happening in town at that time.

Wentworth Cheswell died of typhus fever at the age of 71. He left a legacy as a patriot, a teacher, a historian, a church leader, a judge, and a father of the community. His life was one of honor and service.[2]

Wentworth served as Newmarket's unofficial historian, copying town records from 1727, including the records of various church meetings. He also recorded old stories of the town, as well as its current events. In addition, he investigated and wrote about many artifacts and relics he discovered in the region around Newmarket. He is considered the state's first archeologist.

In 1801, Wentworth helped start the first town library "to preserve and disseminate useful knowledge and virtue." He had become a schoolteacher in 1767. In 1776, he was elected as one of five men to regulate and oversee the schools of Newmarket.

JAMES ARMISTEAD LAFAYETTE — DOUBLE SPY

James Armistead was a slave when the Revolutionary War began. He wanted to fight with the Americans against the British. He asked his owner, William Armistead, for permission to join the army. His master agreed, so James enlisted to serve under the Marquis de Lafayette, a young French general.

James lived in Virginia. There were two British generals attacking in Virginia. They were the British general Cornwallis and the American traitor Benedict Arnold. Lafayette needed to be clever in order to fight well. He needed to know as much as possible about the British plans. That way he could be prepared for anything the enemy might try to do.

He decided to send a spy into the British army. Who would be a good man for the job? It would have to be someone who would not be suspected. He needed a man who did not appear to be a patriot. James Armistead said he would be willing to go.

Continental Army general Horatio Gates, c.1793 (PD-Art).

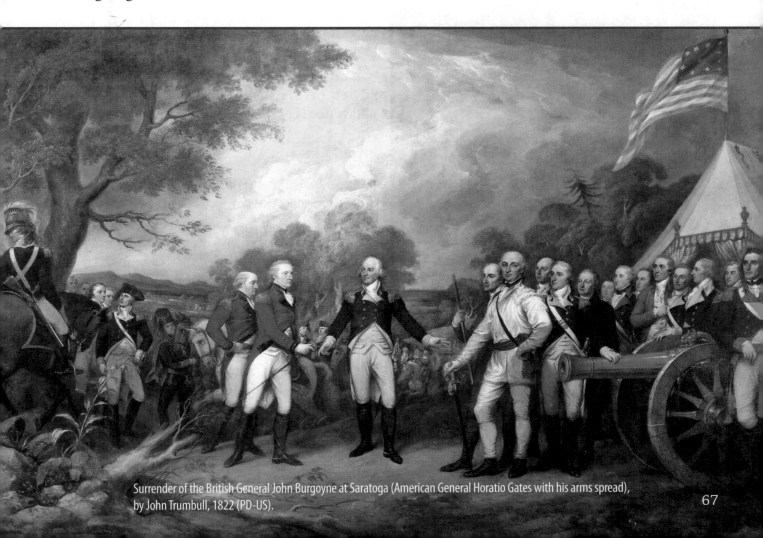

Surrender of the British General John Burgoyne at Saratoga (American General Horatio Gates with his arms spread), by John Trumbull, 1822 (PD-US).

Lafayette dispatched Armistead to the camp of the patriot-turned-traitor Benedict Arnold (then a British general). He posed as an escaped slave looking for work. Arnold accepted Armistead and allowed him to work in the camp. His work brought him around other British generals, including British Commander-in-Chief Lord Cornwallis. Armistead obtained vital information about British plans and troop movements, which he reported to General Lafayette.

Lafayette thought James was perfect. He could enter the enemy camp pretending to be a runaway slave looking for work. If the British would give him a job, he could listen when the leaders talked about their plans. Then he could send messages to the Americans.

James traveled to the army of Benedict Arnold and found jobs to do in the camp. Somehow, he won Arnold's confidence. Because James was a native of Virginia and knew the territory, Arnold gave James the job of guiding British troops as they traveled through the countryside.

As Arnold grew to trust James more and more, he asked James to spy on the Americans and bring back information. James was delighted! Now he could freely pass from the American camp to the British camp with passes from both armies. When he heard what Arnold planned to do next, he would simply go to the American camp and report to General Lafayette. Then he would take information about American plans back to Arnold — but of course, the information was false.

When Arnold returned to the north in 1781, James went to the camp of General Cornwallis and played the same trick there. He moved between British camps often. The officers paid him no attention as they talked about their plans right in front of him. Armistead would sneak away to a hidden place and write reports. Then he would pass the reports to other spies, and they would deliver them to the patriots.

The information that James Armistead provided was a great help to the patriots. It was a great help to Lafayette and General Washington in winning the battle of Yorktown. That was the last great

Portrait of Gilbert Motier the Marquis De La Fayette as a lieutenant general, 1791, by Joseph-Désiré Court, 1834 (PD-Art).

land battle of the war. Cornwallis surrendered to General Washington. When the British king saw that Cornwallis' army was defeated, he agreed to talk about ending the war. In 1783, a treaty was signed, and America was free.

But James Armistead was not free. Virginia had passed a law that said all slaves who were soldiers in the patriot army would be set free after the war. But James was not a soldier. He was a spy.

But James' owner, William Armistead, was a member of the Virginia House of Delegates. With his help, James petitioned the Virginia government to set him free. General Lafayette wrote a testimonial of the fine service James had given in the war. In January 1787, Virginia made James Armistead a free man. Then James added Lafayette's name in honor of the General. He became James Armistead Lafayette.

In 1824, General Lafayette returned to America. He made a tour of all 24 states. Huge crowds met him everywhere. America was thankful for the help of Lafayette and France. In Virginia, he visited Washington's grave and made a speech to the House of Delegates. Passing through the streets of Richmond, he saw James in the crowd. Quickly stopping his carriage, he ran to embrace his old friend.

James Armistead Lafayette got married, had several children, and became a successful farmer. He died on August 9, 1830.[3]

Statue of Lord Charles Cornwallis, engraving by George Dawe; statue by John Bacon Sr. and Jr., 1803 (PD-Art).

> But James Armistead was not free. Virginia had passed a law that said all slaves who were soldiers in the patriot army would be set free after the war. But James was not a soldier. He was a spy.

One day, James learned that the British navy was moving Cornwallis and his troops to Yorktown. He quickly passed on that information to Lafayette and Washington. They gathered the American forces at Yorktown. After the British troops landed, their ships unsuspectingly departed from Chesapeake Bay. Then the Americans attacked the British, and the French navy blocked the bay. Now the British navy could not come back to help Cornwallis. The British were defeated at the Battle of Yorktown because the British ships could not come back with extra soldiers or supplies. They finally surrendered. James Armistead had risked his life to get information that helped end the War of Independence.

Front page to Phillis Wheatley's *Poems on Various Subjects...*, by Scipio Moorhead, 1773 (PD-US).

PHILLIS WHEATLEY — PATRIOT POET

Phillis Wheatley was born in Senegal, Africa, in 1753. She was only eight years old when she was kidnapped and sold as a slave. A ship took her to Boston. There she was purchased by a wealthy tailor, Mr. John Wheatley. Phillis was trained as a personal servant for Mr. Wheatley's wife, Susannah.

But Mrs. Wheatley did not treat Phillis as a servant. She loved Phillis and considered her a daughter. The Wheatleys' daughter, Mary, treated her like a sister. The two girls grew up together, happily working in the home as a team.

Phillis was a quick learner. Susannah and Mary both taught her the Scriptures and how to live a moral life. Within 16 months, Phillis was reading English so well that she could read the most difficult parts of the Bible easily. Mary also taught Phillis astronomy, geography, history, and the English poets. Phillis was so bright at learning hard things and so good at talking with others that the educated people of Boston said she was a child genius.

Phillis started writing poetry when she was 13. Three years later, she wrote a poem about the great evangelist George Whitefield. She admired Whitefield's godly life and powerful ministry. She would become known as America's first African American female poet.

In 1771, Phillis was baptized as a member into the famous Old South Church. This was unusual. It was a rule that slaves would not be baptized into the church.

In 1773, Phillis began to have serious health problems. The doctors said she needed a long sea voyage to get better. So kind Mrs. Wheatley arranged to have Phillis set free. She traveled to England, where she was invited to meet British royalty.

Phillis had returned to America because she heard that Mrs. Wheatley was in bad health. Her adopted mother died soon after Phillis returned. She continued to write poetry.

"But as for you, ye thought evil against me; *but* God meant it unto good, to bring to pass, as *it is* this day, to save much people alive" (Genesis 50:20).

Remember when Joseph's brothers sold him into slavery in the Book of Genesis in the Bible? Many years later when they came to him for food, Joseph realized that although his brothers had done wrong to him, God had used all the experiences for the good of all his people. Remember that God uses what seems to be bad things at the time for our good at a later date. You can trust God to work out what is best for you. You can learn to trust Him as Joseph did.

Kidnapping and slavery did not make Phillis bitter. She considered it God's way of bringing her to where she could hear the gospel. She wrote in a poem:

'Twas mercy brought me from my Pagan land
Taught my benighted soul to understand
That there's a God, that there's a Savior too:
Once I redemption neither sought nor knew.
Some view our sable race with scornful eye,
"Their color is a diabolic dye."
Remember, Christians, Negroes black as Cain,
May be refin'd, and join th' angelic train.[4]

Phillis died at only 30 years of age. She had known many sorrows, but she did not complain. She believed that God meant it all for her good.

For generations after her death, many people still loved reading Phillis Wheatley's poetry. She is still known as a shining example of a great poet, a gracious lady, and a devout Christian.[5]

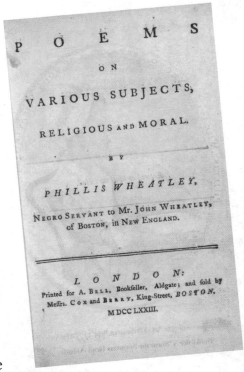

Title page: Poems on various subjects, religious and moral, London: 1773, by Phillis Wheatley (PD-US).

His Excellency George Washington

In 1775, Phillis was still away from America. She heard about the siege of Boston and the new American army that was forming. She wrote a letter of encouragement to General Washington, the new Commander in Chief. She also sent him a poem she had written to honor him:

His Excellency George Washington

Thee, first in place and honors, — we demand

The grace and glory of thy martial band

Fam'd for thy valor, for thy virtues more,

Here every tongue thy guardian aid implore!

Proceed, great chief, with virtue on thy side,

Thy every action let the goddess guide.

A crown, a mansion, and a throne that shine,

With gold unfading, Washington, be thine ...[6]

General Washington was touched by the poem. When Phillis came back to America, he invited her to his camp at Cambridge to honor her with his staff officers.

Morgan's rifleman

CHAPTER 9

DANIEL MORGAN

From Teamster to Major General

NOT AFRAID TO FIGHT

It Was July 3, 1775. A tall man sat straight and dignified in his saddle. He surveyed the troops gathered under the great elm tree on Cambridge Common near Boston. George Washington was officially taking command of the patriot army. The siege of Boston was under way. Washington was living in the fine old mansion known as the Craigie House. Many famous patriots would visit that house.

There were some also some bad men in the group that passed through Craigie. Horatio Gates, a selfish general who could not be trusted, was a visitor. So was General Charles Lee of Virginia. He was restless, adventurous, and a bit lazy. He would soon fail General Washington miserably in the Battle of Monmouth. The great general, who very seldom lost his temper, would become raging mad at Lee. Finally, there was young Benedict Arnold. He would win Washington's admiration through his courage in battle. But later he would be known as the man who went over to the enemy.

But there were far more great men gathering at Craigie. Rough and ready John Stark came from the granite hills of New Hampshire. He would be the hero of the fight at Bennington. From Rhode Island came the Quaker Nathaniel Greene. He had started out working as a blacksmith but would become one of the greatest generals of the war.

Portrait of Daniel Morgan, by Charles Willson Peale, c.1794 (PD-US).

In Dan Morgan's day, people knew that honesty is very important. Thomas Jefferson said, "Honesty is the first chapter in the book of wisdom." Ben Franklin said, "Honesty is the best policy."[1] It is just as important today.

Major General Charles Lee

Also in this honored group was Daniel Morgan, a Virginian. We know little of his background. He seldom spoke about his family. It was said that he came from a Welsh family and was born in New Jersey in about 1737.

Morgan was not educated. He could barely read or write, even when he was a young man of 17. He did not speak English well, and he had not been taught fine manners.

But Daniel was eager to learn. By the time he was 19, he had found time to study. He had grown to over six feet tall, and his muscles were very strong. He had a brave and honest heart. His word could be counted on. People began to see that this young man just might become someone special.

Morgan had enlisted to fight in the French and Indian War. There was bitter fighting in the Ohio Valley. When Daniel heard of it, he joined the army right away. He was given the job of driving a wagon. Even then, Daniel began to make a name for himself.

There was a bully in Morgan's company. He was a big, strong man who was a good boxer. He gave the captain of the company trouble with his brawling and angry manners. The captain of the company knew this man had to be stopped. He decided he had to fight the bully and whip him. It would not be easy. But at the next place where the wagon train stopped, the captain stepped out to meet the bully.

Daniel Morgan stopped him, trying to tell his boss not to fight the man, insisting that it would disgrace the whole company if their captain lost the fight, but if Daniel fought it would be okay whether he won or lost.[2]

The captain was a man who was willing to handle his own trouble. But he agreed to let Daniel handle the fight, which he won.

After the defeat of General Braddock by the French and their Indian friends, the Indians went on a rampage against the English settlers. They were killing people of all ages, burning cabins, and scalping. Something had to be done.

A regiment of 1,000 men was raised with young George Washington as its colonel. It was not a very big force to guard 250 miles of frontier border.

General Benedict Arnold, by Thomas Hart, 1776 (PD-US).

Daniel Morgan was a wagon driver in this regiment. His job was to carry supplies from fort to fort along the frontier. Nearly every day brought many dangers. It was a hard, tough life, but it made Daniel Morgan a strong man. He mastered the rifle and the tomahawk. He became expert in Native American warfare. That knowledge would serve him well in the years ahead.

One day, a British officer got angry at Daniel. He struck him with the flat side of his sword. Daniel knocked him down with an iron fist. Daniel was tried and convicted of striking an officer. He was tied up and given 100 lashes with a heavy leather whip. Again and again, the whip slashed across his bare back. But even that did not finish Daniel Morgan. His wounds healed and he grew tougher than ever. He later joked that there had been a wrong count and that he had only received 99 lashes.

He would remember this unjust punishment. Years afterward, the British and the Americans would be fighting against each other instead of the French. When that time came, Daniel's memories of British cruelty would drive him to fight with determination and courage.

Driving a wagon is not a very exciting job. But God was preparing Daniel Morgan for future work. He grew tough and learned endurance, which made him stronger to endure the hardships ahead in the War of Independence.

DANIEL BECOMES A LEADER

Shortly after this, Daniel was a private serving in the militia. When the French and Indians attacked Fort Winchester, Dan made a name for himself. It was said that he killed four men in four minutes. Daniel never drove an army wagon again.

From that day, Daniel Morgan was known as a born fighter and leader. He was cool in the face of danger. He had good judgment, even in the midst of battle. He also had great influence over the other men. Someone told Governor Dinwiddie that Daniel Morgan should be given a commission in the army as captain. The governor was a little hesitant, since Morgan was a camp boxer and teamster.[3]

But the best men of Virginia encouraged it, so the royal governor of Virginia agreed to commission Daniel Morgan as an ensign. It was not as high as a captain, but it put Daniel Morgan in a place to show what he could do as a leader.

When God saves a person, his or her life changes. That's what happened to Daniel Morgan.

Soon after, Daniel Morgan was in a bloody fight with the French and Indians. He got a terrible wound from a bullet that struck him in the back of the neck and came out through his mouth. It knocked out all his teeth on the left side.

Daniel Morgan knew he was badly wounded, and he suspected he was dying. But he still meant to keep his scalp, so he clung to the neck of his horse and galloped away. He was pursued by a very fast Indian on foot, but the man could not catch him. He threw his tomahawk as he gave up the chase.

For months, Daniel's life seemed to hang in the balance. But finally his tough body healed. As soon as he was strong again, he returned to action. Years later, he would tell the story of the battle and the chase by the Indian warrior.

Image of Morgan's escape.

Finally, the war ended and the settlers lived in peace. Daniel Morgan returned to his farm. He brought with him some bad habits from his days of war making. He was a drinker and a gambler. He loved to fight and was always ready to box or wrestle. Men came from miles around to try their strength against the young giant. Daniel weighed over 200 pounds, and it seemed to be all muscle. But inside his giant body was a tender heart.

Morgan, in his own journal covering his military career, wrote, "we, as an army victorious, formed ourselves into a society, pledging our words of honor to each other to assist our bretheren Boston in case of hostilities should commence."[5]

That big heart was captured by a farmer's daughter named Abigail Bailey. Abigail was a beautiful young woman and a devout Christian. She was just what tough Daniel Morgan needed. Soon they were happily married, and Daniel gladly gave up his wild ways. He stopped drinking and gambling. He left his tavern friends and stayed at home with Abigail. To the day of his death, Daniel Morgan lived a good and God-fearing life.[4]

Daniel and his young bride worked hard and did well. They studied books to learn the things they had missed as children growing up on the frontier. They were blessed with two little daughters. For nine happy years, Dan and his family lived in the joy of a Christian home.

View of the Potomac River from the Mount Vernon plantation, Virginia, by tomf688, 1994 (CC BY-SA 3.0).

DANIEL MORGAN GOES TO WAR AGAIN

But the storm clouds of war were gathering fast. Independence was on the lips of everyone. Events happened one after another. Daniel watched keenly as the country seemed to slide quickly down a slope to war.

After the battles at Lexington and Concord, Congress called for volunteers. Companies were formed from Virginia, Maryland, and Pennsylvania. Daniel Morgan was made a captain five days after the fight at Bunker Hill. Calling for volunteers to join him, Morgan shouted, "Come, boys, who's for the camp before Cambridge?"[6]

It seemed every man in the section was eager to fight with "old Dan." In ten days, he had raised his company of 96 expert riflemen. He marched at their head for the 600 miles to Boston. It was a long, hard journey. But they made it in only 21 days and did not lose a single man along the way.

One day as Daniel's company was marching along, they saw General Washington on his horse. Daniel stopped the march and saluted the famous general. "From the right bank of the Potomac, General!" he shouted.[7]

Then something happened that every man in the company would always remember. General Washington got off his horse. Most officers would just have returned Morgan's salute and ridden on. But George Washington was as humble as he was great. He took time to walk along the line and shake hands with every last man.[8]

Whenever he passed, Washington always stopped to shake hands with them.

We, as an army victorious, formed ourselves into a society, pledging our words of honor to each other to assist our brethren of Boston in case hostilities should commence.

Daniel Morgan

HIS EXCELLENCY GEORGE WASHINGTON

Abigail's faith in God took hold of Daniel. He became a man of prayer. He told the story of how he knelt in the snow just before the attack on the fort of Quebec and prayed. He felt that God gave him the strength to fight. Later, riding across the field after his famous victory at Cowpens, the warrior was seen stopping his horse and praying aloud. Tears streamed down his face as he thanked God for the victory.

Some men might have scoffed at Daniel's prayers, but not those who fought beside him. They noticed that the harder "old Dan" prayed, the sooner they were led to victory. Prayer seemed a good idea when they knew they were about to face death.[9]

Daniel Morgan

CHAPTER 10

DANIEL MORGAN

Sharpshooter

EARLY BATTLES

Late in 1775, Morgan's sharpshooters joined about 1,000 other men to attack the fort at Quebec in Canada. The attack failed, but it was a famous battle. Benedict Arnold had not yet become a traitor. He and Montgomery bravely led the assault. First, Arnold was wounded and carried from the field. Then, Montgomery was killed. Daniel Morgan stepped forward to replace Arnold. He and his men fought well. They forced their way into the city so far that the other Americans could not keep up with them. Finally, Morgan's men were surrounded by the enemy and Daniel had to surrender so his men would not all be killed.

A British officer had noticed Daniel's bravery. He offered Daniel good pay and the rank of colonel if he would leave the American army and fight for the British. Daniel turned down the offer. He felt insulted that any man would think he would desert his country.

After some time, Daniel was released by the British. The Continental Congress made him a colonel in the army. He raised a regiment of men and reported for duty at Morristown in New Jersey in the winter of 1776. Knowing Morgan was an excellent leader and fighter, the army gave him a special force to lead. Five hundred excellent riflemen were selected from and put under his command.

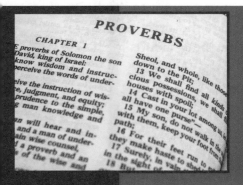

Loyalty means being committed to the welfare of those we serve, even if it costs us our own comfort. Daniel Morgan was a loyal man. Proverbs 20:6 says, "Most men will proclaim their own goodness, but a faithful man who can find?"

Portrait of British General John Burgoyne, by Joshua Reynolds, c.1766 (PD-Art).

He was ordered always to be at the front. He was to watch the enemy closely and report all news of his movements to Washington. They were to harass the British outposts whenever they could.

In the fall of 1777, the British general Burgoyne marched south from Canada. He had with him British, Indian, and Hessian troops. They swept down through the valley of the Hudson. The country was frightened. Washington had to send help, but he needed to keep as many men with him as he could. He sent Daniel Morgan and his riflemen. He knew their straight-shooting rifles would take the place of many ordinary soldiers.

There were two great battles, first at Freeman's Farm and then at Saratoga. In both battles, Morgan's riflemen did great service. Their deadly long rifles chopped up the ranks of redcoat officers, whose red uniforms made them perfect targets. The Hessians were terrified of the sharpshooters as well. They had never seen such perfect shooting. Morgan often said, "The very sight of my riflemen was always enough for the Hessian pickets. They would scamper into their lines as if the devil drove them, shouting in all the English they knew, 'Rebel in de bush, Rebel in de bush!'"[10]

After the surrender, when Burgoyne was introduced to Morgan, he shook his hand warmly. "Sir," he said to Morgan, "you command the finest regiment in the world."[11]

For over a year and a half after Saratoga, Morgan and his men served with Washington's troops, fighting in many small battles. They were constantly attacking enemy outposts. They took part in many picket skirmishes. Because these were not large battles, not much was ever written about them. History has lost track of them.

Just before the battle of Monmouth, Daniel Morgan left the army and went home. He was sick with a painful disease known as sciatica. It had come upon him because of living outdoors so much in all kinds of weather. Also, he was discouraged with the army. He had seen other men promoted to higher jobs that he should have received. He did not like the practice of promoting men just because they had friends in the Continental Congress.

The Death of General Montgomery in the Attack on Quebec, December 31, 1775, by John Trumbull, 1786 (PD-Art).

BACK TO WAR

But in 1780 his fighting blood rose again. He had heard the news of the battle of Camden, where General Horatio Gates had lost a major fight to Cornwallis. He put his personal feelings aside because his country's cause was in trouble. He hurried south, joined the army of Gates, and took his old place as a colonel. He fought in the battle of King's Mountain and showed himself so brave and skillful that the Continental Congress promoted him to the rank of brigadier general.

In January of 1781, there was a battle that was to make Morgan famous. It was called the battle of Cowpens. It was not one of the largest battles of the war, but it was the first battle that Morgan had planned himself. Before, he had always served under other officers. This time, he was the top commander. The battle would go down in history as one of the most brilliant fights the Americans won in the entire war.

Richard Montgomery, by G. R. Hall from painting by Alonzo Chappel, c.1924 (PD-US).

General Nathanael Greene had led 1,100 troops into northern South Carolina. His goal was to keep cut Cornwallis off from the seacoast, where he could get supplies. He sent Morgan and his 1,000 men southwest. They were to threaten the British posts farther from the coast.

Cornwallis did not know what to do. Soon he would have an American army between him and his supply base and another between him and his inland forces. He would not be able to get help from either direction. So he did what Greene had done. He divided his army and sent Colonel Tarleton to crush Morgan.

Tarleton thought he was quite a mighty man. He had won many battles. But the Bible has a warning for men like that: "Pride goeth before destruction, And an haughty spirit before a fall." —Proverbs 16:18

Tarleton was a brutal man. He had ordered his soldiers to kill surrendering patriots. He had burned patriot homes. He had left women and children homeless. He was a bold fighter, and he was sure he could whip Daniel Morgan, the "Old Wagoner."

Portrait of Sir Banastre Tarleton, by Joshua Reynolds, 1782 (PD-Art).

Off galloped Tarleton, full of confidence. He had more men than Morgan. He thought he could quickly catch him and beat him. But Morgan had learned much by fighting under Washington and Greene. He refused to fight Tarleton. He kept retreating until he could find just the right place to arrange his men. He wanted to fight his own way.

What Morgan needed was a place where he would be hard to attack. He also needed a place that would be hard to run away from. Many of his men were militiamen who did not have a lot of battle experience. They might run instead of fighting when the well-trained British redcoats got close.

He finally stopped retreating at a place called Cowpens. This was an area where cattle were often gathered together to be branded. In the back of it was a broad, deep river that would help keep the militia from trying to escape. There was a long, wooded slope in front in the direction from which Tarleton would be coming. Morgan chose the spot carefully.

The night before the battle, the patriot army built campfires and prepared. That evening, General Morgan walked around the camp and visited the men at each fire. He talked to them about the coming battle in his blunt, fatherly way. "Stand by me, boys," he told them, "and the old 'wagoner' will crack his whip for sure over Tarleton tomorrow."[12]

Tarleton was eager to give him his chance. At 3 a.m., he put his army in motion. But even that was not early enough to catch the old rifleman napping. He had given his men a good night's rest and a hearty breakfast. When Tarleton's men arrived at sunrise, they found the patriots ready.

In the skirmish line, Morgan placed 120 men who could shoot a squirrel out of the top of the tallest tree with the first shot. He had Colonel Pickens line up his militia about 300 yards in front of the hill. Across the top of the hill, the veteran Continental soldiers lined up behind the militia. Just over the hill in the rear, he placed his cavalry. The commander of these horse soldiers was Colonel William Washington, a cousin of George Washington. The cavalry was out of sight of the enemy but ready to move quickly at a moment's notice.

The militiamen were ordered to "Be firm, keep cool, fire two volleys at killing distance, then fall back."
Morgan told the regular army soldiers, "Don't lose heart when the militia and skirmishes fall back. 'Tis a part of the plan. Stand firm and fire low. Listen for my turkey call."[13]

THE BATTLE BEGINS

Tarleton had called Morgan's retreat somewhat sullen, stern, and dangerous. His own men were tired from marching all night through the mud. But Tarleton was determined to crush the old wagoner first, then eat breakfast and rest later. He could hardly wait to arrange his lines to attack.

> Morgan was in the habit of using a turkey call, like the ones hunters used to draw turkeys. In the midst of a battle he would blow a loud blast. This was to let his boys know that he was in the battle with them.

The battle began as the British moved forward. The militia fired some well-timed volleys, then moved back behind the regular soldiers. The redcoats thought they were retreating. Tarleton's men gave a wild cheer and started running forward. They were met with a deadly volley from the Continental regulars. They slowed but kept pushing forward. The Continentals dropped back a little to keep their line straight and keep the British from turning their flank.

Then Tarleton hurled all his lines at the patriots. But the veterans stood their ground. They kept reloading and firing steadily. The British lines began to fall apart. Then Morgan saw his chance.

He shouted to Colonel Howard, the commander of the regulars, that they were coming like a mob. Then his men heard the shrieking of the turkey call. The old teamster's voice rang out above the battle noise that one more good fire and the victory would be theirs.[15]

Colonel William Washington at the Battle of Cowpens, by S. H. Gimber, date unknown (PD-US).

Colonel Washington's men galloped into action. Flying their crimson battle flag, they swept around the hill and slammed into the redcoats from the right. At that moment Colonel Howard ordered, "Charge bayonets!" The veterans fired one more volley and charged toward the British lines with their bayonets lowered.

The redcoats were trapped. They had charged ahead into the American line, thinking it would crumble. But it had stood its ground, and now Washington's horsemen were hitting them from the side. It seemed the Americans were everywhere. Soon, 600 redcoats dropped their muskets and surrendered. The rest escaped on horseback. Tarleton was among them, riding in panic.

This untutored son of the frontier was the only general in the American Revolution, on either side, to produce a significant original tactical thought.[16]

John Buchanan
(in *The Road to Guilford Courthouse*)

Nine of Tarleton's cavalry in sight of a troop of four hundred men, design'd by Warrell ; drawn by Barralett ; engraved by D. Edwin, 1814 (PD-US).

AFTER THE BATTLE

Colonel Washington and his troopers wanted to capture Tarleton. Washington got ahead of his men. Tarleton and two of his assistants turned to fight him. Just as one of the assistants was about to strike him with his sword, a trooper rode up and struck the man's arm down with his own blade. Before the other assistant could strike, Washington's bugle boy shot him with a pistol.

Tarleton swung his sword at Washington, but the colonel blocked the blow with his own sword. His blade left a bloody wound on Tarleton's hand. Finally, Tarleton broke away and rode off with his hand bleeding.

The British lost 230 men killed and wounded at Cowpens. The patriots had lost only 73.

But there was more work to do. Morgan knew that Cornwallis would try to crush him before he could get back to Greene's army. He marched hard toward the crossings of the Catawba River. When Cornwallis reached the river, he learned that Morgan had crossed two days before. He was well on his way to join Greene.

Seldom has a battle, in which greater numbers were not engaged, been so important in its consequences as that of Cowpens.[17]

John Marshall
(in *The Life of George Washington*)

Shortly after the Cowpens battle, Morgan had another attack of sciatica. He had to retire from the army and go back home to Virginia. Later that year, Cornwallis invaded Virginia. By then, Morgan had recovered enough to go to war again. Fighting with Lafayette and Mad Anthony Wayne, he helped capture Cornwallis in Yorktown.

Then sciatica struck again and Morgan went home crippled and in pain. He believed he had struck his last blow for liberty.

> After fighting in 50 battles, Daniel Morgan was elected by his neighbors to represent them in Congress.

But his life of service was not over. After fighting in 50 battles, he was elected by his neighbors to represent them in Congress. Today his memory lives on in the north by his statue at the Saratoga monument. In the south, he is remembered with a statue in Spartanburg, South Carolina. America still reveres the memory of "the old wagoner of the Alleghenies," the hero of Cowpens.[18]

IF YOU HAD LOOKED BEHIND YOU

The story is told how two young patriot sisters once reminded Tarleton of his battle with William Washington. Tarleton remarked to one of the sisters that he had heard that Colonel Washington was an ignorant man who could hardly write his name. One sister replied, "Ah, Colonel, you ought to know better." She looked at his wounded hand. "At least you can testify that he knows how to make his mark."[19]

Tarleton told the other sister that he would like to see Colonel Washington. She replied, "If you had looked behind you at the battle of Cowpens, Colonel Tarleton, you would have enjoyed that pleasure."[20]

Storytime with Uncle Rick

Fight for Freedom

Daniel Boone
American Pioneer

CHAPTER II

DANIEL BOONE

Hunter And Pioneer Of Kentucky

ITCHING FEET

At the beginning of the Revolutionary War, the American colonies were on land between the Atlantic Ocean on the east and the Allegheny Mountains on the west. By the end of the war, American territory stretched far beyond the mountains and all the way to the Mississippi River. This story is about a man who helped make that growth happen.

Of all the brave pioneers who explored the land beyond the mountains and made settlements on it, none is more famous than Daniel Boone is. He was born in Pennsylvania in 1735. He cared little for books. He spent most of his time in hunting and fishing. He loved to roam the woods, and he became an expert shot with the rifle. When he was just a small boy, he wandered into the forest a long way from home and built a round hut as a shelter. He would go there for days at a time, camping out with only his rifle and his dog for company. He shot game and cooked it over an open fire. He loved camping alone in the wilderness. This wild, free life prepared him for a future career as a fearless hunter and woodsman.

When Daniel was about 13, his father moved the family to North Carolina. There they settled on the Yadkin River, and Daniel grew into a young man. He

Engraving of Daniel Boone, by Alonzo Chappel, c.1861 (PD-Art).

Daniel and Squire were brave men, but they were not foolish. They moved carefully and quietly through the wilderness, always on guard. They knew there were many dangers in the forest. Proverbs 22:3 says, "A prudent *man* foreseeth the evil, and hideth himself: but the simple pass on, and are punished."

Daniel Boone's Arrival in Kentucky, by Ward Lockwood, 1938 (PD-US).

We were then in a dangerous, helpless situation, exposed daily to perils and death …[1]

Daniel Boone

married Rebecca at the age of 20, and they settled down in a cabin they built far from the other settlers.

Boone was a restless young man. For years, he looked with longing eyes toward the rugged mountains on the west and wondered about the country beyond. It seemed that every day he was more curious about that land. Was there game there? Were the streams full of fish? Were the Indians friendly? Was the land fertile and good for growing crops? He had to find out.

He was about 25 when he headed west from the Yadkin Valley. He explored his way as far as Boone's Creek, which is a branch of the Watauga River. This was in what is now eastern Tennessee. There he shot a bear and carved on a tree: "D. Boone cilled a bar on this tree in the year 1760." Daniel still could not spell his words well, but he knew how to shoot a bear.

Nine years later, Daniel Boone and five other men started out to cross the Alleghany Mountains. For five weeks, the explorers picked their way through the trackless forests. But when they reached Kentucky in June, they were glad they had made the hard trip. Here they found beautiful country with plenty of game, including deer, bear, and great herds of buffalo.

They built a shelter of logs, open on one side. The floor of their cabin was leaves and twigs. But it was enough for these frontiersmen.

Six months after this, Boone and a man named Stewart had a bad scare.

While out hunting, they were captured by Indians. For seven days, the warriors carefully guarded their prisoners. But on the seventh night, they got careless. They had a big feast on some game they had killed. Then they went to sleep. But Boone did not sleep. When he was sure that the Indians were all asleep and there were no guards, he woke Stewart and the two men slipped quietly out of camp. Moving slowly and silently, they snuck farther and farther from the Indian camp. Then they ran like deer and returned to their own camp. They wanted to warn their friends.

But their camp was deserted. Their friends were gone. Had they been killed? Had they given up the wilderness and returned home? Boone and Stewart never found out. They stood looking at the deserted camp and felt alone.

Some weeks later, Daniel Boone got a happy surprise. His brother, Squire, arrived with a friend. They joined Daniel

Boone and party see Kentucky.

and Stewart in their hunting and exploring. But one day, Stewart was surprised by Indians and killed. This frightened Squire Boone's friend so much that he went back to the settlements in the east. Daniel and Squire lived in the forest together.[2]

This went on for three more months, but they were running out of gunpowder and bullets. So Squire left and went back to North Carolina for fresh supplies and horses. Daniel was left alone 500 miles from home. But he was a strong man, and he could survive. He had grown up in the woods, and he knew how to take care of himself.

Daniel did not sleep in his camp. The Indians might sneak up on him there. So at night he would slip into a canebrake or thicket where no one could come close to him without making noise to wake him. He did not even light a fire at night, which could have shown the Indians where he was.[3]

These months were not an easy time. Daniel had no salt, sugar, or flour. He had little to eat besides berries and the game he could shoot with his rifle. But in July, Squire returned with a load of supplies.

> *The land belonged to no one tribe, but was hunted over by all, each feeling jealous of every other intruder; they attacked the whites, not because the whites had wronged them, but because their invariable policy was to kill any strangers on any grounds over which they themselves ever hunted, no matter what man had the best right thereto. The Kentucky hunters were promptly taught that in this no-man's land, teeming with game and lacking even a solitary human habitation, every Indian must be regarded as a foe.*[4]
>
> Theodore Roosevelt

MOVING THE FAMILY

After two years in the wilderness, Daniel Boone returned to his home in the Yadkin Valley. He wanted to move his family to Kentucky. By September 1773, he sold his farm and was ready to go. His reports of the fertile country he had explored were exciting to his neighbors. When he headed west again, his family was followed by five other families and 40 men.

But trouble was waiting. They were attacked in the hills by Indians, and six men were killed. The group turned back for the settlements, and for a while the westward movement was stalled.

Boone was determined that Kentucky would be settled. It was too beautiful, too rich for settlers not to build homes among its hills and woods. It was already a historical place, and not for a good reason. It was called "the dark and bloody ground" because of all the fighting that had taken place there. No Indian tribe could claim Kentucky. There were several tribes who hunted there. They fought each other for the right to use Kentucky as their own.

Map of Kentucke published in 1784 along with The Discovery, Settlement and Present State of Kentucke by John Filson (PD-US).

One of the strongest of these tribes was the Cherokee. A friend of Boone's, a man named Henderson and other white men, made a treaty with the Cherokees. The Cherokees agreed to let the white men settle in Kentucky. But one of the chiefs told Boone as they parted that though his land was fine, he might have a hard time selling it. Henderson and the others hoped that the other tribes would leave them alone. Boone and 30 other men went to open a pathway from the Holston River over the Cumberland Gap to the Kentucky River. This is still known as the Wilderness Road. Thousands of settlers traveled along it to their new homes in the west.

There were many great woodsmen in America at this time. Some of them grew up with the Indians and knew the forest as well as they did. But only a few could have done what Daniel Boone did. He was not only a pioneer, but also a leader.

On the Kentucky River, Boone and his men set to work to build a fort. It was called Boonesborough. It had four strong walls made of logs. Part of the walls were the back walls of cabins. Other parts of the walls were big logs, stuck upright in the ground and sharpened at the top end. The walls were about 12 feet high to make them hard to climb.[6]

Daniel Boone was the leader of the settlement. He was a tall, slender man with iron muscles. He had a strong nature that made him able to stand great hardships. He was quiet and serious and had a great courage that never failed. Other men had confidence in him because he had confidence in himself. They liked him because of his kind heart and his concern for others. He usually dressed like a Indian in a long hunting shirt and leggings. His shoes were moccasins made of animal skin.

Daniel built a cabin for his family a short way from the fort. It was simple, with simple furnishings. A pole ladder was the stairway to the loft. The children slept there. There were pegs driven into the walls for the family's clothes. The dining table was a rough board on four wooden legs.

The food was simple too. There was little beef or pork, for cattle and hogs were hard to come by in the west. But there was plenty of deer and bear instead, and all the settlers grew corn. Corn could be ground in a hand mill and made into meal for corn bread. Or it could be parched by the fire and carried in a leather bag by men out on long hunting trips.

Daniel Boone escorting settlers through the Cumberland Gap, by George Caleb Bingham, 1851 (PD-Art).

Pioneer boys grew up quick and strong. They were trained in imitating the calls of wild birds and animals. They learned how to set traps and how to shoot rifles with deadly aim. At 12 years old, they became soldiers of the fort. Each boy had his own loophole in the fort wall. If Indians attacked, he would run to the loophole and shoot any Indian he saw. He also was taught to follow Indian trails and hide his own trail as he moved through the woods. This kind of training was necessary for pioneer boys. They had to guard their families against Indians who might creep stealthily up on settlers working in the clearings or hunting in the forest

A settler's home in Kentucky.

The girls of the settlement were strong as well. They tended gardens, cooked over fireplaces, made their own clothes, did their laundry on rocks by the creek, and helped the men and boys in the fields.[7]

Captured by the Indians

These girls were brave as well as strong. This was shown when three of them got captured by Indians.

One of the three girls was Daniel Boone's daughter, Jemima. She was out with her friends, Betsy and Frances Callaway. The three were floating on the river in a canoe one day. They drifted near to the other shore, and their boat got stuck on a sand bar. The girls sat there, teasing each other about who would have to get out in the mud and push the boat off the sand bar. Suddenly, five Indians rushed from the forest and grabbed the girls. They screamed and fought the Indians. The oldest girl, Betsy, hit an Indian on the head with her boat paddle. But very quickly, the braves dragged the girls up the bank and into the forest

The girls knew it was foolish to fight any more. The Indians knew the frontiersmen in the fort would soon be coming to find the girls. They must travel quickly with their captives. If the girls fought, or if they did not walk fast enough to keep up with the Indians, they would be killed.[8]

I have never been lost, but I will admit to being confused for several weeks.

Daniel Boone

Once, Daniel Boone was wandering on the top of a cliff 60 feet above the forest floor below. Suddenly, he was horrified to see a party of Indian braves closing in on him. The braves were sure they had their man trapped. There was no place to go but down. Boone leaped off the cliff and landed in the top of a sugar maple tree far below. The branches broke his fall enough so that he was not hurt. He scrambled to the ground. Quickly, he crossed a nearby stream and disappeared into the underbrush on the other side. The Indians stood at the edge of the cliff, staring down in amazement.[9]

But these were pioneer girls. They watched their captors carefully. When the Indians were not looking, one would scuff her foot on the ground. Another would break a branch. One of them tore small pieces from her dress and left them on the trail. They knew the sharp eyes of their fathers and brothers would spot these marks so they could chase the Indians faster.

No one in the fort knew the girls were missing until they failed to come home in time to milk the cows. Then one of the men discovered their canoe and their footprints beside the river. He knew they had been taken by Indians.

When he shouted to the fort, everyone dropped what he or she was doing. Men grabbed their rifles and tomahawks. Soon two groups set out after the girls. One group was led by Mr. Callaway. Those men rode horses and headed for a crossing on the Licking River. They thought the Indians would try to cross there.

Daniel Boone and eight other men started through the forest. Their eyes were alert from many years of hunting and fighting in the wilderness. Carefully, they watched for signs of feet on the trail. The Indians were good at hiding their trail, but the Boonesborough men were determined to get their girls back. The girls had left as many signs as they could. This helped the men to follow the track.

But it was late in the day. It was growing dark. Even these expert woodsmen could not see tracks in the dark. As soon as the sun came up they were on the trail again. For 30 miles, they followed like bloodhounds. The Indians had used every forest trick to hide their tracks. Even though the trail had been hidden carefully, Boone and his men found it. They moved even faster than the Indians. The girls kept leaving marks without the Indians knowing.

Daniel Boone could tell the Indians were not being as careful now. They were not

Alertness — The girls knew their fathers would be alert to any signs they could leave for them. Their alertness saved their lives. Alertness means being aware of what is taking place so we can be prepared with a right response. "Be sober, be vigilant; because your adversary walketh about, seeking whom he may devour." —I Peter 5:8

The Abduction of Boone's Daughter by the Indians, by Karl Ferdinand Wimar, 1855 (PD-US).

hiding their tracks as well. They must have thought they were far enough ahead to be safe.

Boone led his men across the country in the direction he thought the Indians were heading. They could now run through the woods much faster. They were not close behind the Indians, so they did not have to worry about the braves hearing them as they ran.

Daniel Boone had guessed correctly. He found human footprints in a buffalo path. They had saved time. Now the Indians were not hiding their tracks at all. They thought they were safe.

The Boonesborough men were now encouraged. They pushed on even faster. After ten more miles, they caught sight of the Indians. They were making camp to cook a meal.

They had to be more careful than ever. Daniel Boone knew the ways of the Indians. He knew that the Indians would try to kill their captives to keep their families from getting them back. He would have to plan his attack so the warriors would not have time to kill the girls.

Daniel chose three of his best men. They were good shots with the rifle and were the best woodsmen. They would have to sneak up close, and every shot had to take down an Indian. They slipped very slowly through the bushes. Soon they could see the three girls sitting on the ground near a tree.

The girls were tired. Their hair was tangled. Their dresses were torn. They were afraid. They did not know if they would be rescued. Together, they sat huddled, hoping and praying that their fathers would soon find them.

Just a few yards away, the woodsmen crept forward. They were moving toward warriors with the sharpest senses in the world. Each man knew he could not rustle a leaf or break a twig. If a single sound was heard, tomahawks would slash through the air and strike the helpless girls. The sneaking men held their breath. The advance seemed to take hours. Finally, Boone's rifle roared, and the other three fired as well. Then the men in the rear rushed forward to help.

Two of the Indians fell dead. The other three leaped into the depths of the forest and disappeared. They were so terrified that they left their moccasins behind. None of them had even a knife or tomahawk as he fled.

There was great rejoicing as the little party returned to Boonesborough.[10]

The religion I have is to love and fear God, believe in Jesus Christ, do all the good to my neighbor, and myself that I can, do as little harm as I can help, and trust's God's mercy for the rest.

Daniel Boone

Daniel Boone & his friends rescuing his daughter Jemina, artist unknown, 1851 (PD_US).

Daniel Boone,
the Pioneer of Kentucky

CHAPTER 12

DANIEL BOONE

Captured by Indians

INDIAN TROUBLE

But there would be more trouble with the Indians soon. The War of Independence had started a few months before. Now, British agents were making friends among the Indians and giving them gifts for attacking Americans. There were no large armies of Indians in Kentucky at that time, but many small raiding parties roamed the hills. They hoped to find white men alone or in small groups. Then they could strike from ambush and take scalps.

Life was tense in the little frontier forts. Everyone was always on the watch for Indians. It was dangerous to go outside the fort walls. Daniel Boone organized a team of scouts in Boonesborough. He told them to scout the woods around the settlement and watch for Indians. One of these was Simon Kenton, who became nearly as famous as Daniel Boone. He was a great woodsman and hunter, too. He was captured by the Indians many times but always escaped death.

But there were happy times on the frontier as well. Three weeks after Jemima Boone and the Callaway girls were rescued, Betsy Callaway was married to Samuel Henderson. Within the next year, Jemima Boone married Flanders Callaway, and Frances Callaway married John Holder. Both of those young men had been in the party that rescued the girls from the Indians.

In one of the many Indian attacks that year, Daniel Boone was shot. It started when a man named Goodman was walking

Daniel Boone

Why was salt so important? Remember the pioneers had little food. They ate only venison, cornbread, and turnips. They were very tired of eating the same food every day. Without salt, the food was even worse. Besides, they needed salt to cure meat and make it last longer. Salt was also used to cleanse wounds. It was a very important item to the settlers. This need for salt led to one of Daniel Boone's most exciting adventures.

across the clearing around the fort. Suddenly, an Indian jumped from behind a tree and killed him with a tomahawk. When he yelled and began to take Goodman's scalp, straight-shooting Simon Kenton raised his rifle by the fort's gate. A second later, the brave lay dead beside his victim. At the sound of the shot, several braves leaped from cover and fled away into the woods.

Most of the men in the fort ran out through the gate and ran after them. But it was a trick. There were many more Indians hiding nearby. Suddenly, they rushed from cover and attacked the white men. Daniel Boone was in trouble. He had fallen with the first shots. His ankle had been broken by a bullet.

Just a few steps away, an Indian rushed toward the wounded man. He raised his tomahawk to kill Boone. But one of Simon Kenton's quick rifle shots dropped him in his tracks. Then the young giant ran to Boone and picked up his leader with one arm. With his other, he fought his way through the fighting crowd. He dragged Boone back to the fort's gate, and Boone told Simon that he was a fine fellow.

> Greater love hath no man than this, that a man lay down his life for his friends.
>
> John 15:13

The other Boonesborough men fought their way back into the stockade, and the Indians gave up the attack. They disappeared back into the wilderness. But the British agents were hard at work trying to bring the tribes into the war on the king's side. Peace would not last for long.

It had been a hard summer for the pioneers in Kentucky. There were two other small settlements besides Boonesborough, both protected by log stockades. Sometimes they could help each other in case of Indian attacks. But all three had been attacked more than once that summer. They had not been able to go out hunting or work on their farms as much as they needed to. Their food supplies were shrinking as winter began.

In December, Boonesborough was running out of salt. This does not seem like a very big problem to us today. All we have to do is go to the store and buy salt. But Boonesborough did not have grocery stores close by. They had to make the long, hard trip back over the mountains to buy their salt. Or, they could go to the salt springs and boil water to get the salt that it left.[1]

Indians attacking.

It was a cold winter. That meant that the Indians would probably stay close to their villages until spring. Daniel Boone decided to make a trip to a place called Blue Licks. There were salt springs there. He would take 30 men and go to boil down salt for the settlement. This was a big job. To get one bushel of salt, they had to boil down over 500 gallons of water. That would fill many, many bath tubs! Can you imagine how long it would take to boil away that much water to get the salt at the bottom of the pot? And to do this out in the winter cold would be even harder. But Boone and the other men were strong enough to do what had to be done.

So, with 30 men from the three forts, Boone set out to Blue Licks. In the winter cold, they gathered wood and built fires. Then they set out their pots and began the long process of boiling water. After a few weeks, they had enough salt to send a load back to their families. Three men left with a pack horse while the others stayed on to make more salt.

As the days went by, Daniel Boone left the camp on hunting trips. There was nothing to eat but the game his rifle brought down. He hunted even when the weather was cold and there was snow on the ground. In the second week of February, something happened that stopped the salt making in its tracks.

Daniel was hunting in a blinding snowstorm. He knew he would have to get very close to a deer in order to be able to shoot it. But the storm made it easy for him to slip along quietly. He was sure he could move without the deer hearing him.

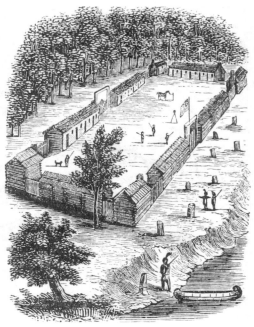

Old Fort at Boonesborough, 1775.

CAPTIVE

But he was not the only one who could move quietly. Suddenly, Boone found himself surrounded by Indians! He had walked right into a Shawnee war party. At another time, Daniel would have run away as fast as lightning. But now he was cold and could not move quickly. He knew his only chance was to act friendly.

It was a huge surprise to find a large group of Indians marching in such weather. But Daniel Boone was a fast thinker, and he quickly knew what to do. Setting his long rifle down, he leaned on the barrel and laughed good-naturedly. He acted as if he had been caught by friends in a joke.

All the braves crowded around. They recognized the famous Daniel Boone, and they were very excited to know they had caught him. He was so famous in Kentucky that his captors would rather have bagged him than George Washington. Instantly, Daniel recognized some of them. He had been captured by this very tribe eight years before. They had adopted him into their tribe as a brother. He had pretended to be happy to live with them so they did not watch him too closely. They still remembered him.

As Boone looked around at the many curious, happy faces, his usual wisdom served him well. First, he acted happy to see his

Daniel Boone

Boone grabs his rifle.

old friends. Then, he noticed details. These men were painted for war. He saw that there were too many for a small raiding party. It was against all customs to be so far from their village in the depths of winter. They must be on their way to attack Boonesborough.

Even as Boone leaned on his long rifle and smiled, he knew what he must do. Boonesborough must not be attacked. Its defenses were weak because some if its men were with the salt-gathering party. There were women and children in the fort. One of its walls was rotten and being repaired. The fort could not stand against a large war party like this one.

Boone cheerfully greeted Blackfish, the Shawnee chief. As the two men talked, Boone convinced the chief that he was happy to be with his Indian friends again. Even though he had fought against the Shawnee, he said he was tired of fighting. It would be nice to go with the braves and live in peace among them. He would go along to their village, Chillicothe.

Somehow, he was able to make the Indians believe him. Boone was known to all the tribes as a man who fought fairly and bravely. He had a reputation for wisdom and fair dealing. He fought for his home and his friends. He did not fight for hatred and revenge. Even though he had sometimes fought against them, the Indians respected him.

Now he suggested to the Shawnees that there was a better way to take Boonesborough. If they would wait until spring, they might be able to convince the people there to give up their homes and move to a new home with the Shawnees. They could go to Boonesborough with horses to carry the women and children. In the spring, the weather would be warm, and the march would be easy. The settlers could live among the tribe as adopted Shawnees, rather than staying in dark and bloody Kentucky where there was always fighting and bloodshed.[2]

The Shawnee Prophet

To convince Blackfish that all this was possible, Boone suggested a test. He asked Blackfish to allow him to go back to his friends at the salt springs. If he could convince them to give up without a fight, he could probably do the same thing at Boonesborough. He made the plan sound very reasonable. Boone had always had an influence over the Indians that was remarkable. He had all the qualities of courage and boldness that they admired. He was also calm and merciful.

Finally Blackfish agreed to capture the salt-makers and leave Boonesborough alone for the present. Boone promised he would get the men to surrender without a fight if the chief would promise to treat them well. Leading the warriors back to his camp, Boone was allowed to approach it alone, showing how much the Indians trusted him. His men trusted him too, and they agreed to surrender. They believed him when he said it was the only way to delay the attack on their homes and families.

But now there was a problem. Some of the Shawnee warriors said that they had not been consulted. They had not agreed to the deal between Blackfish and Boone. They had come many miles on the warpath. They did not want to go home without scalps. There was a two-hour meeting to discuss this. Chief Blackfish spoke strongly against killing the prisoners. He said he had given his word to Boone, and he could not break it. Of course, no one wanted to kill the famous Boone, but many spoke in favor of killing his men.

Running the gauntlet, by Edward Eggleston and Elizabeth Eggleston Seelye, 1878 (PD-US).

Finally, a vote was taken. A war club was given to a warrior. If he struck the ground with it, that meant he voted for death. If he passed it on to the next man, that meant he voted to keep the prisoners alive. When the votes were counted, the prisoners were allowed to live. Even though nearly half of the votes had gone against them, the vote was honored. The men were treated well for the entire journey to Chillicothe.

Boldness: The Indians spared Boone's life because they admired him. When surrounded by Shawnees, he acted as happy and comfortable as he could have been at home. This boldness was a quality the braves appreciated.

When the party arrived at the Indian village, there was a great celebration. The Indians always celebrated the capture of prisoners. But when word passed through the village that the famous Boone had been captured, the people went wild for joy. Blackfish was proud of his prisoners, especially Boone.

The old chief decided to make a trip to Detroit to allow the British soldiers to see his prize. He took Boone and ten other white men along with his warriors. First, they visited all the Shawnee villages. In each village, all the people turned out to praise Blackfish for having such a famous prisoner. After 20 days, they reached Detroit.

All this time, Boone never stopped trying to win the trust of his captors. He charmed the British as well. Detroit was a big fort with many British officers and women. Boone charmed them just as he had the Indians. They all wanted to meet the famous Daniel Boone. When they did, he

The capture of Boone and Stewart.

LIFE & TIMES OF COL. DANIEL BOONE.

BOONE'S INDIAN TOILETTE. PAGE 192.

Illustration of Daniel Boone's ritual adoption by the Shawnees, from *Life & Times of Col. Daniel Boone*, by Cecil B. Hartley, 1859 (PD-Art).

treated them with such courtesy that he won their hearts. These were educated and refined people. They usually had no respect for unschooled backwoodsmen. But Daniel Boone was different.

General Hamilton was so impressed with Boone that he offered Blackfish a fortune in silver to buy him. Blackfish refused. He left the other white prisoners with the British, but Boone belonged to him alone. They returned to Chillicothe and Boone was adopted into the tribe.

The adoption ceremony was painful. First, an old Indian dipped his fingers in ashes and pulled out almost all of Boone's hair. He left only three scalp locks remaining. Boone felt like a turkey being plucked. Next, he was told to remove his clothes and put on a breechcloth around his waist. His face and body were painted with bright colors. A necklace of wampum (Indian money) was put around his neck, along with bracelets on his arms.

Next, Blackfish took him outside and called the whole village. He made a speech, telling them that he was adopting Boone as his own son. Then the squaws took him to the river where they scrubbed him from head to foot. This was supposed to wash out all the white blood. He was taken to the great council house, where many people brought him clothes and gifts. He was named Big Turtle and introduced to the men of the tribe.

Blackfish made a grand speech, telling Boone that he was now Blackfish's own son and would be loved and respected in the tribe. From that time on, he was treated as a member of the tribe. All the time, he pretended to be happy to be there and entered into the life of the Shawnees. He was friendly and cheerful to everyone. No one suspected that he was thinking of escape every minute.

> Resourcefulness — Daniel Boone could not let the Indians know he was saving powder and bullets. But by cutting his rifle balls in half and shooting half charges of powder he was able to store a resource they did not expect.

He was trusted enough to be allowed to go hunting by himself. But the Indians counted the bullets he was given and measured the powder. They wanted to make sure he brought back game every time he used powder and bullets so that he could not be saving up ammunition.[3]

But again, Boone outsmarted them. He found that he could cut his bullets in half and fire them with a half charge of powder. At close range, he could still kill game. So he was storing up the powder and shot he had left. He would need them when he made his break for home.

After four months of living as a Shawnee, Boone saw that the tribe was preparing to attack Boonesborough. Warriors were gathering. War dances were held. Weapons and food were prepared. Boone acted as if he was happy for the attack. In council, he made some suggestions for the raid, which were accepted. He took part in the war dance. He never gave a word or a look that showed he was not pleased with the plan.

The Indians were so deceived that he was allowed to go out hunting for deer to feed the war party. He was given the day's supply of powder and bullets. Walking calmly out of the village, he headed for the woods. He was also carrying his stored powder and shot in his pouch. When he was far enough away from Chillicothe, he struck out boldly for Boonesborough.

Daniel Boone by James Longacre (1835), from 1820 painting by Chester Harding (PD-Art).

The Race for Boonsborough

Soon his absence was discovered, and the Shawnees flew into a rage. He had acted like a son of the tribe, even while planning to warn their enemies. Fast runners were sent out to try to find him, while great trackers began to puzzle out his trail. Boone knew the Shawnees were familiar with the country. They knew all the trails. He must travel day and night to stay ahead of them.

Many times, he saw or heard warriors running through the woods near him, but he always slipped through. He ran and walked for five days, covering 160 miles. He used every trick he knew. He did not dare to fire his gun to bring down game, so he went hungry. He could not even take time to search for roots or bark that he could eat. Finally, he came to the Ohio River. On the other side was Kentucky.

But how was he to get across? It was a huge river. It was running deep and swift because of recent rains. Even an expert swimmer might not make it without drowning.

He looked for a dead log on which he could float across. This would be very slow, but he could not find any other way. But then his eye fell on something that amazed him. There was a canoe on the bank of the river! It had floated down on the current and washed ashore. Out of hundreds of miles of riverbank, the canoe had floated to the very spot where Boone needed it to save his life and Boonesborough. This was one more proof to his simple faith.[4]

United States postage stamp honoring Daniel Boone a frontiersman and trapper, which was issued in 1968.

A wild turkey during mating season, by Riki7 (PD-US).

There was a hole in the bottom of the canoe, but Daniel found a way to patch it. It was not a good patch, but it would last long enough. Across the mighty river he went, struggling with a branch for a paddle. On the other side, he felt that there might be enough time to hunt for some food. A wild turkey fell to his deadly rifle, and he stopped long enough to build a fire and eat. It would be his only meal on the five-day race.

When Boone arrived at Boonesborough he was skinny, hungry, and exhausted. But the people were happy to see him. He was disappointed to find that his family was not there. Becky had missed him badly and feared that he was dead. She had taken her children and made the long wilderness trek back to North Carolina to see her family.

Boone longed to go to her, but his duty came first. Quickly, he set the men to repairing the fort. The walls were rebuilt and supplies of food and water were stored. Everything was made ready to defend the fort. But the attack was delayed.

Shawnee runners arriving at Boonesborough saw that Boone had arrived. They returned to Chillicothe and reported that the fort was being repaired and made ready. The young braves wanted to attack immediately. But the older and wiser men told them that now was not a good time. The chance of a surprise attack had been lost. The thing to do now was to prepare carefully for a long attack.[5]

> Daniel Boone had said that he felt "ordained by God to conquer the wilderness" and this providential supply made him even more sure of it.

After the battle, some people accused Boone of being a traitor. They said that he had surrendered his salt-makers without a fight. They also said he had offered to surrender Boonesborough to the British when he met Hamilton in Detroit. There was a trial, and Daniel Boone was declared to be innocent. In fact, he was promoted to be a major in the Virginia militia.

As soon as he could leave, Boone went to bring his family to Kentucky. This time, he did not settle at Boonesborough. He started another settlement called Boone's Station. Later, he continued to explore. He had moved all the way to Missouri before he died at the age of 86 in 1820.

Shawnees Arrived at Boonesborough

After long preparation, the Shawnees arrived at Boonesborough in September. They had been joined by Indians from several other tribes. They also had with them 12 white men. These were French-Canadian militiamen who were now fighting for England against the colonies. Their commander was Lieutenant de Quindre. There were nearly 500 attackers.

Inside the fort, there were only 60 men and boys who could fire a rifle. It seemed impossible to hold the fort. But God had chosen to protect the little settlement. The Indians had received reports that there were many more men in the fort than there really were. To encourage this belief, Boone had the women and the larger children wear men's hats and shirts. Then he told them to show themselves above the fort at different times. The trick worked.

The Indians at first tried to talk Boone and the others into surrendering. But Boone just stalled for more time. He had sent for help, and he hoped that more men would arrive in time. He kept talking and tried to keep the Indian leaders talking. Meanwhile, the defenders inside the fort were still working to make it stronger. They kept molding bullets and preparing food and water.

Finally, Boone told the Indians that Boonesborough would not surrender. The battle started, and thousands of bullets were fired. The Indians tried to burn the log walls, but rain came suddenly and put the fire out. They pretended to leave, hoping the settlers would open the gates. But the pioneers were not fooled. Finally, the Indians gave up. The battle had lasted for nine days. It was the longest siege in the history of the Indian wars.

103

General Francis Marion's Lunch Party

CHAPTER 13

FRANCIS MARION

The Swamp Fox

A SOUTH CAROLINA BOY

Francis Marion was born in 1732, the same year as George Washington. Both men grew up to be great soldiers and great leaders. But their roles in the War of Independence were very different.

George Washington was the commander of all the American armies. He had thousands of men with trains of wagons to carry their supplies. He also had hundreds of cannons and other weapons of war. His army met the British army in great battles on open fields and in forts.

Francis Marion was the leader of a small group of militiamen who were very poor. He seldom had as many as 100 men. They had to supply their own guns, gunpowder, and food. They brought their own horses. Some of them carried swords that were made from the blades of long crosscut saws by local blacksmiths. They got no pay for their service.

George Washington is known as the Father of Our Country. Francis Marion is known as the Swamp Fox. The story of how the Swamp Fox got his name is one of the most exciting stories in American history.

As a boy, Francis was small and quiet. Most people who knew him would never have dreamed that he would grow up to be a leader. But early in his life, God began to prepare him for the hard and dangerous work that he would be called to do in the war that gave America her freedom.

Just as in the life of Washington, young Francis Marion barely escaped death in his youth. This is another example of how God's Providence spared the life of a boy because God had a plan to use him for an important job as a man.

A New and Accurate Map of the Province of South Carolina in North America, 1779 (PD-US).

Francis was the grandson of Huguenot (hyoo-guh-not) people. The Huguenots had been chased out of France many years earlier by the king. Like the Pilgrims in England, the Huguenots in France had wanted to worship God in the way they believed the Bible taught. But the king wanted the people to worship in the way the Pope taught. So he treated the Huguenots badly and killed many of them. Many of them escaped to America. It is not surprising that young Francis wanted people to live in freedom and was willing to fight for liberty.

Francis grew up on his family's farm in South Carolina. His father died when he was a boy. When he was a young teenager, Francis went to sea on the *May Queen*, sailing from Charleston Harbor to the West Indies. But the *May Queen* was shipwrecked! The small crew drifted for days without food or water. Some of the men were so thirsty that they drank the salty seawater and died. Finally, a ship came along and found the little boat. Francis barely escaped with his life.

When he finally got home, Francis Marion was a strong boy who had grown up a lot in his months away from home. He went to live on his brother Gabriel's farm and worked long, hard hours. He never again said he wanted to be a sailor, but he was still eager for adventure and was always willing to face danger.

When he grew up, Francis bought a farm of his own. He was still small and thin, but he was strong and brave. He joined the militia that protected the settlers from Indian attacks. Twice each month, he joined his friends to train and march, always preparing to fight if the Cherokees attacked. Francis was a friend of Colonel Moultrie, the leader of the militia. Moultrie made Francis a captain in his brigade.

FIGHTING INDIANS AND REDCOATS

In 1761, the Cherokees were attacking settlers to the west. This was when South Carolina was still an English colony. The English governor in Charleston called on Captain Marion to help.

"Captain, I need you and your brigade to join Colonel Grant in fighting these Indians. You know the country. You will be a great help to Grant." Francis Marion began his first campaign as a soldier.

In May, the army marched out of Charleston. The weather was hot and steamy in the South Carolina swamps. Soon, the army was marching through steep, rocky hills. Still, they saw no Cherokees.

One day, they came to a narrow pass. The men had to walk in single file. It was dangerous because the men were scattered along the pass. If the Indians attacked, it would be hard for them to help each other.

Suddenly, a man in the front yelled that Cherokees were attacking. Then shouts and gunshots filled the air. Many soldiers were killed before they could even use their guns. Then, the Indians broke off and disappeared up the hill.

Francis Marion took 30 men and moved forward. They had only gotten a short distance when the Cherokees attacked again. Marion and his men fought back bravely, running between rocks and trees to shoot as the Indians did. Marion was brave and calm. "Keep to the cover, men," he ordered. "Shoot only when you see an Indian."

Most of Marion's men were killed, but they kept the Indians busy until other soldiers could move up to help. Finally, the soldiers drove the Indians away and marched into their village.

The next day, something happened that Francis Marion would never forget. Colonel Grant ordered his men to burn the Cherokee village and destroy all their food. Marion thought this was terrible. Grant wanted to destroy everything that could help the Cherokee warriors fight and kill the white settlers. But he was also destroying all the food the Cherokee women and children needed to live through winter. Smoke rose in great clouds from the Indian cabins. Soldiers walked through the cornfields, slashing with their swords to chop down the green stalks of corn that meant life to the Indians. Some of the men liked this work. The Cherokees had killed many innocent white people, and this was a chance to get revenge.

> While the British enjoyed destroying the Indian towns, Francis Marion was saddened. He feared that the Indian children would blame Christianity for what had happened to their homes.

Francis Marion thought with horror of the suffering that would visit the Indian families in the coming winter. This, he thought, was not the way Christian people should treat their enemies. He wrote a long letter to Gabriel back home.[1]

Francis vowed that he would never volunteer to fight the Cherokees again. He kept his vow.

Sgt. Jasper raising the battle flag of the colonial forces over present-day Fort Moultrie on June 28, 1776 during the Battle of Sullivan's Island, by Johannes Oertel, 1858 (PD-US).

And be ye kind one to another, tenderhearted…

Ephesians 4:32

Returning home, he spent the next 13 years quietly, working hard to make his farm healthy and productive. His neighbors elected him to serve in the colony's government.

During those years, affairs between England and the colonies in America became worse and worse. One day, news came to South Carolina that the British army had attacked Americans at Lexington and Concord in Massachusetts. Suddenly, everyone was talking of war. Marion and his friends were patriots. They wanted America to be free from the English king. Other people were loyal to the king and did not want the colonies to leave England. These people were called loyalists or Tories.

Francis found himself in the army again, but this time it was the Carolinian army. In June of 1776, word came that the British were going to attack Charleston. Charleston was the capitol of South Carolina. It was an important American city. Colonel Moultrie ordered Major Marion to build a fort on Sullivan's Island to protect the city.

Marion and his men built a double wall of logs on the island. Then they filled the wall with sand. When the British ships came, they fired cannons at the fort. The cannonballs sank into the wall of sand and got buried. They did not hurt the men in the fort.

One lucky cannon shot knocked down the flagpole. Sergeant Jasper bravely leaped up on the wall to save the flag. Cannonballs and rifle bullets flew all around him. But he picked up the flag and tied it to another pole. Soon it waved again from the top of the wall.

The cannons of the South Carolina men answered those of the ships. Their shots tore away sails and knocked holes in the hulls. Ship after ship was damaged and had to stop fighting. Finally, the British commander, Sir Peter Parker, ordered the ships to sail away. The Americans had won!

There were other battles after that. In the north, General Washington had fought many hard battles. He had lost most of those fights. His men had suffered through a terrible winter at Valley Forge in Pennsylvania. But the brave soldiers would not give up.

"The lands were rich and the season had been favorable; the corn was bending under the double weight of lusty ears and pods of clustering beans… The furrows seemed to rejoice under their precious loads — the fields stood thick with bread." He went on, "The British seemed to enjoy the cruel work, laughing very heartily at the curling flames … crackling over the tops of the huts, which had only been a few hours before the residences of happy Cherokees. To me it was a shocking sight … But when we came, according to orders, to cut down the fields of corn, I could scarcely refrain from tears."

He went on, "We are sowing the seed for a terrible harvest. When we are gone, the children who have so lately played under the shade of the rustling corn will return and ask their mothers: 'Who did this' And the mothers will reply: 'the white people did it, the Christians did it.' Thus, for cursed Mammon's sake, the followers of Christ have sown the hellish tares of hatred in the bosoms of these … children."[2]

In the south, the British had captured the city of Savannah, Georgia. Francis Marion had been made a lieutenant colonel in the Continental army. He knew the enemy would soon be back again to attack Charleston. He warned the planters near the city to hide their money and drive their cattle into the swamps where the British could not steal them. He told the people in the city to protect their houses with sandbags.

Winter in Valley Forge.

One evening, he was having dinner with some friends in Charleston. They were on the second floor of a wealthy home, and everyone was happy. Someone asked Marion to have a glass of wine, but he declined.

And his friends were not ready to let him leave. With grins, several of them rushed to the door and locked it, one saying that every drop of wine would have to be gone before he could leave.[3]

But Francis Marion was not a man to be stopped easily. He ran out onto a balcony, climbed over the rail, and dropped to the ground. As he landed, a terrible pain shot through his ankle. It was broken! How could he fight now?

Because he was hurt too badly to fight, Colonel Marion was ordered to leave Charleston. Experienced officers were too valuable to be lost in case the city fell. He returned home to his plantation, Pond Bluff. He was there when Charleston was captured by the British. Nearly the whole American army in the south was captured. But Francis Marion was not there.

A Strange Beginning to an Unusual Career

He heard cannons in the distance when the British attacked Charleston in April of 1780. On May 12, the city surrendered. Still unable to move well on his injured ankle, Francis Marion left his plantation and rode into the Carolina swamps to hide from the British until he could fight again. Things were looking bad for the patriots in South Carolina.

Late in the month of May, the British Colonel Tarleton defeated an American force at the Battle of Waxhaws. A white flag of surrender had been offered, but the victorious British Legion (a group made up mostly of South Carolina Tories) had slaughtered many wounded patriots as they lay helpless. The patriots of South Carolina were discouraged, but the cruelty of Tarleton's men made many people bitter enemies of the king. The

Total rout of the loyal recruits.

feeling spread as British troops and Tories throughout the colony attacked their patriot neighbors. People were murdered, houses were burned, and livestock was stolen.

But Marion's ankle was healing. Though he was still limping, he could ride a horse. He began to gather men around him and organized a small militia group. He began to strike at scattered British units. He only had between 20 and 70 men most of the time. But he would hit the redcoats when they were least expecting an attack, then disappear into the swamps he knew so well. He found a good hiding place deep in the swamps on Snow's Island. Here his men would gather and camp when they were called for a raid.

Most of the American army had been captured at Charleston or driven out of South Carolina. Yet Marion's men and a few other small bands of patriot raiders made life hard for the redcoats. Once they attacked a group of 500 British and set free the Americans they were holding as prisoners. Many times they would suddenly storm into a British camp at night, shouting and blazing away with their pistols. They captured prisoners, supplies, horses, and guns. Then, while the shocked redcoats were trying to figure out what had happened, Marion's men would go back into the swamps. Patriotic country people would help Marion when they could, giving his men a safe place to sleep for the night or providing them with a meal.

"The devil himself could not catch that old fox," Tarleton grumbled.[4] Soon everyone was calling Francis Marion the Swamp Fox.

Colonel Tarleton wanted to capture Marion and his men. Once he and his men chased Marion for 26 miles through the swamps before finally giving up.

Later that summer, Marion heard good news. He was going to get some help in South Carolina. George Washington had sent General Horatio Gates south to North Carolina. Still partly crippled in his ankle, Marion resolved to join Gates. He mounted his horse and headed north to Charlotte.

Colonel Marion was joined by some of his men. They were a ragged, hungry set of men. They carried clumsy swords made by local blacksmiths. They had no regular uniforms. On their caps was written, "Victory or Death." That was the motto of Marion's men.

When he met Marion, General Gates was surprised. He had heard of the Swamp Fox and his daring deeds. He expected to see a tall soldier in a fine uniform. Instead, he looked at a small, dark, quiet man in ragged clothes. Marion offered to help Gates fight Cornwallis.

But Gates did not want help from the Swamp Fox. As he looked over the small officer and his men, Gates saw a ragged, mixed-up crew. Some were African American, some were white, and some were Indian. Most were dressed in tattered clothes, carrying a strange assortment of weapons. Surely this

Marion's brigade crossing the Pedee River, S.C., 1778, on their way to attack the British force under Tarleton (PD-US).

ragged bunch could not fight like trained soldiers with good army equipment. So he ordered Marion south to Williamsburg. There was a group of patriots there who wanted a leader to organize and lead their militia.

In August, Gates found out that he could have used some more help. Cornwallis met him at Camden and thrashed his army. Gates fled on a horse and was three days ahead of his army's stragglers when they caught up with him at Charlotte, North Carolina.[5]

A Redcoat Resigns

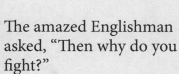

Marion took British prisoners in his battles. He wanted to exchange them for American prisoners held by the redcoats. A British officer came to Marion's camp to talk about it. After they talked, Marion invited the redcoat to stay for a meal. When the food was served, it was only sweet potatoes roasted in the campfire. There was water to drink. The British officer asked Marion if this was all his men usually had to eat.

"Oh, yes," replied Marion. "Although there is often not enough of the sweet potatoes."

"Then surely you must be paid very well, to fight and live such a hard life."

"Actually," Marion said, "we are paid nothing at all."

The amazed Englishman asked, "Then why do you fight?"

Marion answered, "Because, sir, I am in love with Liberty."[6]

The redcoat went back to his camp and resigned from the army. He told his commander that they would never defeat men who were willing to live on roots and river water while fighting for their freedom.[7]

Francis Marion

CHAPTER 14

FRANCIS MARION

The Tables Turn in South Carolina

MARION'S NEW BAND

With the defeat of Gates, the Continental Congress now turned to George Washington. The Continental Congress had sent Gates to South Carolina instead of asking Washington to make the choice of generals. Washington was a humble man, so he did not complain. But when Gates was so badly beaten, Congress decided that it was best to let General Washington decide who should replace him.

Washington chose Nathanael Greene the, "Fighting Quaker." Many historians now believe Greene was the wisest general in the Revolutionary War, next to Washington. Greene started south, sending out messengers along the way to find supplies and volunteers to build up his small force.

When he arrived and met Gates in Charlotte, North Carolina, Greene found a discouraged and injured army. There were fewer than 2,000 men. Many of them were poorly trained. They were short on food, equipment, weapons, and training. They had lost much of their supplies in the battle at Camden.

Greene knew he was not ready to face Cornwallis. He needed time to rebuild the army in the south. He needed time to get the supplies he needed and to train his men to fight well together. If Cornwallis followed up his victory over Gates at Camden by moving north to attack the Americans now, Greene would have a big problem.

But Cornwallis did not move north. A big part of the reason was the Swamp Fox.

It is hard for us to imagine living as the followers of the Swamp Fox did. But as Christians, we are striving for a prize even higher than that of freedom. We are fighting the good fight for the high calling of God. Our battle is to live in a way that is pleasing to Christ. No sacrifice is too great for God.

Major General Thomas Sumter

When Marion had arrived in Williamsburg County, he had received a different welcome than the one he had received from Gates. Major John James, the commander of the Williamsburg militia, was overjoyed to meet Marion. His citizen-soldiers pressed around, shouting and grinning. Some of them had served under Marion before. All of them had heard of his raids and his victories over Tory and British armies. Here was a man who could lead them!

Marion did not waste time. Right away, he led his men up and down the Santee River burning boats and destroying rafts. He would take away the means the British would need to cross the rivers.

While they were busy at their work, news came of the American defeat at Camden. The patriot army had suffered a bitter blow. Then more bad news came. Militia leader Thomas Sumter's raiders had been defeated by the brutal Tarleton at Fishing Creek. Sumter's men had been scattered, and he had barely escaped. It would take time for him to rebuild his militia. For now, the Swamp Fox and his men were the only significant force left in South Carolina to battle Cornwallis.

Marion's men lived in well-hidden camps deep in the swamps. They slept in the shady marshes by day and moved out to attack during the night. They made life hard for the British and Tories, attacking their camps, taking prisoners, and seizing their supplies.

Marion had a network of friendly Carolinians who scouted and spied for him. They told him the movements of the enemy. But no one knew the plans of the Swamp Fox. He kept his plans inside his head until it was almost time to move. Then he ordered his men to get ready and led them to battle.

Marion's spies had told him that a small British unit was at Nelson's Ferry, a place where armies could cross the Santee River. There they were guarding prisoners and supplies for the British army. Quietly, the swamp raiders approached the British camp at dawn's first light. Suddenly, a shout was heard. Horses charged, shots rang out from everywhere, and the British camp was full of wild struggle. Many Tories and redcoats were captured or killed. Marion's triumphant men captured horses, wagons, weapons, and supplies.

Fishing Creek (north branch Susquehanna River), photo by Ruhrfisch, 2012 (CC BY-SA 3.0).

Best of all, they freed 150 American prisoners. They had been captured at Camden less than a week before. Marion hoped these prisoners would join his group, but most did not. Marion's best fighters continued to be the men who had grown up in South Carolina and knew the swamps well.[1]

FIGHTING WITH THE SWAMP FOX

It was not easy living as a member of Marion's band. Men slept on the ground and drank swamp water. Their food was grits, sweet potatoes, or whatever they could capture from the British. Once in a while, a trooper would get a good meal from some patriotic farm family. But most of the time, pickings were slim. Only their patriotism and loyalty to their dedicated leader kept the men fighting.[2]

Marion sent reports of his missions to General Gates. This was not easy for him. He did not read or write well. He reported his victories without bragging.

Gates was delighted to hear about the triumph at Nelson's Ferry. It was not often that there was good news about the war in the Carolinas. He sent the report on to the Continental Congress, who reported it to the newspapers throughout the colonies. Soon the name of the Swamp Fox was known all through the struggling new country.

The Swamp Fox was hard to catch. His men never stayed long in one place. After a battle, the troop would often scatter to their homes or the homes of friends and stay there until the call once again went out from their leader. A small core group of loyal men went with Marion almost everywhere. No matter where he went, the Swamp Fox always attracted a good group of fighting volunteers when he needed them. As he had more and more victories, it became easier to get recruits.[3]

Marion's men loved him because he cared about them. He knew most of them had families and farms to look after. He also knew that they were volunteers and fought for patriotism instead of for pay. He appreciated their willingness to fight. They appreciated his concern for them. They followed the Swamp Fox because they believed in his courage, wisdom and judgment.

The brigade moved easily through the swamps. His spies and scouts roamed for many miles to check up on the enemy and report to Marion. But the British never knew what to expect from the Fox. They and their Tory friends stayed nervous and fearful, wondering where he would strike next.

There were rivers and creeks to cross in the swamp country. Sometimes the men rode across on horses. At other times, they poled flatboats

> Marion's men loved him because he cared about them. He knew most of them had families and farms to look after. He also knew that they were volunteers and fought for patriotism instead of for pay.

Francis Marion talking with British officer in forest camp, by W. Ridgway, 1860 (PD-US).

or rafts across carrying supplies. Marion could not swim. Sometimes he would cling to his horse's saddle as the swimming animal towed him across.

> Marion and his men fought all through the War of Independence without ever being paid for their services. They even had to provide their own food, guns, and horses. Yet they fought on. Their sacrifices won freedom for you and me.

There were many Tories as well as patriots in South Carolina, so the countryside was divided in loyalty. They had all lived as neighbors before the war. But war always brings out the worst in people. Some of the Tories and patriots became bitter enemies once the fighting started. Sometimes communities were torn apart because of the disagreement. Sometimes some family members favored independence and other members were loyal to the king.

Sometimes people changed sides. As the war went on, many people decided to be on the patriot side because the British were being cruel. They raged through the countryside, hanging patriot farmers, burning homes, and destroying crops. Even women and children were sometimes abused. In a way, the British hurt themselves more than the patriots did. Their cruelty turned people against them.[4]

Some of the patriots responded to the cruelty with more cruelty. Sometimes they burned the homes of Tory neighbors who had worked with the British. But Marion was not one of those. He knew that the war would be over someday. Then the former Tories and the patriots would have to live together as neighbors again. It was best to fight and forgive. Many times he saved Tories from death when they had been captured by patriots.

One day, Marion's spies told him that the Tory leader John Ball was camped with is men at Black Mingo Swamp. The Swamp Fox decided to plan a night attack.

This time, the Tories were not completely surprised. Even though Marion's men attacked from three sides, Tories in the camp heard hoof beats crossing a wooden bridge. They were making ready when the attack came. Still, the wild patriot riders drove them into the swamps. Some of them were killed. Colonel Ball left behind his beautiful thoroughbred horse. Marion claimed the horse and named him Ball as a joke. He rode Ball through the rest of the war. After that battle, Marion always used blankets on wooden bridges to muffle the sound of the horses' hooves.

Rear-Admiral Alexander John Ball, by Henry William Pickersgill, c.1805 (PD-Art).

A month after that battle, Marion struck again at Tearcoat Swamp. He had 150 men, his largest force yet. Again, they struck from three sides. Not a single one of Marion's men was killed. They captured horses and supplies. Now they could support even more volunteers.

After so many patriot militia victories, Tory support for the British began to fade in the area. Cornwallis was frustrated. Marion could strike British and Tory camps and then go back into the swamps. Cornwallis could not safely send messengers and supplies between his forces. He sent Tarleton and other cruel raiders to punish the patriot farms and settlements. Yet, that only seemed to make more people take sides with the rebels.

But Charleston was still in the hands of the British. And Gates had been badly beaten at Camden. The British still held the upper hand in the Carolinas.

> Colonel Tarleton was one of the cruelest of the British officers. But his outrages against the patriots turned much of South Carolina against the British. It got harder and harder to get Tories to help the redcoats. Tarleton should have learned the lesson of Proverbs 26:27:
>
> "He who digs a pit will fall into it, And he who rolls a stone, it will come back on him."

GREENE TAKES OVER

But Nathanael Greene had come. The "Fighting Quaker" now took over command from Gates and began to organize his army.

He sent Dan Morgan and his riflemen southwest, where they would face and defeat Tarleton at Cowpens. He sent "Light Horse" Harry Lee (the father of Robert E. Lee) southeast to join with Francis Marion. Now Marion could attack larger British forces than ever before.

Cornwallis had hoped to subdue the Carolinas quickly. He wanted to march north and help the other British armies fight Washington. But now he had to give up on that plan. He had his hands full in South Carolina. Greene had divided his army. Now Cornwallis had to divide his army, also.

News came of the patriot victory at Cowpens. Now the Tories grew more discouraged. Greene's army had moved south into South Carolina and Cornwallis wanted to attack him. But "Light Horse Harry" and Swamp Fox kept hitting him from every direction.

Greene and Cornwallis finally met in a battle at Guilford Court House in North Carolina. Both armies were tired and sick. When the smoke cleared, the British held the field. They had driven the Americans out. But Greene knew what he was doing. He withdrew after having cost the British many men and supplies.[5]

Henry Lee, by William Edward West, c.1838 (PD-Art).

With a smaller force and never enough supplies, Greene would fight several battles. He lost most of them. But he was so clever

Surrender of Lord Cornwallis, painted by John Trumbull, c.1820 (PD-US).

that even when he retreated, he left the enemy with more men killed and wounded than the Americans. He was wearing down the British army in the Carolinas.

Cornwallis gave up on South Carolina and pushed north into Virginia, where he would be trapped by Washington at Yorktown. Greene let him go and returned to South Carolina. At his camp, he met the Swamp Fox for the first time. The two men talked for hours and grew to respect each other.

Greene told Marion and Lee of his plan to take back South Carolina. Cornwallis was gone with the main British army, but the British still held Charleston. There were also British posts in various parts of the state.

Lee and Marion banded together to attack Fort Watson on the Santee River. The fort was well protected. It had log walls and sharpened logs stuck in the ground and pointing outward. There was a deep ditch outside the logs to trap attackers where the defenders could shoot them from the walls. It seemed that the British and Tories inside were safe.

Cornwallis said, "Another such victory would ruin us."[6]

But then a militia officer named Hezekiah Maham had an idea. Why not build a tower high enough to shoot over the fort walls? Marion liked it. During the night, his men built a tower of logs. In the morning, the British looked out and were amazed. The patriots in the tower could shoot right into the fort! The British could not go out in the open to get ammunition or fire their cannon. They had to surrender.[7]

Greene wanted to force the British to surrender Charleston. With Cornwallis moving away toward Virginia, the Charleston redcoats could not count on help from him. Greene started moving east. Marion and Lee joined him. At Eutaw Springs, they were met by a British force that had marched out of Charleston to stop them. There was a sharp battle, and then both sides withdrew.

Greene intended to move ahead with an attack on Charleston. A few weeks after the fight at Eutaw Springs came the news that Cornwallis had surrendered at Yorktown. Now both sides knew the end of the war was near. France had sent many men and ships to help America. England was fighting the French and the Spanish as well, so she was worn out with fighting. It was not until the next year that the British finally gave up Charleston. The commander promised the patriots that he would not destroy the city if his army was allowed to leave in peace.

Wee Tee Lake, an oxbow of the Santee River, South Carolina (CC BY-SA 3.0).

General Greene held his army back as the British boarded ships and set sail.

There was a great celebration in Charleston when the British left the city. The city leaders invited General Greene's army to parade through the city. Marion and his men were not invited to parade. They were considered too ragged.

Francis Marion did not care about that. He just wanted to go home to his farm at Pond Bluff. He said a fond farewell to his ragged, brave soldiers and headed home.

When he got to Pond Bluff, he found the place in ruins. Soldiers on both sides had ransacked it for supplies. He borrowed money and bought livestock, feed, seed, and tools to start over.

At age 50, Francis Marion finally got married. He did not have any children, but he and his wife lived happily on their farm and sometimes enjoyed camping in some of the places where he had camped with his men during the long war for liberty.

Siege of Fort Watson, 1781, artist unknown, 1879 (PD-US).

THE BATTLE OF FORT MOTTE

The British set up their headquarters on the plantation of Mrs. Motte, a patriot. She had been moved out of her mansion and made to live in a small cabin on the property. The redcoats built a stockade around the buildings to defend themselves in case of attack.

Marion secretly sent one of his men to talk to Mrs. Motte. He told her he was going to attack the fort and that he might have to set her mansion on fire to drive the British out. She replied that she would gladly sacrifice her home to help the cause of independence. She even gave Marion a quiver full of arrows that she had received as a gift. She said he could make flaming arrows and shoot them onto the wooden shingles on the roof.

The attack started, and the patriots sent the flaming arrows and balls of sulfur flying toward the roof. Soon it was burning wildly, and the British saw that they had to surrender or burn to death.

As soon as he saw the white flag, Marion ordered his men to put out the fire. Their British prisoners helped them to do so. Then Mrs. Motte prepared a great dinner and invited officers from both sides to dine. Patriots and redcoats sat down and enjoyed a meal together in peace.[8]

119

Isaac Shelby,
first governor of Kentucky

CHAPTER 15

COLONEL ISAAC SHELBY

The Battle of Kings Mountain

A THREAT THAT BACKFIRED

Isaac Shelby was born in 1750 and lived until 1826. He was a great man in many ways. During his life he fought in three different wars. He held political office in three different states. He was the governor of Kentucky twice. But he is most remembered for his leadership in the Battle of King's Mountain.

The year was 1780, and the War of Independence was going badly for the southern colonies. British General Sir Henry Clinton had been defeated in his first attack on Charleston, but he came back with more soldiers and captured the city. Most of the American army in the south had been taken prisoner. There was no American force left that was large enough to stand against the British. Clinton had gone back to New York and left Lord Cornwallis to wipe out the few small bands of patriots that still fought.

The death of British Major Patrick Ferguson at the Battle of King's Mountain, by Alonzo Chappel, 1863 (PD-US).

Congress sent General Gates to fight Cornwallis, but he was a weak general. His men retreated before the British. Gates retreated fastest of all. He did not stop his galloping horse until he reached Charlotte, 70 miles from the battlefield.

The times were dark for the patriots. Only small groups under clever leaders such as Marion, Sumter, Pickens, and Davie were left. The British Red Dragoons overran North Carolina, South Carolina, and Georgia.

Then the king of Israel replied, "Tell him, 'Let not him who girds on his armor boast like him who takes it off.'" – I Kings 20:11, NASB

The Tennessee men might have thought of this verse when they heard the message from Ferguson. A pagan king had threatened Ahab, the king of Israel. He told Ahab his army was so large that Israel could not hope to stand against him. He found he was wrong when God gave Israel a smashing victory over him. The same thing happened to the boasting, threatening Ferguson.

Sir Henry Clinton, by Andrea Soldi, 1762 (PD-Art).

The British soldiers and their Tory friends were brutal to the patriot settlers. They wanted to show that the king was still master in the southern colonies. This cruelty only made the patriots more angry and determined. Some of them lived a long way from the towns and did not have much to do with the government. Some did not know much about the reasons that started the war. They had been busy clearing the forests for farms and building their cabins. But when the redcoats and Tories swept through the south, burning houses, stealing cattle, and abusing women and children, the men of the forests came out in force. Under the Swamp Fox and other brave leaders, the men fought many battles with the invaders.

Colonel Ferguson was a British officer. His regiment had been recruited in America, not England. Most of his men were Tories. Ferguson was a loyal Englishman and a good soldier. He was famous for boldness in battle and swift movement of his men. He was just the man to recruit Tories and train them for battle.

With his many Tories and a few regulars, Ferguson pushed toward the mountains of western North Carolina. He began to hear that over the mountains were many of the men who had been striking him in sneak attacks. Some of them had lived over the mountains all their lives. Others had retreated there as Ferguson marched westward. All of them were tough woodsmen.

Now Ferguson made a great mistake. He sent a messenger over the mountains with a message for Colonel Isaac Shelby. He threatened Shelby and the other patriots. He said if the "backwater" men did not stop fighting the king's soldiers, he would march over the mountains and attack them. He said he would lay waste their farms, burn their homes, and hang their leaders.

Ferguson did not understand the men of the mountains. His threats only made the patriots angrier. They had challenged the wilderness and carved out homes for themselves. They had built log cabins, schools, and churches. Their lives were full of danger and hardship. The preacher kept a gun handy as he preached, and the men brought their rifles to church with them.

Gathering of Overmountain Men at Sycamore Shoals, by Samuel G. Heiskell, 1915 (PD-Art).

122

They were used to dealing with trouble, and they were not at all afraid of Ferguson.[1]

These settlers knew the British paid gold to the Indians to attack and murder the colonists. They knew the British also hired the wild and dishonest men among them to join the redcoats and kill their neighbors.

When the war had started, the over-the-mountains men had been busy fighting the Indians and had not been able to help the other patriots fight the British in the east. But now these hardy backwoodsmen heard Ferguson's threats and replied with defiance. They looked to Colonel Shelby to lead them across the mountains against Ferguson.

MUSTERING THE TROOPS

When he received the message from Ferguson, Shelby's blood boiled. He mounted his horse and traveled 60 miles to meet with John Sevier. Sevier was a man known for his fighting ability and his hospitality. When Shelby arrived, he found a barbecue going on. Whole oxen were being roasted, and all the neighbors had turned out for feasting, dancing, and horse races. When Shelby shared the news with "Nolichucky Jack" Sevier and his friends, all the men agreed to turn out and fight.

Shelby then rode home to muster his own neighbors. He sent an urgent call for help to Colonel William Campbell, a well-known Indian fighter. Campbell lived 40 miles away on the Holston River. He said would call out the Holston Virginians and meet the other forces at Sycamore Shoals on September 25.

When the day came, Shelby and Sevier brought 500 men. Campbell brought 400 Virginians. McDowell was there from North Carolina with 160 Carolinians who had been driven west by Ferguson's larger army. A message was sent to Colonel Cleveland, a hunter and Indian fighter of Wilkes County in North Carolina. They asked him to raise all the men he could and join them.

Colonel Sevier hurriedly went about trying to borrow enough money for supplies. But most of the people had spent all their money just to buy land. The only large amount of money in the region was kept by the county government. Sevier approached

Colonel Cleveland's war prize, October 7, 1780, by Don Troiani, 2012 (CC BY-SA 3.0).

123

John Adair, by Nicola Marschall, 1908 (PD-Art).

John Adair, a county official. Would the county loan them the money? Adair's reply was given in true patriotism.

He told Sevier that he did not have the authority to give the county's money to the soldiers. But if the British took over the country, the money would be stolen by them. He told Sevier to go ahead and take it and use it to defend the settlers. He would trust the country and his neighbors to agree that he had done what was right in the end.

Shelby and Sevier promised to pay back the money out of their own fortunes if the legislature did not approve of Adair's act. The $13,000 in silver and gold bought loads of supplies for the fighting backwoodsmen. They were ready to start.

Excitement was in the air on September 25. The entire fighting force of Tennessee turned out at Sycamore Shoals. They agreed that the younger, stronger men would march against Ferguson, and the older men would stay behind and defend the settlements in case of attack.

Crowds of men milled around, talking with each other and saying sad good-byes to wives, children, and sweethearts. Neighbors brought food, guns, horses, blankets, and anything that might help the soldiers on their way.

The men wore long hunting shirts and coonskin caps. Some preferred soft hats with a sprig of evergreen on them. Their horses were tough and wiry. Nearly all were armed with the Deckhard rifle, a weapon that could shoot far and straight. Each man had his tomahawk and fighting knife. Nobody had bayonets. A few of the offices carried swords.

Off they went, stringing out over the woodland trails. In three days, they had crossed the Blue Ridge and looked out over the lowlands. The next day, they were joined by Colonel Cleveland and 350 militiamen. Their little army was growing.

The other leaders decided to make Colonel Cleveland their top leader. He said to the men: "Now, my brave fellows, the redcoats are at hand. We must up and at them. When the pinch comes, I shall be with you."[2]

Colonel Shelby gathered his regiment about him. "And now, if there is a man among you who wants to go back home, this is your chance. Step three paces to the rear."[3]

Not a single man moved.

Sycamore Shoals State Historic Park in Tennessee.

124

Reverend Samuel Doake

The next morning, the men formed up to march. First, they gathered in a clearing to hear words from Reverend Samuel Doake. He would send them off with prayer for God's blessing on their battles.

Years before, the God-fearing Mr. Doake had crossed the mountains to bring the gospel to the settlers. He had driven an old gray horse loaded with Bibles. Settling in the Holston country, he had set to work with great energy. He built churches and schools. He helped the people defend themselves against attacking Indians. He won their respect, and they were happy to let him teach them about God. Now, each frontier soldier took off his hat and bowed his head by the muzzle of his rifle as Mr. Doake asked God to give them victory and bring them home safely.

The army moved along, picking up small groups of other woodsmen who had been forced from their homes by the British. On October 3, they reached Gilbert-town, 1,500 strong. They hoped to catch up with Ferguson there, but Tories had warned him that the riflemen were coming. He had retreated and sent to Cornwallis for more men. He asked the Tories for help, calling the over-the-mountain men "the dregs of mankind," "a set of mongrels," and other bad names.

When the Shelby men and their comrades heard this, they knew that Ferguson was afraid. He might have gotten away from regular soldiers, but the woodsmen were made of strong stuff. They had hunted wild beasts and fought for their lives. They had come to fight, and they intended to have their battle.

They sent 700 men on the best horses to catch up with Ferguson. The rest would follow as quickly as possible. When they went into camp for the night on October 6, they were joined by still more militia. They built blazing fires and roasted corn for supper that had been stripped from Tory fields.

The colonels then held a council. They decided to push on all night to catch up with Ferguson. Nine hundred men picked up their weapons, mounted their horses, and moved out. Some of their companions without horses were so eager to fight that they followed on foot and caught up in time for the battle.

THE BATTLE ON THE MOUNTAIN

Meanwhile, Ferguson was preparing to meet them. Several bands of Tories were on their way to help him. He also expected more men from Cornwallis. He just needed a day or two more to prepare to make a stand. He pitched his camp on a ridge near King's Mountain, massing his baggage wagons on the northeast side of the camp. The soldiers camped on the south side of the ridge. Ferguson was confident. He declared that all the rebels and "God Almighty Himself" could not drive him from the ridge. He would find out that he was wrong.[4]

> Colonel Ferguson stated that all the rebels and "God Almighty Himself" could not drive him from the ridge.

Shelby sent out Enoch Gilmer as a spy. Gilmer met a young woman who had been at Ferguson's camp to sell chickens. She said Ferguson's camp was on the same spot where a group of hunters had camped the year before. Some of those hunters were now with Shelby. They knew the ground well and would lead the way. Two captured Tories were forced to tell how Ferguson was dressed. It would not be hard to tell who the leader of the British was.

When the patriots were a mile from the ridge, they got off their horses. They surrounded the hill. Each man was ordered to fight for himself. They had no bayonets, and they would have to retreat when the British charged. But they would soon rally when the British soldiers scattered in the woods, and then they would drive them back.

Some of Sevier's woodsmen rode hard around the ridge, cutting off Ferguson's only escape route. Others surrounded the other sides of the mountain, and Ferguson found himself attacked from all directions at once.

But Ferguson was no coward. Riding back and forth, swinging his bright sword over his head, he shouted to his men to fight for their king. He led a charge down the hillside, which was met by hundreds of Campbell's buckskins. The woodsmen were forced back by the British bayonets, but Shelby's men swarmed up the other side of the ridge.

Ferguson was foolish in saying that even God could not drive him off the ridge. He was like the captain of the ship *Titanic*, which sailed from England for North America in 1912. He said, "God himself could not sink this ship!" He said that because the *Titanic* had many watertight compartments in it. Several of those compartments could fill up with water, yet the others would stay dry and keep the ship floating. But when the ship struck an iceberg, it ripped a long gash down the side. It opened so many of those compartments that the great ship sank in a few hours. There is nothing that God cannot do, and only a foolish and prideful man would ever challenge God.

Ferguson's men turned to meet this new attack and drove the patriots back down the ridge with their bayonets. Soon, their charge was scattered among the trees and rocks, and they had to back up the ridge. Shelby's woodsmen reloaded and came back at them, while other riflemen were hiding everywhere, picking off redcoats with nearly every shot.

Col. Patrick Ferguson grave site on King's Mountain.

Brave Ferguson was everywhere on the ridge, shouting orders and driving his men on. He had two horses shot out from under him, but he would not be stopped. Seeing some of his men raise a white flag, he galloped over and whacked it down with his sword. Then he saw a second one and cut it down as well.

Suddenly, some of Sevier's men appeared at the top of the ridge. Seeing them, Ferguson led a charge against them. But they recognized him from the girl's description and raised their rifles. The young British officer fell from his horse and did not move.

Ferguson's assistant, Colonel De Peyster, took command and fought on bravely, but the patriot rifles had done their work. The British were hemmed in on all sides. They huddled around the baggage wagons as the American colonels led their men to the top of the hill. Finally, De Peyster raised a white flag. Several white handkerchiefs were also raised on ramrods, and the rifle fire died away.

The battle was a great success for the patriots. Ferguson was left with 400 men. The Americans had only 28 men killed and about 60 wounded.

> Col. Issac Shelby continued to serve his country and became the first governor of Kentucky.

The over-the-mountains men quietly buried their dead. Then they loaded their horses with captured weapons and supplies. They had to return home quickly to protect their families. Carrying their wounded on stretchers made from captured tents, they turned their horses west.

Thanks to Colonel Isaac Shelby and the other patriot woodsmen, King's Mountain was a great defeat for the British. It was a decisive battle of the War of Independence. The southern patriots gained new courage from their victory, and the Tories of the Carolinas would never be as powerful again.

Isaac Shelby served in the state legislatures of Virginia and North Carolina. When Kentucky was changed from being a county in Virginia to an independent state, he was elected to be its first governor. He served as a soldier in Lord Dunmore's War and the War of 1812. For the rest of his life, it was for his leadership in the Battle of King's Mountain that people admired him most. He became known by the nickname "Old King's Mountain."[5]

George Rogers Clark

CHAPTER 16

GEORGE ROGERS CLARK

The Hero of Vincennes

THE WARRIOR BECOMES A LEADER

George Rogers Clark was a country boy born in Virginia in 1752. He spent his childhood roaming the Virginia woods. He learned the ways of the forest and grew strong and clever. It was good training for the life he would lead as a patriot woodsman.

Like George Washington, Clark became a surveyor and fighter. Also like Washington, he picked up his axe, rifle, and surveying tools, and he headed into the lonely forests of the upper Ohio River country.

When the governor of Virginia sent an army to fight Cornstalk, the great Shawnee chief, he sent Clark along as a scout. Two years later, Clark ventured alone over the mountains to Kentucky. There he became a leader, along with Daniel Boone. His neighbors trusted him and chose him to be their representative in the Virginia government. At this time, Kentucky was part of the colony of Virginia.

Rogers went back to Virginia to speak to the leaders. He told Governor Patrick Henry that Kentucky was a fine land, and it needed to be defended against the Indians. There were several tribes of Indians who claimed Kentucky as their own hunting grounds. Tribes made war against each other. They also attacked the white settlers who tried to build towns and farms in Kentucky.

George Rogers Clark statue at George Rogers Clark Memorial, Vincennes, Indiana, by Hermon Atkins MacNeil, (CC BY-SA 3.0).

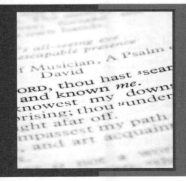

Even as a boy, God was preparing young George for his future work. His early life in the woods prepared him for his tough mission later on the frontier. Isn't it wonderful to know that God has a plan for each of our lives? In fact, God is busy shaping us into the persons He wants us to be, even before we are born. Psalm 139:14-16 says,

" I will praise thee; for I am fearfully and wonderfully made: marvellous are thy works; and that my soul knoweth right well. My substance was not hid from thee, when I was made in secret, and curiously wrought in the lowest parts of the earth. Thine eyes did see my substance, yet being unperfect; and in thy book all my members were written, which in continuance were fashioned, when as yet there was none of them."

Yes, God has a plan for your life, and He has been preparing you for it since before you were born!

The Virginia lawmakers set up Kentucky as a county of Virginia and gave George Rogers Clark 500 pounds of gunpowder to take with him. He took it down the Ohio River to Kentucky. The settlers used it to protect themselves.

Clark made his home at Harrodsburg, Kentucky. For more than a year, he stayed busy helping the settlers fight off the Indians. This was at the same time that Daniel Boone was helping other settlements fight the Indians, also. There was much bloodshed in Kentucky in those days. The American colonies were fighting against the British for their independence. The British officers at Detroit offered money to the Indians for every American scalp they would bring in. This made the fighting between the Indians and the white settlers much worse.

Clark saw good men and women killed by the Indian friends of the British. So he decided to attack the British across the Ohio. But he needed men. There were not enough patriots in Kentucky. He would also need money to build an army. Where would he get it?

He remembered Patrick Henry, the patriotic governor of Virginia. With some other people, he rode back to Virginia. He kept his plans secret, even from the friends who were traveling with him.

It was easy to get help from Governor Henry. Patrick Henry made George Rogers Clark a colonel and ordered him to raise an army to defend Kentucky. He gave him $6,000 to pay for his army's expenses.

> *My name is Clark, and I have come out to see what you brave fellows are doing in Kentucky and to lend you a helping hand, if necessary.*[1]
>
> George Rogers Clark

TAKING THE FORTS

In May of 1777, Clark led an army of about 150 tough backwoodsmen, along with several families, on a flatboat trip down the Monongahela River to Fort Pitt. The riflemen were not told where they were going. Clark did not want to take a chance on word getting to the British. At Fort Pitt, they took on a few small cannons and fresh supplies.

They kept their boats near the middle of the river. This was to keep away from the woods on the bank, where enemies might be hiding. They landed at the falls of the Ohio on Corn Island. Here, the settlers planted corn, while Rogers trained his men in fighting together. It was the beginning of the city of Louisville, Kentucky.

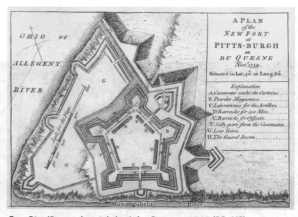

Fort Pitt (Pennsylvania), by John Rocque, 1765 (PD-US).

Clark's plan was to attack the British forts on the Illinois and Wabash rivers. He had kept his plan a secret until now, but one day he told his men. The trip would take them 1,000 miles from home. Some of the men would not go that far from their families. But most of Clark's men were willing to follow their brave leader. In June, Clark and his men floated down to where the Ohio River and the Tennessee River came together. Here, a group of hunters joined them.

The army hid its boats and began its long march. It would take them over prairies and through dense forests. They had to be on the lookout all the time for enemies who might attack them or British scouts who would warn British General Hamilton that the patriot were on the way to attack his forts.

Off for Vincennes!

Father Gibault, the priest of Kaskaskia, went to Vincennes to tell the French people there why Clark had come to their region. He told them that France had taken sides with the Americans. The people rejoiced and ran up the American flag. Clark instructed his men to be kind to the French settlers. He placed Captain Helm in command of the fort.

Up in Detroit, General Hamilton was making plans to attack Fort Pitt and encourage Indians in Ohio to kill American settlers. He thought he was safe and that he was well in control of the upper Ohio region. He was surprised to learn that his forts in the Illinois and Wabash country had been taken by George Rogers Clark and his backwoods riflemen!

The Americans called the British general "Hair-buyer Hamilton" because he paid the Indians for American scalps. He gathered an army of British, Indians, and Canadians, and he crossed Lake Erie on boats. Then they marched and floated on down to Vincennes. "Hair-buyer Hamilton" wanted his forts back, and he wanted to drive the Americans out of the upper Ohio country.

When Clark heard that Hamilton was on his way, he said, "I must take Hamilton, or Hamilton will take me."[3] Word came that Vincennes had been taken back by the British. Hamilton had attacked with over 500 men. Because Clark had left only a few Americans there, there had been nothing for them to do but surrender the fort.

If a country were not worth protecting, it was not worth claiming.[2]

George Rogers Clark

THE CITIES SURRENDER

At sundown on the fourth day of July, the army reached the town of Kaskaskia. It was an old town with a fort that was controlled by the British army. The British commander had more soldiers than Clark did, so Clark planned to take the fort by surprise. Quietly, the patriots surrounded the town. Clark led a group of them to the fort where they heard the sounds of music and dancing. Slipping inside, Clark went to the building where the dance was taking place. He quietly stepped through the door and stood with his arms crossed, watching the dancers.

An Indian saw Clark's face in the light of the torches. He sprang to his feet with a loud war whoop that shocked everyone and stopped the dancers in their tracks. Women screamed. Men started toward Clark to challenge him, demanding to know who he was and what he wanted.

Clark cheerfully said, "Go on with your dance, but remember that you dance under Virginia and not under Great Britain!"[4] Then his men rushed in behind him. The British general surrendered quickly.

The French people who lived in Kaskaskia were afraid. They were shocked to find that their town had been completely surrounded by men who were at war with their British friends. They feared they would be killed.

The French sent some of their leaders to beg Clark not to kill them. They were surprised and happy when Clark told them that no one would be killed. The Americans were friends of the French. He gave them the news that the king of France had agreed to send soldiers and ships to help the Americans fight for their freedom from England. When this news spread through the countryside, the town of Cahokia also surrendered.

Clark's attack on Fort Sackville, Vincennes. February 1779, by Ezra Winter, c.1910 (PD-US).

THE TERRIBLE WINTER MARCH

Hamilton made a big mistake. He decided to spend the winter at Vincennes. He knew he had more men and cannons than the Americans had. He thought he could spend the winter in comfort and destroy Clark's army in the warm weather of spring. Surely he had nothing to fear from the Americans until then. It was winter. No army could brave the harsh frontier conditions to attack him.

But Hamilton did not understand Clark and his men. They were tough frontiersmen who had worked hard all their lives to conquer the wilderness and make homes for their families. They had grown their own food, built their own shelter, and made their own clothing. They were used to taking all the harsh blows that nature could throw at them.

Clark's men were pioneers. They had grown strong by living in the wilderness and facing many dangers. Hard times in life are used by God to make us stronger. "Thou therefore endure hardness, as a good soldier of Jesus Christ." —II Timothy 2:3

Besides that, they were patriots. They had to take care of themselves and help their neighbors, as well. On the frontier, no man ruled over another. Towns had their own laws, and people obeyed them because they had helped make them. They believed in freedom. They wanted to live as free men all their lives, and they wanted freedom for others, too. They knew how to fight, and they were willing to fight for freedom from kings and tyrants.

Clark set to work. He had his men build a makeshift gunboat. He placed his cannons and about 40 men on the boat and ordered them to travel by river to Vincennes. Then he set out with the rest of his men to march through the freezing wilderness to attack the fort by land.

People in the French frontier towns heard about Clark's march. Forty or 50 French men joined his force. Clark divided his men into groups. Each party would take a turn hunting game for food for the rest. At night, they built campfires, sang, danced, told stories, and feasted on wild meat. They enjoyed "bear ham, buffalo hump, elk, saddle, and venison haunch."[5] The mood was merry, and the men looked forward to the fight for Fort Vincennes.

Wabash River, by Lt. Governor Henry Hamilton, 1778 (PD-US).

But it was a different scene when the army reached the low land near the Wabash River. They looked across miles of muddy water with islands of high ground showing in places. It would have been difficult to cross this area of cold water and deep mud, even in warm weather. But it seemed impossible in winter's freezing weather.

The men made a simple boat to carry them through the deepest places. The horses swam. After a few days of suffering terrible cold and struggling through the mud, they heard the boom of a cannon. It was the morning gun from the fort. They knew they were getting close to their goal.

But travel was slow through the swampy land. They were running out of food. Most of the game had been driven away to find dry ground. Starvation began to be a real threat. The men knew they still had a few days to travel, but how could they keep on going? Sometimes they could not even find a dry place to camp at night.

Some men grew too weak to walk. They were carried along in boats pushed by the others. The stronger men sang songs and joked to keep up the courage of the weaker men. Finally, they reached the other bank of the Wabash River. As they struggled up the bank to dry ground, some of the men were so worn out and cold that they fell down while still half in the water. Men built great fires and carried the weaker men near to get warm. They made broth of deer meat and fed the weak ones first. Soon, the army was rested and ready to fight.

One thing that stands out about George Rogers Clark is his boldness. Boldness means "facing confrontation with the assurance that God will bless the outcome if I'm standing firm for the truth."[7]

"The wicked flee when no man pursueth: but the righteous are bold as a lion."

—Proverbs 28:1

George Rogers Clark had to make a decision. He could try to attack the fort by surprise, or he could send a messenger to the people of the town and warn them that a battle was about to happen. Clark decided to act boldly. He would send a message saying that he was about to attack and that he was sure he would win. He would tell the people who were loyal to America to stay in their homes and be left in peace. He would tell those loyal to the British king to go into the fort and fight like men along with the "hair buyer." He hoped that his bold words would discourage the enemy.[6]

Just at dark, Clark's men charged the town. They attacked the fort. The fight went on all night. When morning brought daylight, Clark's men fired through the portholes and drove the gunners away from the cannon. Clark's men begged him to let them storm the fort. Only one American had been killed in several hours of fighting. Several British soldiers had gone down dead or wounded.

Night attack on Fort Sackville, by Edward Mason, 1895 (PD-US).

That afternoon, Hamilton surrendered, and the Stars and Stripes waved once again over Fort Vincennes. Clark placed his men in the forts at Kaskaskia, Cahokia, and Vincennes. He hoped to march against the British stronghold at Detroit, but he was unable to gather the large amount of money and the number of men that would be needed for such a large attack. He said, "Never was a person more mortified than I was at this time, to see so fair an opportunity to push a victory; Detroit lost for want of a few men."[8]

The brave men who had followed Clark on this tough expedition were rewarded. Virginia gave each of the 300 acres of rich Indiana land for their farms. After surveying, the land became known as Clark's Grant.

> *Our cause is just, our country will be grateful.*[10]
>
> George Rogers Clark

FROM THE ATLANTIC TO THE MISSISSIPPI

The British were never able to take back the region that Clark and his men captured. The patriots accomplished one of the greatest feats of the Revolutionary War. They extended the western border of the colonies all the way to the Mississippi River. When the War of Independence ended, England gave up the Northwest Territory, and it became part of the United States.

Clark lived until 1828, and died he on Corn Island. In 1895, his achievements were honored by a monument created in Indianapolis, Indiana. He is remembered as the great and brave leader who opened the Northwest Territory to American settlers.[9]

Lt. Governor Henry Hamilton surrenders to Col. George Rogers Clark, February 24, 1779, artist and date unknown (PD-US).

James Robertson

CHAPTER 17

JAMES ROBERTSON

Tennessee Pioneer

A NEW HOME OVER THE MOUNTAINS

James Robertson was another pioneer who lived in Boone's day. Like Daniel Boone, James came from North Carolina. But while Boone was leading the way for the settling of Kentucky, Robertson was doing the same thing in Tennessee. The story shows that he was one of the most dedicated and resourceful pioneers.

Robertson was born in 1742. He was born ten years after George Washington. But his early life was far different from that of young Washington. While Washington was born on a plantation to a wealthy family, James was a poor child. His father and mother were too poor to send James to school. He was a grown man before he learned to read and write.

But he wanted to learn. He was determined enough to teach himself. When he was grown, he learned to read, write, and spell. If the chance had come when he was a boy, we can be sure that he would have learned well. He showed what a good learner he was by the way he learned the ways of the woods.

It was his skill as a woodsman that first made him a great leader. James was not a tall young man, but he was strong and healthy. He had light skin, dark hair, and blue eyes. He was honest and serious. He was a natural leader.

Like Boone, James was also a great hunter. But what he really wanted in the wilderness was a home. He did not want just to

James Robertson, by Washington B. Cooper, c. 1840 (PD-US).

> **"**
>
> *The door to learning is never closed.*[1]
>
> Benjamin Franklin
>
> **"**

It took a lot of determination for James Robertson and other pioneers to make a home in the wilderness. It was never easy. That's why President Harry Truman said, "America was not built on fear. America was built on courage, on imagination and an unbeatable determination to do the job at hand."[2]

Reconstructed Fort Watauga at Sycamore Shoals State Historic Site in Elizabethton, Tennessee, photo by Brian Stansberry, 2009 (CC BY 3.0).

explore new lands. He wanted rich farmland with nearby springs of water. He wanted a good place to raise his family.

James left his home in North Carolina to seek his fortune among the wooded mountains. He made his way through the wild forests with no companion but his faithful horse. His only protection was his rifle. He crossed mountain after mountain until he came to the region where the westward-flowing rivers began.

On the Watauga River, he found some settlers from Virginia. They gave him a kind welcome. He stayed long enough to plant a crop of corn and see it grow up and ripen. He decided this was a good place for his family.

Late that fall, he started back home. Riding his horse, he carried a leather pouch of corn for his food. His rifle would provide the rest.

All went well at first, but James got lost. The mountains became too steep for his horse. He had to let his horse run free and go ahead on foot.

Soon, his corn ran out. His gunpowder got wet and would not fire. For two weeks, his only food was berries, nuts, and whatever else he could find in the woods.

Nearly starving, he finally met two hunters who gave him food. Then they asked him to join them. The three men took turns riding the two horses, and finally James reached home safely.

What a scary experience! A weaker man might have been afraid to make another journey back through the wilderness. But James Robertson was not a man who was easily beaten. He had found a wonderful home in the wilderness, and he was determined to take his family there. He told his friends about the land over the mountains. When spring came again, 16 families were ready to follow him back to the Watauga.

How the Backwoodsmen Lived

Let's imagine what the trip must have been like for these pioneer families. Each family had a pack horse or mule. Some families had more to carry, so they might have had two horses. On the horses were loaded the family's household goods. Pioneer life was simple, so the horses carried only things the families really needed, like rolls of bedding, bundles of clothes, cooking pots, and bags of seed, corn, and salt.

A pioneer mother might ride on a horse, along with its pack and a small child or two. The boys and men would walk, carrying their rifles. They would go ahead of the women, ready to shoot wild game or Indians if they were attacked.

Once they reached their new home in the wilderness, there was work to do. The younger children would set to work clearing away the dead brush. They would make big piles to burn. The men and older boys would cut down trees. Some of these would be used to build a cabin. Everybody helped. Soon, the new home would be ready.

The furniture was simple, too. Most of it was made of wood found around the cabin. There was a bedstead made of poles and a washstand nearby. They usually had a few three-legged stools. They used split poles to make a table. They would bring water from the spring in wooden buckets, and gourd dippers were in the buckets for drinking and dipping. Pegs driven into the walls held clothes, rifles, and other things. Some families had real blankets, but most slept under skins from a deer, bears, or buffalo.

The food also was simple, but there was plenty of it. Most of it was wild game. Instead of pork and beef for meat, these forest people would eat bear meat or venison. There is no white flour, but they used cornmeal for cornbread. Each family had a little grinding mill for the corn. Some of the corn was boiled to make hominy.

Every pioneer man had to be good with a rifle. He had to get his own meat and protect his family from attack. He needed sharp eyes and ears to find game and to watch out for enemies.

But most important of all, he had to be tough and strong. Sometimes, he had to spend weeks or months living in the

Gourd dipper made from a calabash (bottle gourd).

woods. He might have no food but meat. He might have no shelter but a lean-to made of brush.

There were plenty of deer and bears. There were great, shaggy buffalo. Now and then, there was an exciting battle with wolves, a bear, or a cougar. A man had to be always alert for Indians. Some of them were friendly, but some were not.

Each family depended on itself for most of the necessaries of life. Each member had his own work. The father was the protector and provider; the mother was the cook, the weaver, the tailor, and the housekeeper. The girls were her sturdy helpers, while the boys helped the father outdoors with sickles, hoes, and axes.[3]

But a few things could not always be found or made in the wilderness. Each family would shoot and trap all the animal skins they could. Then, once a year, after the harvest was gathered, they loaded the packhorses with the skins. Back over the mountains they went. They headed for the big towns of the east. There, they would trade their skins for salt, iron, and other things they needed.

Usually two or more families would travel together. Sometimes they would take hogs or cattle to sell.

This free outdoor life developed strong and tough bodies, but there was not much schooling in the backwoods settlements. Most boys and girls learned very little except reading, writing, and simple math. If there were any schoolhouses at all, they were log huts. They were poorly lit, and the furniture was mostly log benches. Most families had no books except the Bible.

In many ways, the life of the pioneer child was different from yours. But it was very interesting. He learned, like his elders, to imitate bird calls, to set traps, and to shoot rifles. At 12, the little boy became a foot soldier. He knew what loophole he was to shoot from if enemies attacked the fort. He took pride in becoming a good shot with the rifle. He was also carefully trained to follow an trails and to hide his own trails from enemy eyes. These skills served him well as a hunter and fighter in the wilderness.

This was the life of these early woodsmen and their families. This was the life Robertson and his neighbors lived year after year. When James brought his party of settlers to the Watauga country, they quickly mixed in with the people already there.

Robertson became one of the leaders of the settlement. His log cabin stood on an island in the river. Some said it was the largest cabin in the settlement. It had several rooms, a loft, and a huge stone fireplace. On cold days, a fire blazed up the chimney. It made the cabin cheery and warm.

James Robertson and his family were prosperous at Watauga. But in 1799, James got the urge to wander again. He left his place of leadership at Watauga, and he went west once more. Deeper into the wilderness, he marched to seek yet another new home.

> *But if any provide not for his own, and specially for those of his own house, he hath denied the faith, and is worse than an infidel.*
>
> —I Timothy 5:8

Moving On Again

In middle Tennessee he found a beautiful country lying along a bend of the Cumberland River. This is where the city of Nashville now stands. Because James had proven himself as a leader, other families wanted to go on the journey with him.

In the early spring, a small group of men went ahead of the rest to plant corn. The rest of the settlers would come in the fall. There would be corn ready for them to eat when they arrived. James led the party. They followed the paths of wild animals through the woods.

When they came to a good place for a settlement, the men built cabins and planted cornfields. Then they left three men to keep buffaloes from eating the corn crop, the others returned to Watauga.

When fall came, two groups started out. One group went down the river on flatboats and in canoes. These people were mostly women and children. That route was longer, but people thought it would be easier than traveling over land with the children. Robertson led the others by land. They planned to get to the new settlement in time to get it ready for the women and children coming by water.

About Christmas time, Robertson and his men arrived. They waited four months for the others to arrive. Finally, in April, the boats came. They traveled down the Tennessee River, then up the Ohio River, then up the Cumberland River.

141

They had been attacked many times by Indians on the shore. The big flatboats were hard to steer, so it was hard to get away from the clouds of arrows hissing through the air.

Finally, all were in their new homes. They forgot their past troubles and took up the work of making a settlement in the wilderness.

However, their Indian troubles were not over. The first group of settlers had seen no troubles with the tribes. But now, spring came, and groups of hunters and warriors became a danger. They did not like the settlers scaring away their game. They also liked to take scalps and steal, just as they did from other Indian tribes.

They became a constant terror. Settlers were killed while working in their fields or hunting in the forests. A shot would sound from out in the bushes, and a bullet would go singing through the air to find its mark. Sometimes a settler would go hunting after a turkey he heard calling in the woods, only to be shot by an Indian who had really given the turkey's gobble.

The corn crop did not grow well. The autumn brought heavy rainstorms that knocked down the stalks. The poor settlers had to live on the game they killed. But they began to run low on bullets and powder. The danger was great. Robertson decided to go to Kentucky for more supplies.[4]

When the Revolutionary War ended, the Indian problems began to die out. No longer was the British government paying them for settlers' scalps. Settlers began to cross the mountains in large numbers as there were fewer dangers. Many made their homes at Nashville, and it became safer to live in the settlement.

The name of James Robertson was now well known. He had planted two successful settlements. He had led them and protected them with wisdom and courage. George Washington heard about Robertson and made him a general in the army in 1790.

When he died in 1790, James Robertson left a good name behind him. He was brave, strong, tough, and self-reliant. He was willing to face the hardships of the wilderness. He was loved by his family, admired by his friends, and thought of as a hero to his country.

SAVING THE FORT

Robertson went alone, and he made the long trip safely. In January, he returned with a load of ammunition. He was welcomed in the fort. Everyone gathered around to hear the story of his adventures on the trail. There was much to talk about, and they sat up late into the night. At last they all went to bed. But they were not worried because it was winter, and the Indians usually did not make trouble then. The settlers did not leave any men guarding the fort that night.

Though he was tired, James Robertson could not sleep. He had a feeling that there was danger about. He was right. Near the fort, lurking in the trees and underbrush, was a group of warriors. They were planning to ambush the fort. They were eager for scalps and plunder.

They crept forward carefully. They had to be careful, for the moon was bright and gave some light in the sleeping fort. The braves crept forward to the attack. A moving shadow fell upon the moonlit clearing outside the fort. An Indian had silently crossed the clearing between the log wall and the woods. Then another crossed, then another. They huddled quietly against the posts. Soon, the entire war party crouched in the shadow of the fort.

The next move was to slide the bar and unhook the chain that fastened the gate. But something made a sound. Perhaps the hinges creaked or the chain links clinked together. Suddenly, Robertson sprang to his feet. His eyes were already used to the dark because he had been lying awake. He saw several shadows moving quietly through the gate.

He alerted the others in the fort. Instantly, every settler snatched their guns. In a second, the shots rang out, and the Indians disappeared through the gate and into the tangled woods. But one brave was dead, and some of the settlers were killed or wounded, as well.

James Robertson, the leader and protector, had saved the fort. He had probably saved many of his friends from death as well.[5]

John Hancock

CHAPTER 18

JOHN HANCOCK

Dedicated Patriot

THE YOUNG BUSINESSMAN

Massachusetts was important in the War of Independence. The city of Boston was the scene of many exciting events. The Boston Massacre and the Boston Tea Party were milestones on the road to independence. The battles at Lexington, Concord, and Bunker Hill took place in Massachusetts. Also, several Founding Fathers were born in the state. These included Benjamin Franklin, John Adams, and Samuel Adams.

Another great patriot born in Massachusetts was John Hancock. He was born in the town of Braintree, near Boston, in 1737. John's father was a good man. He was a preacher of the gospel. But when little John was only seven years old, his father died.

Next, Thomas gave John a job. John was a clerk in his uncle's business. He worked hard in the store. He was always on time, and he learned fast. People said he was a good example to the other young men of the town.

Thomas Hancock was a rich man. He used four large ships to carry goods from England to sell in the colonies. He taught John so well that he was able to send him to England to business for the company.

In 1764, Thomas died. He left most of his fortune to John. People watched John carefully. He was only a young man, 27 years old. Would he have the wisdom to handle so much money? Would he waste it all? He was now one of the richest men in Massachusetts. Would he still be rich in a few years?

John Hancock, by John Singleton Copley, c.1770 (PD-Art).

(CC BY-SA 3.0)

After his father died, John Hancock went to live with his grandparents. His uncle, Thomas Hancock (left), took John under his wing. Thomas had no children of his own. Thomas treated John as a son. He sent John to school when he was a boy. Later, he sent John to Harvard College. This education was expensive, but Thomas was a wealthy businessman.

Portrait of John Hancock, by John Singleton Copley, 1765 (PD-Art).

John did have nice suits and fancy carriages. But those who thought he would waste all of his uncle's money were wrong. He was not selfish or silly. He gave money to help people. Once, several buildings were damaged in a big fire. John gave a large amount of money to rebuild them. Every winter, he gave money to buy food for poor people.

The people of Boston liked John because of his kindness. They trusted him because they saw that he wanted to help people. So they elected him to be a selectman. The selectmen were men who made the laws in New England towns.

Samuel Adams knew John Hancock. He knew John would be even more willing to help Boston now that he was an elected leader. He said Boston citizens had been wise to elect John because "they had made that young man's fortune their own."[2]

In 1776, John Hancock was elected to a higher office. He was made a member of the colonial legislature of Massachusetts. He would help make the laws for the whole colony. In the legislature, he was a friend of Samuel Adams. Adams recruited Hancock to be a member of the Liberty Party. That group in the legislature wanted independence from England. Both men knew it was dangerous to oppose the king. There had been trouble in Boston because of the town's independent spirit. But Hancock was willing to lose his entire business in Boston if he had to. He said to his patriot friends, "Burn Boston and make John Hancock a beggar, if the public good requires it."[3]

A Rising Young Leader

Hancock and Adams were an interesting pair. Adams was poor, and his suit was nearly worn out. Hancock was young and rich. He had many fancy suits. Adams wrote letters to the newspapers arguing for independence. Hancock made speeches and gave money to the cause. People joked that Adams wrote the letters and Hancock paid the postage.

In 1768, one of Hancock's ships came into Boston Harbor with an expensive load of goods. The British officer at the harbor said Hancock had to pay taxes on his cargo. Hancock refused to pay. The officers seized the ship, and Hancock could not get it back. When the people of Boston heard that the British had stolen their leader's ship, some of them attacked the officers' office. Then they burned a boat that belonged to them. Hancock did not take part in the attack, but the British blamed him for it.

Sensible of the importance of Christian piety and virtue to the order and happiness of a state, I cannot but earnestly commend to you every measure for their support and encouragement.

John Hancock

The citizens of Boston elected Hancock to a special committee. This group was formed to persuade the British governor to remove the redcoat troops from Boston after the Boston Massacre. Finally, the governor ordered the redcoats out of town. The people of Boston respected John Hancock even more.

In October of 1774, Hancock was elected president of the Massachusetts provincial congress. This was a group of patriots that met in Concord. The British governor of Massachusetts, Gage, began to think of Hancock as a traitor and an outlaw. Hancock encouraged the men of Massachusetts to organize groups of minutemen.

In April of 1775, the British were concerned about affairs in Massachusetts. They knew the patriots were preparing for war. They knew about the guns and supplies stored at Concord. They knew about the provincial congress meeting there. They had heard that Samuel Adams and John Hancock were staying at the home of Reverend Jonas Clark in Lexington. They sent a troop of redcoat soldiers to capture the guns and supplies. They were also ordered to arrest Hancock and Adams.[4]

Peyton Randolph was elected to be the president of the second Continental Congress. But he was sick and had to resign. The delegates then elected John Hancock president.

In May, 1775 Hancock got married to Dolly Quincy. They would have a son and a daughter. Both of them died as children.

The second Continental Congress voted to fight for liberty from Britain. Thomas Jefferson wrote the Declaration of Independence.

Peyton Randolph, by Charles Willson Peale, before 1827 (PD-Art).

The generous man will be prosperous, And he who waters will himself be watered.

Proverbs 11:25 NASV

HANCOCK AND ADAMS

You already know the story of Paul Revere's ride to warn Lexington and Concord that the British were coming. Hancock and Adams got away before the redcoats could reach Lexington. Young Hancock wanted to stay and fight with the minutemen, but his friends told him he had to leave. He was needed to help lead the colony in the days ahead.

Hancock and Adams left Lexington and headed for Philadelphia where they would attend the second Continental Congress. Shortly after the battles of Lexington and Concord, Governor Gage made a proclamation. He said he wanted peace between the British government and the people of Massachusetts. If the people would lay down their weapons, they would be forgiven for their rebellion. But there were two men who would not be pardoned. They were Hancock and Adams.[5]

After the Continental Congress approved it, John Hancock was the first man to sign his name. This was a brave act. These men knew they might fail in their war for independence. If they failed, the king would hang them as traitors. But John was a brave man. He signed his name in large letters. He joked that the king could read it without his glasses and double his price on John Hancock's head.

Portrait of Dorthy Quincy, by John Singleton Copley, c.1772 (PD-Art).

FINISHING WELL

Hancock served in Congress through some of the darkest days of the Revolutionary War. When the British drove Washington out of New York and New Jersey in 1776, Congress had to flee to Baltimore. In March 1777, Congress returned to Philadelphia. But the members had to run for their lives again six months later when the British took over Philadelphia for their winter quarters. John Hancock wrote letters to leaders of the colonies. He asked for money, supplies, and troops for Washington's army.

He led the Marine Committee. He took pride in helping create a small fleet of American frigates. One of these ships was named the *John Hancock* in his honor.

> John Hancock called on the entire state to pray "that universal happiness may be established in the world [and] that all may bow to the scepter of our Lord Jesus Christ, and the whole earth be filled with His glory."[6]

Massachusetts made Hancock a major general in the militia. He led a command of 6,000 New England troops on a mission to Rhode Island. Their job was to drive the British out of Rhode Island. A fleet of French ships was to sail to Rhode Island and attack the redcoats at the same time. But the French did not do their part. The ships did not come, and the militia had to go back.

Hancock was in the Massachusetts state legislature when they wrote the first state constitution. He was elected the first governor of Massachusetts. He was so popular in Massachusetts that he was elected governor again and again. When America won its independence and wrote the national Constitution, Hancock made a speech urging the other Massachusetts leaders to vote for it. Later, he had to resign as governor because of poor health.

> "
> *The interposition of divine Providence in our favour hath been most abundantly and most graciously manifested, and the citizens of these Untied States have every reason for praise and gratitude to the God of their salvation.*
>
> John Hancock
> (A Proclamation for a Day of Thanksgiving and Prayer to be celebrated on December 11, 1783.)
> "

Hancock died in 1793 at 56 years of age. Acting governor Samuel Adams declared a state holiday on the day Hancock was buried. He was given a large and grand funeral. Thousands of people attended it. There were state leaders, citizens, and militiamen. Samuel Adams walked in front of the coffin. Behind it walked John Adams, the vice president of the United States.

After his death, John Hancock was not remembered as much as he should have been. This was in the early days of America. There were many national heroes still living. George Washington was the name everyone talked about. Years after his death, John Adams said both John Hancock and Samuel Adams had been almost forgotten.

In 1876, America turned 100 years old. There was a celebration called the Centennial all across the country. People took more interest in the history of America's birth. The city of Boston put up plaques in honor of Hancock. Then, in 1896, a big memorial was built over Hancock's grave.

Today, John Hancock has been honored as a patriot in many ways. Several U.S. Navy ships have been named after him. There are counties named after him in ten states. Some cities and other places are named after him, also. John Hancock University is in Illinois.[7]

While in leadership in Massachusetts, John Hancock called on the people of the state to pray:

> that all nations may bow to the scepter of our Lord and Savior Jesus Christ and that the whole earth may be filled with his glory.

> that the spiritual kingdom of our Lord and Savior Jesus Christ may be continually increasing until the whole earth shall be filled with His glory.

> to confess their sins and to implore forgiveness of God through the merits of the Savior of the World.

> to cause the benign religion of our Lord and Savior Jesus Christ to be known, understood, and practiced among all the inhabitants of the earth.

> to confess their sins before God and implore His forgiveness through the merits and mediation of Jesus Christ, our Lord and Savior.

> that He would finally overrule all events to the advancement of the Redeemer's kingdom and the establishment of universal peace and good will among men.

> that the kingdom of our Lord and Savior Jesus Christ may be established in peace and righteousness among all the nations of the earth.

> that with true contrition of heart we may confess our sins, resolve to forsake them, and implore the Divine forgiveness, through the merits and mediation of Jesus Christ, our Savior. . . . And finally to overrule all the commotions in the world to the spreading the true religion of our Lord Jesus Christ in its purity and power among all the people of the earth.

John Hancock's Tombstone in Boston, by Shadow0704, 2008 (PD-US).

Capture of the
Hessians at Trenton

CHAPTER 19

JOHN HART

Honest Patriot

HONEST JOHN

America has a rich history. We have many great men and women to look back to for examples of godliness and virtue. Some of those people are well known. Everybody knows about Washington and Jefferson, Davy Crockett and Robert E. Lee. But there are many great people who are less known. Still, it is worth reading about them and learning to be like them. One of these people is John Hart, a farmer from New Jersey.

Most farmers do not become famous. Most of them just work hard, producing food for the rest of us. But sometimes a farmer is given other important things to do. If a man lives a life of honesty and justice, others will see it. He might be asked to leave his plow for a time to take care of important business where others need him.

It's been said that the most important "ability" is "availability." John Hart had a big farm to run — with no tractors, only horses. Yet he made himself available when his neighbors needed him in public office.

John Hart was born in Stonington, Connecticut, in 1711. Before he was two years old, his family moved to Hopewell, New Jersey. John's father was Edward Hart. He had been a farmer, too. For a time, he had been called to lead a corps in the French and Indian War. His men were called the New Jersey Blues. After the war, Edward and his young family settled down to farm in Hopewell.

Thanks be given unto Almighty God therefore, and knowing that it is appointed for all men once to die and after that the judgment [Hebrews 9:27] . . . principally, I give and recommend my soul into the hands of Almighty God who gave it and my body to the earth to be buried in a decent and Christian like manner . . . to receive the same again at the general resurrection by the mighty power of God.

—John Hart's last will and testament, April 16, 1779

Young John grew up working with his father in the fields. He studied in his spare time and gained a good education. As a young man, he was able to buy a 380-acre farm of his own. Over the years, through hard work and honesty, he became known as the most respected man in his community. When he was 29 years old, he married Miss Deborah Scudder. Together, the happy couple began building their family. God blessed them with 13 children. The family worked as a team, and their farm prospered.[1]

2 Corinthians 8:21 says, "for we have regard for what is honorable, not only in the sight of the Lord, but also in the sight of men." It was the honorable nature of John Hart's life that caused his neighbors to respect him.

Year by year, John's acres brought forth their crops. He led a busy life. He raised a family, helped his neighbors, and improved his farm. He became known as a man of good character, one who could be trusted. His neighbors knew that they could depend on him to do what was right. He was called "Honest John."

In 1755, John's neighbors elected him justice of the peace. People soon saw that even though he had some power, he was still honest. In 1761, he was elected by his neighbors to make their laws for them in the New Jersey legislature.

In 1765, Parliament passed the Stamp Act. It placed a small tax on stamped paper used to do business in the colonies. John Hart believed the act was not legal. He thought the colonies should send a letter to the king telling him so.

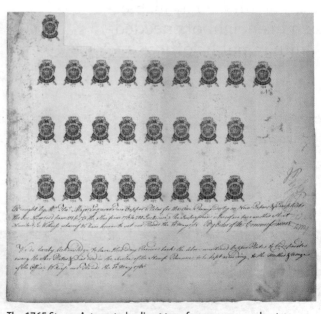

The 1765 Stamp Act created a direct tax of one penny per sheet on newspapers and required that the newspapers be printed on stamped paper purchased from government agents, engraver unknown, 1765 (PD-UKD).

John Hart was a farmer. He did not have much to do with stamped paper. That paper was used for legal documents like wills and licenses. A farmer did not need a license. But some people talked of resisting the king and Parliament. What would Honest John do? He was also getting older. Why should he take a hand in matters that would make little difference in the way he lived his life? Why should he get involved in arguments with England? Why should he be a part of fighting, if it came to that?

John Hart was concerned about justice. Even though he knew war might come to America, even to his peaceful farm, he felt he had to take a stand.

The problem with the Stamp Act was not that it cost anybody a lot of money. The king and Parliament had made it a small tax on purpose.

They hoped the Americans would pay it rather than argue about it. But many of the colonists thought as John Hart did. They did not like the tax just because the king had no right to tax them.

HONEST JOHN GOES TO CONGRESS

Still, most Americans still thought of themselves as Englishmen. They did not want to break away and start a new country. They just wanted to be treated as other Englishmen. They wanted to have a vote on the taxes they had to pay.

John Hart was wise enough to know that this issue could cause trouble. He wanted to live in peace on his quiet farm. He enjoyed the blessings of life and his happy family there. But like many others, he believed the king and Parliament could take all their rights away if they could take away their right to vote on their own taxes.

The Stamp Act did not affect John Hart much, but he was concerned about others. He knew the Parliament had no right to tax the colonists. He stood against the tax because it hurt other people.

This issue was important to both sides. The British were used to a life in which some people were considered better than others because they were nobles. Those people were proud of their birth. They liked being able to make rules for others. The Americans were the children and grandchildren of the early Pilgrims and Puritans. Their forefathers had come to the New World to be able to live and worship as they chose. They had struggled to build homes and communities in the wilderness. The English government had not given them much help. They were free people who stood on their own feet. They did not like it when England passed laws that took away their rights. The colonies decided to send their leaders to decide what to do.

The first Continental Congress met in 1774. New Jersey elected John Hart to be one of its representatives. The British closed the port of Boston so no ships could come and go. England thought it could starve Massachusetts into giving up its rights. But Massachusetts

The First Continental Congress, 1774, by Allyn Cox (Architect of the Capitol), 1974 (PD-US).

King George III in coronation robes, by Allan Ramsay, c.1765 (PD-Art).

would not give in. The other colonies heard what was happening and took a stand with Massachusetts. Their representatives gathered in Philadelphia.

The Continental Congress was an unusual group of men. The colonies sent their best and most honest men. These men were not out to gain anything for themselves. They were not looking for fame. They did not want to separate into groups and fight with other groups to get what they wanted. They were there to give their time, strength, and wisdom for the good of all the colonies.

John Hart was one of those who wanted to appeal to King George. Most of the early delegates did not want war. They did not want independence. They just wanted to be treated like English citizens were treated in England. A letter was written and signed by the members of Congress. It was sent to the king and the people of England, asking them to work with the colonies to fix the problems.

Then Hart went back to his farm. He waited for a reply from the king, hoping there would be a spirit of peace between England and America. But he was not able to stay at home.

In January of 1775, he was appointed to go to Congress again. He was 60 years old, one of the oldest men there. He had wise judgment. That helped calm down some of the younger members who were sometimes too excited to think wisely.

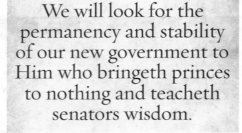

We will look for the permanency and stability of our new government to Him who bringeth princes to nothing and teacheth senators wisdom.

When the Continental Congress allowed the members to go home for a while, Hart went back to his family and his farm. He had been away so much that things were not running as smoothly as they should. It took a lot of care to run a large farm. When Congress started up again in September, he begged the New Jersey legislature to excuse him from going back. He needed more time at home.

During the Revolutionary War, the king of England had to hire foreign soldiers to help him. This was partly because he was also fighting France and Spain. It was also because there were many people in England who did not want to fight other Englishmen in the colonies. Some of them had relatives in America. The king hired men from the German state of Hesse-Cassel to help him. They were called Hessians. King George hired about 30,000 of them.

But the needs of his colony kept calling him back to public service. He was elected to the provincial congress of New Jersey. Then he was elected to go back to the Continental Congress in Philadelphia in 1776.

Hart was still hoping for peace with England. But every friendly bill in Parliament was voted down. The king had been preparing to hire foreign soldiers called Hessians to help him fight the colonies. The British people did not seem to care that the colonies were not being treated fairly. The New Jersey legislature sent John Hart back to Congress in June. He was instructed to join the other delegates in protecting the rights of the colonies, even if it meant declaring independence from England.

When the representatives in Congress signed the Declaration of Independence, the king said they were committing treason, usually punished by hanging. The signers also knew that their homes and farms could be destroyed by the British. Signing the Declaration took a lot of courage.

The Delaware Regiment at the Battle of Long Island, artist and date unknown (PD-US).

Soon, the British General Howe and his army arrived in New York. Then, the Continental Congress passed the Declaration of Independence. A copy was sent to General Washington. He had it read to the soldiers. Other copies were sent to all the colonies. But these copies had only two signatures on them. They were the signatures of John Hancock, the president of Continental Congress, and Charles Thomson, the secretary. When Howe defeated Washington's army at Long Island and drove them out of New York, a new set of copies were published. This time, the signatures of all the signers were on the Declaration. The hard times the army was suffering made all the members of Congress want to remind the soldiers that the Continental Congress was on their side.

John Hart knew what he was risking when he signed the Declaration. His New Jersey home was not far from New York. The British army would be hunting for him and the other men from New Jersey. They would destroy his farm and his family if they could. But he was a patriot. He was not a young man, driven by excitement. He was not a politician, hoping to be elected to some high office in a new country after the war. He was driven by patriotism, love of justice, and trust in God to reward righteousness.

In August of 1776, New Jersey elected a General Assembly under its new state constitution. Hart was elected to that body, and he was selected to be speaker. He soon returned home to attend to family matters. His wife, Deborah, died on October 8, 1776, with John at her side.[3]

> *We will look, for the permanency and stability of our new government, to Him who bringeth Princes to nothing, and teacheth Senators wisdom.*"[2]
>
> John Hart

John did not see the fulfillment of his wish of freedom and independence for Americans, for he died before the end of the Revolutionary War. Nevertheless, he is remembered for having dedicated years of service to his Christian faith, his family, and his country. He died on May 11, 1779, and "was always known as a sincere, but unostentatious [humble] Christian."[4]

> *Thanks be given unto Almighty God therefore, and knowing that it is appointed for all men once to die and after that the judgment [Hebrews 9:27] … principally, I give and recommend my soul into the hands of Almighty God who gave it and my body to the earth to be buried in a decent and Christian like manner … to receive the same again at the general resurrection by the mighty power of God.*
>
> John Hart's
> last will and testament

HART'S SACRIFICE FOR FREEDOM

Storytime with Uncle Rick

Fight for Freedom

Soon, the war was in New Jersey. The British advanced from New York to the Delaware River. The men in Congress were shocked when they heard of the destruction. All those who had signed the Declaration knew they were marked for destruction. Now, John Hart's farm was in the path of the British. They wanted to capture him and punish him.

John Hart was at home one day when some of his neighbors rushed in. "The British are coming down the road! You must run for your life, John!"[5]

But Hart did not want to leave his family. Finally, his friends persuaded him that his leadership was needed too much for him to be captured. They promised to care of things for him as he fled. With deep sadness, he left his farm and ran into the woods.

The British hunted for John Hart. Day after day, he hid out in the nearby Sourland Mountains. Most of the time, he was hungry. He could not seek shelter in a friendly home. He could not even build a hut in the woods because the British might find it. He seldom slept in the same place two nights in a row. Caves, thickets, and even hollow logs became his hiding places. He slept on the ground, nearly freezing to death sometimes. Once, he curled up with a large dog he met in order to keep warm.

When Washington defeated the Hessians at Princeton on January 3, 1777, Hart was able to return home. He found the Hessians had devastated his farm in his absence.

January 1777 was not a cheerful time for John Hart. His wife had died. His family had been scattered. The redcoats had destroyed his farm.

The British published a notice that Hart would be left alone if he would renounce his signature on the Declaration. John Hart would not break his word. He suffered from sickness often, but he worked to rebuild his farm and gather his children. He died in 1779. He did not live long enough to see the end of the war and a new nation born.[6]

Quakers meeting
in 18th century

CHAPTER 20

LYDIA DARRAGH

Petticoat Patriot

THE QUAKER SPY FAMILY

The first few days of December 1777 were important for General Washington. The British had just beaten America in September at the Battle of Brandywine Creek. They had lost another battle at Germantown in October. Washington's army was camped at Whitemarsh, near Philadelphia. His men rested and recovered, waiting for the next orders.

In Philadelphia, the British army under General Howe was having a good time. They had plenty of food and other things they needed. But Howe planned to make a night march and surprise the American army. If he could catch Washington off guard, he might score a victory and defeat the Americans for good. The patriots had lost two major battles in only a few weeks. A hard blow might destroy their army forever.

But Washington had friends in Philadelphia. Some of them had contact with the British officers. They heard that Howe was planning an attack. They began to sneak messages to the patriots so they would not be caught by surprise.

On December 1, Major Clark got a message and sent it on to Washington. It said the British soldiers had received orders to be ready to march. Captain Craig sent word from Frankford, Pennsylvania that Howe had plans to drive Washington out of his camp. He said 500 redcoats had crossed the river nearby. On December 3, Craig sent another message. He said 3,000 British soldiers had now crossed the river. It looked as if they were going to strike the Americans from behind.

Though we consider thee as a public enemy, we regard thee as a private friend. While we detest the cause thee fights for, we wish well to thy personal interest and safety.

Lydia Darragh

Nation Makers, by Howard Pyle, Brandywine Museum in Chadds Ford, Pennsylvania, date unknown (PD-US).

Pennsylvania was established by affluent Quaker William Penn in 1682, and as an American state run under Quaker principles. William Penn signed a peace treaty with Tammany, leader of the Delaware tribe, and other treaties between Quakers and Indians followed.

Later that afternoon, another message came from Major Clark. This time, he said the British were moving and taking horses and wagons from farmers. At 6 p.m., Clark reported again. An American spy had snuck out of Philadelphia to report that the British soldiers were being given food to carry on a march. Later that evening, a note came from Captain Allan McLane, who had been scouting with his cavalry. Howe was about to try a surprise attack.

Several patriots sent information to General Washington about the coming attack. None of them had better knowledge than a quiet woman named Lydia Darragh. She heard the British plans straight from the redcoat leaders. How could she do that?

Lydia Darragh was a Quaker. Quakers do not believe in wars and fighting, but Lydia believed in the American cause. So did her son, Charles. Even though Charles had been raised in a Quaker home, he had joined General Washington's army. He was a lieutenant in the camp at Whitemarsh.

Lydia's house was at Number 177 on Second Street. Across the street stood a large house being used by the British army. A general who was friendly to General Howe was living there.[2]

General Howe

BUTTONS FOR GENERAL WASHINGTON

Lydia heard things from officers who came and went in the neighborhood. When she heard something she thought Washington should know, she sent him a message. She had a clever way of doing this.

Lydia's husband would write the message in code. He would write it in small letters on tiny pieces of paper. Lydia would wrap the paper around large coat buttons. After that, she would sew cloth over the buttons and sew them on her son's coat. They looked just like any other cloth-covered coat buttons.

Her son John was only 14 years old, but he was already an important spy messenger. He would slip out of the city and try not to be seen by the British. If British sentries caught him, they would let him go on. He was only a boy.

John would go to the American camp and find his older brother, Charles. Charles would cut open the buttons, read the code, and write out the message for General Washington. The British never caught the Darragh family spies.[3]

A Watch in the Night, a Journey in the Day

The time for the attack drew near. Lydia received some important information. The British army needed more room for their officers. Lydia's husband was ordered to move his family away and turn his house over to the British. Lydia was upset about this. It was hard to move her family to a different house. She marched to British headquarters across the street. She protested the order to move.

Lydia's protest worked. We do not know exactly why the British changed the order, but the Darraghs were allowed to stay in their home. All they had to do was allow General Howe to use one room for important meetings.

A backwoods girl.

Lydia might have known one of the redcoat officers personally. Her last name had been Barrington before she married her husband. One of the officers was Captain Barrington, so they might have been related. Lydia's husband had been a teacher for the Barrington family in Ireland. Perhaps Captain Barrington knew her husband, too. It might be that this was the reason the Darraghs were allowed to stay in their home.[4]

Whatever the reason was, Lydia made the best of the situation. She gave the British officers a room in the back of the house for their meetings. She sent some of her children to live in the country for a while, but she kept John at home. She would pay close attention to anything she heard. Anything important that was said would find its way into John's coat buttons.

Redcoat officers began to visit Lydia's house often. There were many meetings in the back room. Perhaps the officers were not as careful about speaking as they should have been. They probably thought a family of Quakers would never help an army in fighting a war. How surprised they would have been if they had known that Charles Darrah was an officer in Washington's camp!

"Be sober, be vigilant; because your adversary the devil, as a roaring lion, walketh about, seeking whom he may devour."

—1 Peter 5:8

To be vigilant means to be alert. Alertness is "being keenly aware of what is taking place around me so I can be prepared with a right response."[5] Lydia was alert at an important time. We need to be alert in spiritual things at all times.

Washington had already started to get reports about British movements. On December 2, he was about to get another one. A British officer told Lydia that her family must go to bed early that night. There would be an important meeting in the back

Washington's headquarters at Whitemarsh.

room. The redcoats must not be disturbed. Officers would be coming at about 7 p.m.

The Darraghs left the officers candles for light and more firewood for the fireplace, and then they went off to bed as they had been told. The British officers began to arrive. Mr. Darragh was away, and Lydia lay alone in her bed. She could not sleep. She had a heavy feeling. She felt that the meeting going on downstairs held danger for the American camp, where her son Charles was. What if the redcoats were planning to attack?

Lydia could not sleep. Finally, she slipped from her bed and went quietly down the stairs. She stepped into a closet next to the conference room. The wall between was only thin boards with wallpaper. She could hear the British voices plainly.

Lydia had tossed and turned in bed so long that the meeting was nearly over. But she was in time to hear a British officer read a paper that reported what they had talked about. Lydia listened, holding her breath.

The British were going to attack the camp at Whitemarsh. They would march out of Philadelphia at night on December 4 and surprise Washington's army. They would have more men than the Americans. They would attack without warning, and Washington would be defeated.

Lydia had heard enough. She had to get back to bed before the meeting ended. With her heart pounding, she slipped back

Washington and Lafayette visiting the suffering army, from *A History of Pennsylvania*, 1913 (PD-US).

up the stairs. She heard the scraping of chairs and the rattle of swords. Then boots clumped up the stairs, and someone knocked on Lydia's bedroom door.

Lydia pretended to be asleep. The hand knocked again, louder this time. Lydia called out in a sleepy voice. The officer told her the meeting was over. She could go downstairs to lock the door and put out the fire and the candles. After he left, Lydia went downstairs and took care of things for the night. She had to decide what to do. It was good that she had acted as if she had been awakened from a sound sleep. Later, she was not suspected of spying. The British officer who had knocked on her door remembered that she sounded sleepy.

Availability means being willing to attend to a need when we are called to help. Lydia desired to be useful to the cause of liberty. She did what she could, and her efforts proved to be crucial. Remember, sometimes God will use you to accomplish great things for His purposes. Remember to be willing and available.

Poor Lydia! All through the next day, she struggled to decide what to do. The British guards would really be on the alert with the day of battle so near. She was afraid to trust the mission to John or anyone else. It was too important. She had to handle it herself. But how would she get the British to let her go out of the city? She needed a good excuse. She would have to carry the message in her head so it could not be lost or read by the wrong person.

Finally, she picked up a cloth sack. She also took her British pass, which said she could leave the city when she had business to do. She began walking out of Philadelphia toward the mill on Frankford Creek. If the redcoat guards asked her what she was doing, she would say she was going to buy flour at the Frankford mill. When she came back, she would be carrying a sack full of flour.

The Battle that Did Not Happen

Lydia trudged along. She was stopped at guard stations, but the guards let her go on. She did not appear to be a threat. She was just a woman dressed in Quaker clothes. Everyone knew Quakers did not take part in wars. She was small and slender. She did not look like a dangerous person.

Finally, she came to Frankford. She was past all the redcoat guards. She left her sack at the mill to be filled with flour. She turned on Nice Town Lane, walking westward toward the Rising Sun Tavern.

The Rising Sun Tavern, Fredericksburg, Virginia. Photo by Morgan Riley, 2011 (CC BY-SA 3.0).

Because Washington had already heard that the British were planning on a move, he had riders watching the roads. Lydia met an American officer riding his horse along the road. He stopped her and asked her what her business was. Lydia recognized the man. He was Colonel Thomas Craig, a friend of the Darragh family. He was surprised to see Lydia so far outside Philadelphia.

Lydia told him she had an important message. Craig got off his horse so they could talk quietly. As he led his horse, she told him what she heard from the redcoats. Colonel Craig left Lydia at a friendly farmhouse to rest and get some food. Then he went galloping along the road to deliver the message to General Washington.

But Lydia was not taking chances. She sent a second message to Washington. That afternoon, American colonel Elias Boudinot was at the Rising Sun Tavern, receiving reports from his scouts. A woman walked in and spoke to him. We are not sure whether the woman was Lydia, but she handed Boudinot a message. When Boudinot described the woman later, it did not sound like Lydia Darragh. She was probably a messenger sent by Lydia.

Prudence is exercising caution in all situations. Lydia Darragh demonstrated prudence as she labored to aid the cause of the patriots. "A prudent man forseeth the trouble and hides himself: but the simple pass on and are punished.

—Proverbs 22:3

The woman gave Colonel Boudinot a needle book with several pockets in it. He was surprised, but after the woman left, he looked through the pockets. In the last one, he found a tiny piece of paper rolled up. The message on the paper said General Howe would attack the next day with 5,000 men. He would be bringing 13 cannons, boats on wheels, and baggage wagons.

Colonel Boudinot mounted his horse and went to General Washington. The two men talked about the note and its meaning. Boudinot thought Howe would cross the river on the boats he brought and attack the Americans from behind. Washington disagreed. He believed the boats were just a trick to fool American spies who might see them. He said the British would attack the patriots from the left side. He even said which road they would use.

The British were clever. All night, they kept a train of wagons rolling through Philadelphia. They were headed for the river. It was plain they were going to cross over and attack the patriots. But it was all fake.

At 3 a.m., alarm guns boomed. They were along the road Washington had said would bring the attack. Boudinot had been wrong. He was sleeping in a house on that road. Even though he thought his general was mistaken, he put out extra guards and kept the horses saddled. He was glad he had done so as he and his men scurried down the road to join the others.

The British surprise was ruined. All day long, the two armies looked across at each other, but there was no major attack. General Howe had led the redcoats who attacked Bunker Hill. He knew the Americans could shoot straight. He did not want to try a direct attack again. One British major who tried a small-scale charge lost 100 men in the attempt. At noon the next day, the redcoats turned and marched back to Philadelphia. Thanks to the patriot cavalry scouts and alert spies such as Lydia Darragh, the British looked like a group of fools.

General Howe knew someone had found out his plans and reported to General Washington. But who could it have been? He sent an officer to speak to Lydia Darragh. It was good that he came at night, as Lydia later said to her daughter, Ann. She told Ann that if the light had been strong in the room, the officer would have known Lydia was a spy because she was so pale.

The officer asked Lydia if any of her children had been awake on the night of the meeting. "No, Lydia said. "They were all in bed asleep."[7] That was true.

The Darragh family worked together to help the cause of freedom. The British army never discovered that they were spies.[8]

> "
>
> This quote tells Lydia's perspective on the British.
>
> *"Though we consider thee as a public enemy, we regard thee as a private friend. While we detest the cause thee fights for, we wish well to thy personal interest and safety.*
>
> Lydia Darragh
>
> "

Then the redcoat said, "I need not ask you, for we had great difficulty in waking you to fasten the door after us. But one thing is certain: the enemy had notice of our coming."[6]

Meeting of
patriotic women

CHAPTER 21

TWO PATRIOT WOMEN

Standing Up to Tyranny

NANCY HART — ONE TOUGH LADY

Nancy Hart was taller than most men. She had flaming red hair. She was strong and tough. Her face was scarred from the marks of smallpox.

Nancy was probably born in North Carolina in 1735. She married Benjamin Hart, and they started a family. In the early 1770s, Ben Hart moved his family to the fertile Broad River Valley in Georgia. They cleared land for fields and built a log cabin. Nancy was known for being a strong woman. The Indians called her "War Woman."

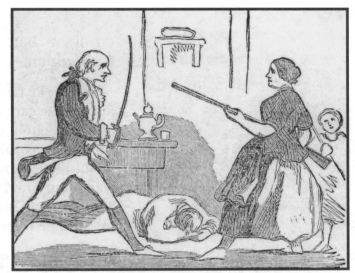

Nancy shoots one and demands the surrender of the others.

The patriots in Georgia had a hard time during the war. The British took the port city of Savannah in 1778. The next year, American and French forces tried to take it back. But their siege failed. The city stayed in the hands of the British until near the end of the war. After the American soldiers sailed away, British soldiers marched through the colony. They destroyed crops, stole horses and cattle, and burned patriot homes. They killed any patriot man they could find.

Aunt Nancy's husband, Ben, fought with the American militia. Because they were outnumbered, the militia could not meet the British in large battles. They had to sneak through the woods

"Aunt Nancy," as she was often called, was just the right woman to be a pioneer wife and mother. She was also just right to be the wife of a patriot militiaman. Nancy had many adventures and faced many dangers during the war. She raised six sons and two daughters in her rough log cabin in the woods.

The She Devil's favorite tree.

and attack small groups whenever they could. When they were at home, they had to watch out for enemy raiders. Many times, Ben and Nancy would hear of soldiers heading their way. Ben would gather his livestock and drive them deep into the swamps where the enemy could not steal them.

Nancy was angry with the Tories. She thought they were traitors because they were Americans helping the British. She knew the wicked things the Tories had done to their patriot neighbors. Near the edge of her cabin clearing, there was a big oak stump surrounded by weeds and bushes. Nancy cut a notch in the top of the stump to hold the barrel of her gun. When she saw Tories crossing the river, she would shoot them. Nancy was a good shot, and she was fearless. She was always ready for a fight. When the war came, she was determined to do all she could to drive the British and Tories out of the Broad River region.

Much of the time, Ben was away with the militia. Nancy was left to take care of herself and her children. She was strong and wise enough to do that. In addition, she served as a spy, sending messages to patriot leaders whenever she heard things about the enemy. Sometimes she dressed up as a man and wandered into British and Tory camps. She would pretend to be a crazy man. The British and Tories were not careful when they talked. She listened carefully and reported important things to the militia leaders.

There were reports that Nancy fought in the Battle of Kettle Creek, a fight in which the patriot militia beat a force of Tories. The battle happened not far from the Hart cabin.

Once, when Ben was away from the house, Nancy was making lye soap. This soap was made by boiling lye from wood ashes with animal fat. As Nancy was stirring the soap over the fireplace, her daughter stepped near her. She whispered that they were being watched. Nancy kept stirring the pot. Out of the corner of her eye, she could see a Tory peeking through a crack between the cabin logs. She acted as if she had not noticed. She kept on stirring the boiling soap. She dipped a big dipper into the pot.

Large pot of soap

Suddenly, Nancy whirled around and threw the contents of the dipper at the crack in the wall. There was a scream as the Tory spy got hot lye soap in his eyes. Nancy ran outside and tied the man up. She sent her daughter to tell Ben. Then the militiamen came and made the Tory a prisoner.

Nancy Hart knew she was strong. Her life on the frontier had made her that way. She was also brave. She often took her corn to the mill to be ground into meal, traveling alone. One day, she ran into a group of Tories. They had their clothes and hats marked with British colors. They knew Nancy was a patriot, so they took the opportunity to make trouble for her. One of them asked her if she had a pass to travel that way. Nancy held up her fist.

Nancy held up her fist. "This is my pass," she said angrily. "Touch me if you dare!"

"This is my pass," she said angrily. "Touch me if you dare!"[1]

The Tories pushed her off her horse, making the heavy bag of corn fall to the ground. This did not stop Nancy. She lifted the bag to her shoulder and walked on to the mill.[2]

Don't nobody move a foot!

Nancy's most famous adventure happened at her home. One day, five Tories came to her cabin. They wanted Nancy to tell them where to find a certain patriot leader. The man they were looking for had just passed Nancy's cabin on a galloping horse. Nancy would not tell the Tories anything about the man.

This made the Tories angry. They told Nancy she had to cook dinner for them. One of them shot one of Nancy's turkeys. She cleaned the turkey and began to cook. The Tories demanded something to drink. Nancy got out a jug of wine and set it on the table.

The Tory men were happy. They had a jug of wine to drink while they waited on their dinner to cook. They stacked their muskets against the cabin wall and began to drink. As they became more and more drunk, Nancy kept passing between them and their guns to put food on the table.

Suddenly, Nancy grabbed one of the guns. "Don't nobody move a foot!"[3] she shouted.

One of the Tories stood up and jumped toward her. Nancy shot him dead. As he fell, she grabbed another gun from the wall. She looked at the other men and threatened to shoot them, too. They all looked back at her. There were still four of them. They could have captured her because she only had one shot in her musket. But which of them would she shoot if they tried?

Nancy sent her daughter to fetch some men from the militia. She pointed her gun at the Tories until the patriots came. One of the militiamen said, "We'll take them out and shoot them, Nancy."

But Nancy answered, "No, shooting's too good for them. Hang them!"[4]

So, off went the men with their prisoners and the dead Tory. They hanged the four remaining ones and buried all five in a shallow grave about a half mile from the Hart cabin.

This story was passed down through the Hart family for 100 years. Some of the details were changed from time to time. Finally, some family members were not sure whether the story was true. They found out in 1912.

In that year, the Elberton and Eastern Railroad was building a track through the Broad River region. Half a mile from where the Hart cabin had stood, workmen found an old grave as they were grading the roadbed. In it were five skeletons buried in a neat row. Some of their necks were broken. They looked as if they had been hanged.[5]

Deborah Sampson — A Woman in Uniform

One of the most interesting mysteries of the War of Independence is the story of a young Massachusetts soldier named Robert Shurtliff. He served in the American army for 17 months and fought in several battles. He suffered from a saber cut, bullet wounds, and fever. Many young soldiers had similar experiences, but Robert was different from the rest.

Robert was a woman.

Robert's real name was Deborah Sampson. She had disguised herself as a man and fooled the enlistment officers. It was not until she was examined by a doctor that the truth came out.

Deborah Sampson

Deborah was born in the village of Plympton, Massachusetts, in 1760. She was the oldest of seven children. Her parents were named Jonathan and Deborah. Her mother was a descendant of William Bradford, the famous governor of the Pilgrims. Her father was a descendant of Myles Standish, the military leader and protector of the Pilgrims.

Deborah's family had a hard time when she was a child. Her father lost most of his money to a dishonest relative. He went to sea to make a better living for his family. On one voyage, he was gone longer than expected. Deborah's mother finally received a message that he had been lost in a shipwreck.

Mrs. Sampson now found herself unable to provide for her children. She began looking for other families who would adopt them and raise them. Young Deborah was sent to live with her aunt. But her aunt soon died, and Deborah was homeless again. Later, at ten years of age, she went to live in the home of Deacon Jeremiah Thomas.

Deacon Thomas did not adopt Deborah. She was an indentured servant.[6]

In the home of Jeremiah Thomas, Deborah received an education. It was not the kind of education most children receive today. She learned how to take care of a home and do farm work. She took care of animals, worked in the garden, and even learned to do some carpentry work.

> An indentured servant is a person who makes an agreement to work for another person for a certain period of time.
>
> Many of the workers who came to early America from England were indentured servants who agreed to work for several years for someone who would pay for their voyage to America.

Deacon Thomas had a large family with ten sons. Deborah often asked the boys to teach her the lessons they were learning. In this way, Deborah worked hard to get a good education, even though she could not go to school.

Deacon Thomas was fond of Deborah. He was also a patriot. As years went by and the War of Independence drew near, he talked about the problems with the British. From Mr. Thomas, Deborah learned that freedom was important.

When Deborah turned 18, she was finished with her indenture. What should she do now? She had learned so much in the Thomas home that she was able to get a job as a schoolteacher part of the time. In the winter, she did weaving work.

In 1781 or 1782, Deborah decided that she wanted to fight for liberty. But women were not allowed to join the army in those days. What could she do?

She had an idea. She would dress as a man and try to fool the enlistment officers. She was tall for a girl, so that would help. She would adopt the name of her brother, who had died. His name was Robert Shurtliff Sampson. She dropped the last name and became Robert Shurtliff. She enlisted in the army and gave her address as Uxbridge, Massachusetts.

Siege of Yorktown (1781), by Auguste Couder, 1836 (PD-Art).

Death of Col. Scammell at the Siege of Yorktown, by Alonzo Chappel, 1858 (PD-US).

The other soldiers noticed that Robert never shaved. Deborah pretended that she was a teenage boy and did not need to shave yet. But what would she do when the other soldiers bathed together in the river? Somehow, she managed to be away when that happened.

When Deborah joined the army, most of the fighting had moved from Massachusetts to New York. She was sent to fight in the Hudson Valley in the infantry. Later, she said she suffered more from the fatigue and heat than she did from the fear of being killed. In one battle, she got two holes through her coat and one hole through her cap. Three of her friends were killed. Years after the war, Deborah still had sad memories of all the suffering she had seen. Many times, she would tell stories of her time in the army while tears fell from her eyes.

"Robert" fought in several battles. During the first battle, Deborah took a severe cut on her forehead. She also got a musket ball in her leg. She was afraid her secret would be found out. She begged the other soldiers not to take her to the hospital, but they would not let her die. At the hospital, she let the doctor take care of the cut on her head. She managed to walk away from

House of Deborah Sampson Gannett in Sharon, Massachusetts, from *Some Events of Boston and its Neighbors*, 1917 (PD-US).

the hospital before anyone looked at the bullet wound in her leg.

Deborah tried to get the musket ball out of her leg with a penknife. She could not get it out, but she did not go back to the doctor. The ball stayed in her leg and caused her pain for the rest of her life.

Deborah was in the last big battle of the war at Yorktown. After the British army surrendered, she marched north again. The army was not sent home because there was still fighting going on in a few places.

In 1783, Deborah's unit was ordered to go to Philadelphia to put down a rebellion. Some former soldiers were angry and threatening to make trouble. The fighting was over when Deborah got to Philadelphia, but the danger was not. She got sick with a bad fever and had to go to a doctor.

The doctor who took care of her was Dr. Barnabas Binney. Deborah was so sick that she was unconscious. She did not know when Dr. Binney removed her clothes to examine her. When he found that she was a woman, he kept her secret. He took her to his home to take care of her. There, she could keep her secret and get well in the peaceful home with his wife and children.

Patterson said, "Don't be afraid. You have been a good soldier. I will keep you safe. You should not be punished. You should be generously rewarded. I will get you a discharge very soon and you can go home."[7]

Dr. Binney kept Deborah's secret until she could get well and strong again. Then he asked her to deliver a personal letter from the doctor to General Patterson. The letter told the general that "Robert Shurtliff" was really a woman. Her secret was discovered at last!

Deborah was afraid she would get in terrible trouble. She had lied to the army. Would she be punished? Army punishments could be bad. She begged General Patterson not to treat her harshly.

General Patterson was kind.

Deborah was discharged in October of 1783, and she went home to Massachusetts.

After the War

After her discharge, Deborah dressed and acted as a woman again. She fell in love with a farmer named Benjamin Gannett, and in 1785 they were married. They had three children and lived on a farm near Sharon, Massachusetts.

Deborah kept a journal of her life in the army, but it was lost when a boat she was riding sank. In 1797, a man named Herman Mann wrote her biography. When the book was published, people wanted to see Deborah. She went on a tour to give speeches. During her tour, she sometimes dressed in her army uniform and performed soldier movements from the manual of arms.

Later in life, Deborah was in poor health. She was still carrying a bullet in her leg from a battle. She wrote to Congress, asking to be granted a soldier's pension. At first, she found it hard to get her request considered. The famous Boston patriot Paul Revere wrote to Congress on her behalf.

Paul Revere wrote to Congressman William Eustis and asked for help in getting a pension for his friend, Deborah. This had never been done for a woman. But Revere knew the Sampson family needed help.

On March 11, 1805, Congress granted the request and placed Deborah on the Massachusetts Invalid Pension Roll. This plan paid her $4 a month.

Deborah Sampson died in April 1827 of yellow mountain fever. She was buried in Rock Ridge Cemetery in Sharon, Massachusetts. Several monuments to her were built in Sharon. More than 100 years later, Massachusetts named her the official state heroine and declared May 23 "Deborah Sampson Day."[8]

> *I have been induced to enquire her situation, and character, since she quit the male habit, and soldiers uniform; for the more decent apparel of her own gender ... humanity and justice obliges me to say, that every person with whom I have conversed about her, and it is not a few, speak of her as a woman with handsome talents, good morals, a dutiful wife, and an affectionate parent.*
>
> Paul Revere

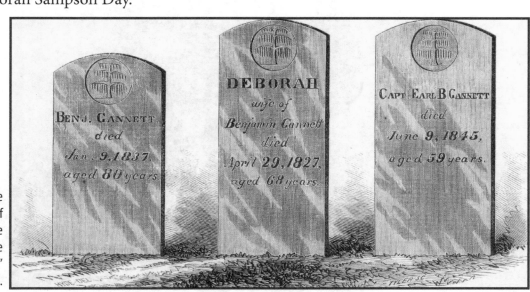

Image from "The female review. Life of Deborah Sampson, the female soldier in the War of Revolution," 1866 (PD-US).

Nathan Hale

CHAPTER 22

NATHAN HALE

Patriot Spy

HELP WANTED

It seemed to the people of New England that the war had gone on a long time. The British tried to take guns and supplies at Concord, Massachusetts. The minutmen pushed them back into Boston. Then the patriots strengthened Breed's Hill outside the town and fought the redcoats there. The redcoats won the hill, but only because the patriots ran out of powder. The battle was named after Bunker Hill, which was close by. Far more British soldiers died in the battle of Bunker Hill than Americans.

Later, General Washington went to Boston and took command of the army. He fortified Dorchester Heights above the city. When the British commander saw how Washington's cannon could fire right down onto his army in Boston, he put his soldiers on ships and sailed away.

Washington knew the British would be back. They would not give up their colonies in America just because they had been driven out of one city. Where would they strike next?

In late June of 1776, the answer came. People on the wooded islands around New York looked over the ocean and saw the tops of white sails appear above the blue waves. Ships! There were many sails, so the people knew it was not just a merchant ship. It had to be the English navy.

It was a wise move for the British. New York's harbor was large and deep. It was a good place for many ships to anchor together. The wide Hudson River flowed down from the north. The British

Sometimes there are jobs that need to be done that are not desirable. Such was the job that General Washington needed done. Nathan Hale understood the concept of duty to one's country. He volunteered because he knew the whole outcome of the war depended on proper information, and he was determined to be useful to his country.

The attack on Charles Town.

could travel up the river and attack patriot forces. When they fought their way through the countryside, they could meet up with another British force coming down from Canada. Then they could join. There would be a big British army separating New England from the other colonies. The patriot country would be cut in half and easier to defeat.

First, the British landed on Staten Island. There was no patriot army there to fight them. In August, they invaded Long Island. King George hired soldiers called Hessians from Germany to help him fight the patriots, so there were both Hessians and British soldiers on Long Island. They attacked the Americans from two sides. Washington had to cross the water to Manhattan Island. In September, the patriots retreated again. Now the British were in control of New York.

What would the British do next? Where did they plan to go? How many men and cannons did they have? General Washington needed to know.

The Americans should have already had spies in place. They should have located civilians on Staten Island, Long Island, and Manhattan. That way, they would have had a team of spies getting information and sending it back to Washington. This was what Paul Revere and others had done in Boston. It was a spy network. There

178

were a few loyal people in New York who watched the British and wrote down what they saw going on. But there were no messengers who could collect the notes and get them to Washington.

Everyone knew the Americans did not have enough men to hold New York. If they had a spy network put together, the spies would have already been in place when the army pulled back and left the islands to the British. But this was early in the war. Washington's army did not know as much about spying as they would later. Besides, they had not had much time to prepare. They did not know the British were coming to New York until the first ships appeared.

Hale receives his orders.

Washington called his officers together. He told them he needed to find out more about the British army in New York. Someone had to go into the town as a spy. He had to find out how many soldiers were in the city and how many cannons they had. Where were the cannons placed? When and where would they make the attack on the Americans on Manhattan Island?

It was a dangerous job. If an American was captured in battle, he would be held as a prisoner of war. But if he was caught spying, he would be hanged. There was no second chance for a spy.

There was another problem, too. Most people did not like the idea of being a spy. They felt that spying was not as honorable as being a soldier. Some men were willing to die on the battlefield, but they thought it would be shameful to be hanged as a spy. Who would be willing to take on this mission?

A Brave Man Steps Forward

A young man offered himself. His name was Captain Nathan Hale. He had only been in the army a short time. He had never been in a battle, but he was brave. He would take the risk of going into New York dressed as a civilian to find out what General Washington wanted to know.

Nathan Hale loved America. He had been born in Coventry, Connecticut, in 1755. When he was only 14 years old, he attended Yale University. He graduated with high honors when he was 17. He became a schoolteacher. When the war began in 1775, he enlisted in the Connecticut militia and became a lieutenant. When his friends marched off to fight in the siege of Boston, Nathan stayed behind, perhaps because his teaching job did not end until the end of the school term.

> Talmadge wrote, "Our holy Religion, the honour of our God, a glorious country, and a happy constitution is what we have to defend."[1]

His friend Benjamin Talmadge wrote him a letter after seeing Boston. He said Nathan should go into the regular army.

Nathan agreed. That summer he joined the Seventh Connecticut Regiment as a lieutenant. Later, he transferred to Knowlton's Rangers.

They marched northward to help General Washington at New York. Here, Nathan met General Washington and many other American officers. There was much concern at headquarters. They knew the British would move again. They needed to know what their plans were. So far, no patriot on Staten Island or Long Island had been able to get messages out to Washington. No Tory had been found who would report on the British. Washington was getting more and more concerned. He said, "I was never more uneasy than on account of my want of knowledge."[3]

> Nathan replied, "Every kind of service, necessary for the public good, becomes honorable by being necessary."[2]

Even though Nathan was still pale from a long sickness, he heard that Washington needed a spy, and he volunteered to go.

Nathan Hale was not the right man for the job. He stood out in a crowd because he was tall, sturdy, and good-looking. He also attracted

Historic homestead of American Revolutionary War hero Nathan Hale in Coventry, Connecticut.

attention because of an unusual mark on his face. He had been burned by exploding powder when he was younger. In addition, he had a cousin who was a Tory. That man was now serving with the British army. What if he saw Nathan and exposed him? It would be certain death.

Nathan's friend Captain William Hull tried to talk him out of it. Hull had gone to school with Nathan at Yale. They had served together in the army since Hale had enlisted. As they talked the plan over, Hull tried to convince Nathan not to go.

Nathan felt it was his duty to go. Washington needed information. Hull told him it was not a duty. Soldiers could not be ordered to be spies. That was why they were always volunteers. Hull said it was dishonorable to be a spy. They were not respected like other soldiers.

That was the last time William Hull and Nathan Hale saw each other.

Portrait of John Montresor, by John Singleton Copley, c.1771 (PD-Art).

Nathan Hale left the north end of Manhattan on September 12, 1776. He had been given a general order that told all American war ships to take him anywhere he wanted to go. Captain Charles Pound of the sloop *Schuyler* carried Nathan across Long Island Sound. Careful to stay out of sight of British ships, the captain dropped Nathan off in a lonely place. He would have to make his way through the British camps on his own.

Nathan removed his army uniform and put on a plain brown suit. He decided to pretend to be a schoolmaster looking for work. Since it was September, it was not unusual to meet a teacher looking for a school. It was good that he had been a schoolmaster in Connecticut. He knew how they dressed and talked. If anyone suspected him and asked tricky questions about the life of a schoolmaster, Nathan would know the right answers.

"Have not I commanded thee? Be strong and of a good courage; be not afraid, neither be thou dismayed: for the LORD thy God is with thee whithersoever thou goest."

—Joshua 1:9

Courage means standing alone for what is right and yielding our fears to God. Nathan Hale was truly a man of courage. We should all try to be like him when God calls us to face danger.

DEATH OF A HERO

But it was all for nothing. We do not know what happened right after Captain Pond dropped Nathan off, but we do know he was

New York Harbor, just after the Battle of Long Island, NYPLDC.

captured by the British and hanged as a spy. He was hanged without a trial, so there were no written court records. But the evening after Hale was hanged, a British officer named Captain Montresor came into the American camp under a flag of truce. We learned more from him.

Montresor had come to tell Washington that his spy had been caught and hanged. He had been with Hale just before his execution. He told Washington that Hale passed through the British lines on Long Island and in New York City. He made sketches of their defense. He wrote down the number of cannons and soldiers he saw. It was just the information that Washington needed. But Hale would not live long enough to get it back to headquarters.

Three days after Hale landed on Long Island, he heard that Manhattan had been taken by the British. Hale boldly went on to Manhattan to spy there as he had spied on Long Island. He passed through the lines of Lord Percy, Sir Henry Clinton, and Lord Cornwallis. He observed carefully and took notes of all he saw. The information he had would be helpful to General Washington. But how was he to get through the British outer lines?

That is the story of how Nathan Hale, a Connecticut school teacher, became a symbol of courage and noble character. His story is still read across America.

If the British thought that hanging Nathan Hale would frighten other Americans away from being spies, they were wrong. Less than a week after Nathan's death, a patriot named Joshua Davis snuck into New York and returned safely with the information Washington needed.

As for the cruel William Cunningham, who denied Nathan Hale a Bible or a preacher, we know what happened to him. Years after the war, he was convicted of a crime in London. It was his turn to hang.

"I only regret that I have but one life to lose for my country."[4]

Nathan Hale

One Life to Lose

On the night of September 21, Nathan Hale was walking along the waterfront. It was dark, and he hoped no one would see him before he found a boat that would take him off the island. Perhaps he hoped to borrow a boat tied to the shore. Perhaps he hoped to find a friendly person who would row him across the water.

He met a rowboat bringing an officer ashore from a British war ship. Because it was dark, he did not see the British uniforms until it was too late to run away. Since there was no reason for a schoolteacher to be so near the battle line, the sailors were suspicious.

They seized Nathan and turned him over to the British army. He was taken to the headquarters of General Howe. When he was searched, the soldiers found the papers he had hidden on him. He did not deny that he was a spy.

General Howe looked at the handsome young man. Howe was a good-natured officer, and it touched him to see this young patriot showing such courage. His simple loyalty to his country touched the older man's heart, but the rules of war could not be broken. The king expected all spies to be hanged. Howe gave the order for Nathan Hale to die the next morning at dawn.

Captain Montresor told the entire story to Captain Alexander Hamilton and Hale's friend, Captain William Hull. Montresor said Nathan had been handed over to British officer William Cunningham. Cunningham was known as a cruel, heartless man. When Hale asked for a preacher, he was refused. He was also refused when he asked for a Bible.[5]

The next morning, Hale waited in Captain Montresor's tent before his execution. Montresor felt sorry for the young man. He gave him materials to write two letters. The letters must have been turned over to Cunningham because they were never delivered. William Hull claimed that Cunningham had destroyed the letters, "that the rebels should never know they had a man who could die with so much firmness."[6]

When he was taken out to the tree to be hung, Nathan Hale spoke his last words:

"I only regret that I have but one life to lose for my country."

Death of General De Kalb
at the Battle of Camden

CHAPTER 23

RICHARD CASWELL

The Father of North Carolina

THE STAGE IS SET

Richard was born on August 3, 1729, in Hartford County in Maryland. He was one of 11 children. Richard was only 16 when he left home and went to seek his fortune. He settled in the colony of North Carolina.

Shortly after the end of the French and Indian War, there was already trouble between the American colonies and England. Caswell was an officer in the North Carolina Militia. At that time, the militia was still loyal to the king. A group called the Regulators refused to obey the colonial government. Caswell fought against the Regulators in 1771.

As time went by, there was more and more arguing between the king and the colonies. Caswell began to believe that the colonies needed fight for their liberty. North Carolina sent him to the Continental Congress in 1774 and 1775. When war between England and the colonies came, Caswell was the commander of the minutemen in New Bern. Later, he was promoted to major general in the Continental army.

In 1775, news came of the battles in the northern colony of Massachusetts. The country was preparing for war. All across North Carolina, groups of men began to prepare to fight. Some of the groups were patriots. Others were loyal to the king. These were called loyalists, or Tories. The king's governor, Josiah Martin, wanted to build a large force of loyalists to keep the patriots from taking over his colony.

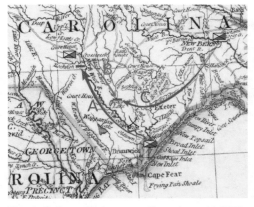

Map depicting preliminary marching prior to the 1776 Battle of Moore's Creek Bridge, 1794 (CC BY-SA 4.0).
Letter key:

A: Continental Army movement under James Moore from Wilmington to Rockfish Creek

B: Loyalist force's movement from Cross Creek to Corbett's Ferry

C: Richard Caswell's North Carolina militia movement from New Bern to Corbett's Ferry

American history is full of stories of men who served their country and their communities. Richard Caswell is one of those selfless men. He was the governor of North Carolina two times. Caswell County and Fort Caswell are named after him. He held many important jobs in North Carolina. He is one of the state's greatest heroes.

Allan Maclean

To do this, he made friends with men who had once been in the Regulators but did not want to separate from England. He also sent messengers around the colony to recruit other Tories.

There was another Tory force being raised. It would bring many men to fight against the patriots in North Carolina. The man who was building this group was named Allan Maclean. He was a British soldier who had been born in Scotland. He had gotten permission from the king to raise a company of Scotch Tories in the colonies. He was looking for men who had been soldiers and had battle experience.

Maclean was an experienced soldier. He had fought in several battles in the French and Indian war. He was smart and tough. His regiment was known as the Royal Highland Emigrants. Many of these men had been given land by the king and had settled in North Carolina. With Maclean leading them, they would be a tough regiment to beat in battle.

While Maclean was recruiting Tories in New York and Canada, he sent two men south to recruit North Carolina and other southern colonies. When they arrived in New Bern, the local Committee of Safety was suspicious. They began to suspect what the two men were doing. Still, they were not arrested.

On January 3, 1776, Governor Martin learned that General Henry Clinton was about to bring more than 2,000 redcoats to the southern colonies. They were going to arrive in the middle of February. He sent a message to Maclean's recruiters. He told them to bring their recruits to the coast by February 15. He sent one of them to Cross Creek to find men there. This man reported to Martin that he would gather a large group of Tories. He said he could raise 5,000 Regulators and 1,000 Scots. Martin was happy to hear this news. He thought the British could defeat the patriots in the Carolinas for good.

There was a meeting between the Regulator leaders with the Scots leaders at Cross Creek. They could not agree on what to do. The Scots wanted to wait until the British came before gathering their men. The Regulators wanted to move right away. The Regulators claimed they could raise far more men than the Scots could. The Regulators had their way.

When the loyalist forces gathered on February 15, there were about 3,500 men. Many of them began to leave when they found out that the British had not come yet. They had hoped to join up with the British as soon as they gathered. They did not like the idea of having to fight their way through the patriots to meet the British at the coast. When they marched three days later, Brigadier General Donald MacDonald led about 1,500 men.

This is the moment when this country may be delivered from anarchy.[1]

Governor Josiah Martin

Most of them were Scots. But over the next several days, he lost more men who left the army.

The patriot Provincial Congress got word of the of the Cross Creek meeting. They wanted to stop the Tories from joining up with General Clinton's redcoat army when it arrived in North Carolina. They needed to gather all the patriot forces to fight the Tories and defeat them before they could get to the coast.

The Provincial Congress had one regiment of Continental Army soldiers led by Colonel James Moore. The Committees of Safety in Wilmington and New Bern had militia forces to send. Richard Caswell led the New Bern troops. On February 15, the Patriot forces began to move.

General Henry Clinton

ARMIES ON THE MOVE

Moore led 650 Continentals out of Wilmington to stop the Loyalists from reaching the coast. His men camped on Rockfish Creek about seven miles from the Tory camp. When the Tory general heard of this, he sent a message to Moore.[2]

MacDonald's message came with a announcement issued by the Tory governor Josiah Martin. The proclamation called on the rebels to lay down their weapons and obey the British government in the colony. Colonel Moore was not frightened by this.

Courage is standing up for what is right and yielding our fears to God. Men of courage have fear. They just learn that God is in control and will protect them to do the job he has for them to do.

Moore sent a message back to the Tories. He told them to lay down their weapons and support the Continental Congress. In the meantime, Richard Caswell was leading 800 New Bern militiamen to the area.

General MacDonald decided to move around Moore rather than fight him. He chose another road that would bring his forces to the bridge on Moore's Creek. The Tories packed up their guns and tents and marched off through the woods.

On February 20, MacDonald crossed the Cape Fear River. He destroyed the boats so that if Moore tried to head him off, he would have a slow river crossing. His men crossed the South River and headed toward the Black River. He would still have to cross that river to get to the coast. There was a crossing called Corbett's Ferry. MacDonald decided to cross there.

Colonel Moore sent Richard Caswell's troops to stop him. Caswell reached the crossing first and blocked the entrance. What if MacDonald defeated Caswell? What if he suddenly went to another crossing place? Moore decided to send more troops to help Caswell.

Alexander Lillington was sent with 150 militiamen from Wilmington. Colonel John Ashe brought 100 men from New Hanover. These small groups could travel faster than a large army. By marching hard, they arrived at the Widow Moore's Creek Bridge ahead of the Tories. If MacDonald decided to avoid Caswell at Corbett's Ferry, there would be other patriots waiting to stop him at Moore's Creek Bridge.

When MacDonald and his force reached Corbett's Ferry, Caswell and his men blocked the crossing. The loyalist leader had a decision to make. Should he fight Caswell and try to cross there? Should he look for another crossing?

SHOWDOWN AT MOORE'S CREEK BRIDGE

MacDonald heard from a local slave that there was a bridge over the river a few miles away. He sent a small group of his men to pretend that they were about to attack Caswell and cross the river. This was just a trick. MacDonald led most of his force away toward Moore's Creek Bridge.

MacDonald sent a man to Caswell's camp under a flag of peace. The man gave Caswell a message from MacDonald. The Tory leader demanded Caswell's surrender. Probably, MacDonald knew Caswell would never surrender. But the messenger he sent was also a spy!

Caswell soon figured out that the Tories had slipped away. He hurried his men on a ten-mile march to Moore's Creek Bridge and got there just a few hours ahead of MacDonald. He put his men to work building fortifications. Moore was marching toward him with his Continental soldiers. They did not arrive in time for the battle.

MacDonald sent a man to Caswell's camp under a flag of peace. The man gave Caswell a message from MacDonald. The Tory leader demanded Caswell's surrender. Probably, MacDonald knew Caswell would never surrender. But the messenger he sent was also a spy! When he returned to MacDonald, he gave him a detailed description of the patriot defenses.

Caswell's defenses were on the west side of the bridge. This was the side where MacDonald would approach. He decided to move back across the river. That would make it harder for MacDonald to attack him. Would MacDonald attack at all? Would he decide to move on up the river and try to cross at another place?

The Battle at the Bridge

During the night, the Tories decided to attack. They figured that if they took time to find another place to cross, Moore might catch up with his additional troops. They would face a much larger force than Caswell's.

General MacDonald would not lead the charge. He was an elderly man, and the hard marching wore him out. He was tired and sick. He turned the command over to Lieutenant Colonel McLeod.

By the time they arrived at Moore's Creek, the Loyalist force had shrunk. More men had deserted. There were now about 700 or 800 men. On February 27, they marched the few miles from their camp to the bridge. Just before dawn, they arrived at the bridge. A patriot sentry heard marching men and fired his musket to warn Caswell. When he heard the musket shot, MacLeod realized that his surprise attack was hopeless. He ordered a charge. He and Captain John Campbell led a group of swordsmen across the bridge.

Bridge over Moore's Creek in Pender County, North Carolina, photo by Billy Hathorn, (CC BY-SA 3.0).

Scene at the Signing of the Constitution of the United States, painted by Howard Chandler Christy, c.1940 (PD-US).

It was a great mistake to send men armed only with swords. Perhaps MacLeod thought muskets would be useless in the dim light before dawn. After all, the patriots would be huddled down behind dirt walls and logs. The patriot marksmen were in a better position. They only had to fire toward the bridge. With the Tories massed to charge across the narrow span, they would be hard to miss.

The battle had some lasting effects. Later in the war, many Scots refused to join when the British army sent out calls for volunteers. They remembered that their patriot neighbors knew how to fight.

> Now each colony was an American state. They had to form a new government because they were no longer governed by the king.

Five months after the battle, America declared independence from Britain. Now each colony was an American state. They had to form a new government because they were no longer governed by the king. Caswell was elected to be the president of the Provincial Congress. This group wrote the first state constitution of North Carolina. They elected Richard Caswell to be the state's first governor. Years later, he would be elected governor again. In between, he did many things to serve the new state and America.

Caswell was a state senator in North Carolina. He was chosen to be one of his state's delegates to the Constitutional Convention. After a second term as governor, he served as speaker of the state senate. He died on November 10, 1789. Today, in his home town of Kinston, North Carolina, there is a memorial to him. A nearby museum tells his story. Richard Caswell has been called, "The Father of North Carolina."[3]

Caswell once owned Harmony Hall in Kinston (Peebles' House), photo by Tradewinds, 2013 (CC BY-SA 3.0).

CANNONS AND CAPTURE

During the night, Caswell and his men built barriers around their end of the bridge. They mounted two small cannons on them. When the Scots were within 30 paces, the patriots opened fire. Many Tories fell. MacLeod and Campbell both went down in a hail of gunfire. Later, Colonel Moore reported that MacLeod had been struck by over 20 musket balls. The Scots had no choice but to retreat. They rushed back, and the loyalist force retreated. Soon, Moore arrived with his Continentals. He estimated that the patriots had killed about 50 loyalists. The patriots had only one man killed and one wounded.

Over the next several days, the Patriot forces captured most of the fleeing loyalists. In all, about 850 men were taken. Most of them were released after signing a paper called a parole. A parole was a promise not to fight any more. Their leaders were kept as prisoners so they could not start trouble again.

The patriots also captured 1,500 muskets, 300 rifles, and $15,000 in Spanish gold. The battle encouraged more colonists to join the patriot forces. Even though there were hard feelings on both sides, the Tory prisoners were treated with respect. This helped convince them not to fight against the patriots in the future.[4]

Storytime with Uncle Rick

Fight for Freedom

191

Nathanael Greene

CHAPTER 24

NATHANAEL GREENE

The Fighting Quaker

WASHINGTON'S BEST GENERAL

You have probably read many books or stories about George Washington. You know that he was a great man and a great general. Many people have written about him because he was the top general in the War of Independence and our first president. But you might not know as much about Nathanael Greene. Many people in his own lifetime thought he was the greatest general of the war, after Washington. Many historians still believe the same.

Without understanding the work of General Greene, it would be hard to understand how our independence from England was won. Washington fought mostly in the northern colonies. Greene was the greatest general in the south.

The first battles of the war took place in New England. When the British saw it would be hard to defeat the patriots there, they turned their attention to the southern colonies. The believed that if they could take Virginia, North Carolina, South Carolina, and Georgia, they could weaken the patriot forces. There were many people in the southern colonies who were still loyal to the king. They wanted to remain part of England. If the English could get these loyalists to join their army and fight against their neighbors, they would have many more soldiers. Then they could move north and join the other British fighting against Washington.

Nathanael Greene started out as a private in the militia. A private is the lowest rank of soldier. Yet, by the end of the war, Greene was a general. That is a high rank. What happened? Greene loved learning. He read all the good books he could find. He watched other soldiers drill so he could drill like them. Always remember that you can learn in many different ways. Keep reading and watching. Someday you may be a great leader too!

Ezra Stiles, by Samuel King, 1771 (PD-Art).

King George hoped to conquer the southern colonies for another reason. He believed that, even if he lost the war, he could hold the colonies in the south. Beginning in 1778, the British army attacked the cities of the south. They captured Atlanta in Georgia that year. In 1780, they made a second attack on Charleston, South Carolina. The fight was a disaster for the Americans. General Lincoln, the top general of the American army in the south, surrendered his entire force there. Then, General Washington sent General Gates down to fight in the south.

General Gates was not one of the best generals. Washington wanted to send Nathanael Greene. But Washington worked for the Continental Congress, which ordered him to send Gates. Soon, they wished they had listened to Washington.

Gates suffered a crushing defeat by the British in the battle of Camden. That left the patriot cause in serious trouble. Everybody knew a great military leader was needed. Otherwise, the British would have total control in the south. Washington knew exactly whom to send and this time, and Congress listened to him. Nathanael Greene gathered his troops and headed south.

Greene was born in 1742 in the town of Warwick, Rhode Island. His father was a blacksmith and a miller. On Sundays, he was a Quaker preacher. He trained his son to be a strict Quaker. The Quakers were not lovers of books and school, so Nathanael's training was mostly in the work of the field and the mill. But he loved to study and learn when he had spare time.

> Everybody knew a great military leader was needed. Otherwise, the British would have total control in the south.

Nathaniel was also strong and athletic. He was better than most of the other boys when they played at outdoor sports.

As a young man, Greene met the Reverend Ezra Stiles, who would someday be the president of Yale University. Stiles was a godly man who had a good education. He encouraged Nathanael to keep reading books. Whenever Nathanael would go to town, he would try to visit Reverend Stiles and talk with him about what he was learning.

In 1774, it was plain that there might be fighting between the king's soldiers and the Americans. Nathanael Greene helped organize a militia troop in Rhode Island. He was a private in this militia. He got books about military tactics and studied. He did not have a musket, so he had to travel to Boston to buy one. While he was there, he watched the British soldiers as they trained in their drill. He wanted to learn all he could about being a soldier and training other soldiers.[1]

Traveling back to Rhode Island, Greene hid his new gun under straw in the bed of his wagon so passing British soldiers would not see it and take it away. He met a soldier who deserted, or left, from the British army. This man agreed to help Greene drill the militia.

Then came the news of the battle at Bunker Hill. Rhode Island raised a group of three regiments, and Nathanael Greene was promoted to lead it. He had shown such leadership and military knowledge that he was promoted from private to brigadier general. He marched his brigade to Boston. When General Washington arrived to take command of the American army, General Greene had the honor of welcoming him on behalf of all the soldiers.

Nathanael Greene, by C.W. Peale, date unknown, (PD-Art).

A BIG JOB FOR A BIG MAN

Greene was 33 years old at this time. He stood six feet tall. He had a strong, active body and an honest, intelligent face. He became Washington's friend and won his confidence as a leader. Washington later placed him in positions of responsibility. All through the war, Greene stayed active. His campaigns showed him to be a man of energy with a smart military mind. He could keep his troops ready to fight where they were most needed. When a new commander was needed in the south, Greene was the best choice.

In 1780, General Greene reached the Carolinas. He found the army in a sad condition. There was only one blanket for every three soldiers. They never had enough food for more than three days in advance. The men were discouraged because they had been beaten in their battles. They were angry because they had not been paid. Because of the poor food, their health suffered,

*A **prudent** man foreseeth the evil, and hideth himself: but the simple pass on, and are punished.*

Proverbs 22: 3

and many were sick. All they had for shelter were huts made of cornstalks, brush, and fence rails. The men did not feel or act like soldiers.

> A good leader always tries to take care of the people he leads. If the soldiers know their general is doing his best for them, they will do their best for him.

Greene knew how to build an army. He won the confidence of his officers and soldiers. They believed he was doing his best to help them and to take care of them. Once, he came across a soldier standing guard duty. It was winter, and the man had no shoes. He stood shivering on bare feet. The general was wrapped up in his cloak, so the sentry did not know who he was.[2]

"How you must suffer from cold!" exclaimed the kind general.

"I do not complain," said the soldier. "I know I should fare well if our general could procure supplies."[3]

Soon after taking command, Greene sent Daniel Morgan with 900 picked men toward the mountains of the Carolinas. He was to threaten the British posts in that region. Greene posted the rest of the army nearer to the coast on the Pee Dee River. The British General Cornwallis sent Tarleton to attack Morgan.

Tarleton was a brutal man who killed prisoners who surrendered. He was confident he could beat Morgan. He made a hard night march and attacked Morgan at Cowpens, even though his men were tired. The Americans fought off the attackers and won. Two hundred thirty of the British were killed and wounded. Six hundred were captured. It was nearly all of Tarleton's force.

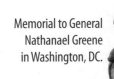

Memorial to General Nathanael Greene in Washington, DC.

This was an unhappy surprise for Cornwallis. He had expected Tarleton to beat Morgan. He started to march across country to fight Morgan himself. He knew he needed to defeat Morgan's smaller force before Greene could join him. It would be harder to beat Morgan and Greene together.

Morgan was a skillful fighter. He guessed Cornwallis would attack him and try to take back his soldiers who had been captured. Morgan marched at top speed to the northeast. He hoped to cross the Catawba River before Cornwallis could catch him.

Greene heard the news of Morgan's victory and was delighted. But he knew Cornwallis would attack Morgan again. He had a plan to prevent that and to draw Cornwallis farther away from the coast. Cornwallis had most of his supplies near the sea at Wilmington.

He would be easier to fight if he could not get food and ammunition quickly.

Greene ordered General Huger to march north with the army. Then he took a few men and rode 150 miles across rough country to join Morgan. On January 31, he reached Morgan's army and took command.

Cornwallis had been marching as quickly as possible to attack Morgan. Greene knew he had to keep Morgan's men ahead of Cornwallis until he could join up with Huger. They crossed the Catawba River, which he hoped would slow Cornwallis down. But there was still a chance the British would catch up to them.[4]

> General Greene showed PRUDENCE in mounting boats on wheels. He did not need boats as he marched along the roads. But he was thinking ahead. He knew he would come to rivers to cross. PRUDENCE made him plan for those river crossings.

Greene sent some men ahead to look for boats. He was carrying some boats with him. The prudent general had boats mounted on wagon wheels so they could be pulled along the road by horses. When they came to a river, the boats floated across with the wheels hanging underneath. When they reached the shallow water on the other side, they could be pulled on to solid ground.

Greene sent Morgan and his riflemen toward the town of Salisbury. Greene waited for a militia unit. He was going to have the militia to guard the fords on the Catawba. These untrained militia men could not hope to stop Cornwallis, but Greene hoped they could slow him down. This would give Morgan's troops more time to get away.

Then bad news came. The militia was scattered. Cornwallis crossed the Catawba with little trouble from the Americans. There was nothing for Greene to do but catch up with Morgan. He went alone through a heavy rainstorm and thick mud.

A RACE FOR LIFE

When Greene arrived at Salisbury, he did not know where Morgan was. He stopped at an inn to rest. The inn had been turned into a hospital for soldiers. A doctor saw him and asked how he was.[5]

The soldier stated that he was fatigued, hungry, alone, and penniless.[6] He was heard by the landlady, Mrs. Elizabeth Steele. She brought the general two bags of coins. It was money she had saved from years of hard work.

Lord Cornwallis, by Peter Lightfoot, 1798 (PD-US).

She told Greene to take them because he would need them more than her.[7]

With such sacrifices as this, how could the Americans fail to win their freedom?

It must have been hard for Mrs. Steele to give up her savings. It was wartime. Things were hard. She probably did not know how long it might take to save up more money. Yet, she gave General Greene all she could. Many patriotic women like Mrs. Steele helped during the War of Independence.

Greene found Morgan, and the army crossed the Dan River. When Cornwallis reached the river, he found that the heavy rains had made the water too deep and swift to cross. The Americans used all the boats in the area to cross the river. Now they were on the other side when the British arrived. Greene had won the race. He had united the two parts of his army and could now let his men rest a few days without fear of attack.[8]

Nathanael Greene withdrew from the field. He knew he had damaged the British force. Three days later, Cornwallis pulled his beaten army back to Wilmington.

Home of Major-General Nathanael Greene at Coventry, Rhode Island, from *The Remains of Major-General Nathanael Greene* 1903 (PD-US).

Greene turned south once more and fought more battles against other British armies. He did not win every battle, but he fought so hard and so wisely that the British gave up the Carolinas and retreated to the coast. They were never able to control the Carolinas or march north to help in the fight against Washington.

After the war, Nathaniel Greene was rewarded with large amounts of land and money from North Carolina, South Carolina, and Georgia. He sold some of his land to pay debts from the supplies he had bought for his army during the southern campaign. He was twice offered the post of Secretary of War, but he did not accept. Like most great men, he was also a humble man. He remained a faithful patriot to the end of his days.

Burial site of Nathaniel Greene in Johnson Square, Savannah, Georgia (PD-US).

STRIKING AT THE BRITISH

They were joined by reinforcements. Now Greene's army had hundreds more men. He was strong enough now to fight Cornwallis. When the river went down, he crossed back to the south side. Now it was Cornwallis who was running for his life. The Americans caught up with him at Guilford Court House, and the battle began.

The Americans were tired of being chased. They wanted to strike at the British. In the midst of the battle, they drove back the enemy's left flank. Cornwallis committed one of the cruelest acts of the war. He ordered his cannon in the rear to fire grapeshot into the middle of the fight. Thousands of lead bullets roared from the cannons, striking many British and American soldiers. Cornwallis killed many of his own men in order to drive back the patriots.

Battle of Guilford Courthouse

199

The Battle of Cowpens

CHAPTER 25

JOHN SEVIER

Nolichucky Jack

GROWING UP EARLY

John Sevier's life began in the beautiful Shenandoah Valley of Virginia. As a boy, his mother taught him to read. He got some years of schooling in Fredericksburg, Virginia, but he did not like school. When he was 16, he quit school and went back to Shenandoah. There, he built a store and called it New Market. Later, the town of New Market, Virginia, would grow. He was still only 16 when he married Sarah Hawkins.

There were still hostile Indian tribes in Shenandoah. Sevier helped defend other settlers as well as his own home. His store was the only store in his part of the valley, so many people came to him to buy supplies. John had built a good business by the time he was 26. He was respected as a fighting man, as well. The governor made him a captain in the militia led by George Washington.

John Sevier was tall, lean, and graceful. He had blue eyes and a friendly face. He had learned manners from his mother and father, so he charmed all those who met him.[1]

Virginia seemed to offer a bright future to young Sevier, but he had an urge to see new country. He and his brother visited the Holston River area in what is now Tennessee. He eventually moved his family to the Holston country and later to the settlement called Watauga. He became the clerk of the court. Later, he was elected to be a judge. Even though he had not been in the settlement long, his neighbors liked and trusted him.

John Sevier, by Charles Willson Peale, 1792 (PD-Art).

Few men in the history of Tennessee have been as loved and respected as John Sevier. He lived for a long time near the Nolichucky River, where he earned his nickname, Nolichucky Jack. He was a hero of the Revolutionary War.

When the colonies declared independence from England, the British wanted the Indians to help them fight the Americans. They sent agents among the tribes and gave them guns and ammunition. The Cherokees planned an attack on Fort Watauga. Early one morning, they came creeping through the woods toward the fort. They were quiet, hoping to surprise the Americans. Suddenly, 40 rifles blazed from the stockade, and Indians fell to the ground. The others rushed back into the woods.

A man that hath friends must shew himself friendly: and there is a friend that sticketh closer than a brother." There is a reason everyone like John Sevier. Remember, in order to have true friends, you must be friendly to others.

The siege of the fort lasted for three weeks. The people began to run out of food. Some of the men snuck out of the fort. Some were killed by the Cherokees.[2]

Sevier left the Watauga settlement and went to live on the Nolichucky River. There he built a two-part log cabin. The parts were connected by a roof over an open space between. The house had large fireplaces and room for guests. Here, John and Kate welcomed strangers, as long as they were honest. Sometimes he invited all the neighbors for barbecues. At other times, a family of neighbors or new settlers would join them for supper. They dined on wild game, corn bread, hominy, and cider. Some people came for his advice. No one was turned away. John became known as Nolichucky Jack. Everyone in the countryside liked and respected him.

RUNNING FOR THE WALL

There is a story told about a young woman who was outside the fort milking a cow when the first shots were fired. Katherine Sherrill ran, but could not reach the fort before the gates closed. Seeing her run across the clearing, some of the Indians ran out of the woods to catch her. John Sevier saw her from the wall of the fort. He shouted and told her to run.[3] He shot the Indian closest behind her. Then, as she jumped for the top of the wall, he pulled her over. She fell into his arms. Later, after Sevier's wife died, he fell in love with Kate.

Storytime with Uncle Rick

Fight for Freedom

We do not know if all of the story is true, but we do know that after Sarah's death, John and Kate were married, and she was his First Lady when he was later the governor of Tennessee.[4]

OVER THE MOUNTAINS

In 1780, British General Cornwallis was winning battles in South Carolina. Many patriots who had fought against him had to flee ahead of his armies. Some of them crossed the mountains into the settlements. Cornwallis sent Colonel Ferguson and 1,000 soldiers into the western part of Carolina. He wanted to punish the backwoodsmen. Ferguson grew bold. He sent word over the mountains that the settlers should stop resisting the king's army. He said that if they did not, he would cross the mountains and destroy their homes.

Hospitality - The character quality of hospitality is making those who visit our home feel comfortable. John and Kate certainly did just that with their many visitors. Romans 12:13b encourages us to be "given to hospitality."

This independent frontiersmen did not like this. They had braved storms, wild beasts, and hunger to build their homes and towns. They were not afraid to face Ferguson. Sevier and Colonel Shelby of Kentucky agreed to disturb the frontiersmen. They would cross the mountains and show Colonel Ferguson how real fighting men acted.

They were joined by Colonel Campbell and his men from the Holston country in Virginia. Soon, 1,000 backwoodsmen started the march over the mountains.

Once over the mountains, scattered Carolinians joined them. There were hundreds of men who had fought Ferguson. They had been beaten because Ferguson had many more men.

Fort Watauga reconstruction at Sycamore Shoals State Historic Park, photo by Brian Stansberry, 2009 (CC BY 3.0).

The Battle of Cowpens

Ferguson was outnumbered. He asked Cornwallis for more troops. Before help could arrive, he was trapped by over 1,000 riflemen on a ridge of King's Mountain. He boasted that he could not be driven from his ridge by all the rebels or even God Himself. Ferguson thought that he could easily hold out until help came.

One side of the ridge was too steep to climb. Three divisions of woodsmen marched up the mountain on the other three sides. They had no bayonets on their rifles, so after firing their guns, they turned and ran down the slope. They reloaded their rifles as they went. The Tories followed in an angry bayonet charge. They were soon separated and scattered in the woods.

Each time a division charged, it would be driven back down by the bayonets. But then a division on another side of the ridge would move upward. When that division was driven back down, a third would advance. Each time, the woodsmen got closer to the top. Finally, the Tories could not drive back a patriot division without being shot at. The Americans began to appear at the top of the ridge. They drove Ferguson's men into a group around the baggage wagons. Ferguson tried to gather his men. He led a charge against the nearest group of patriots coming over the the ridge. Several woodsmen got him in their rifle sights. He fell from his horse, dead.

The battle was soon over. The men rested and took a meal of British rations. They soon started back home. Many of them would be back three months later to help Daniel Morgan win the battle of Cowpens.

I am in suspense as to the probable or improbability of being called into the Army, a station I would prefer to any other that of being in arms to defend an injured and grossly insulted country.[5]

John Sevier

SEVIER THE STATESMAN

After the battle of King's Mountain, John was kept busy fighting Indians on the western side of the mountains. He fought battles in places that are now in the states of Tennessee, Georgia, and Alabama.

Finally, the war was over, and the colonies were free. The land that is now Tennessee was then a part of North Carolina. In 1784, North Carolina offered the land west of the mountains to Congress for a new state. For a time, the area did not seem to belong to any government. At first, Congress did not set up an American government there. But North Carolina did not consider it its land, either. John Sevier and others set up a new

government and called it the state of Franklin, after Benjamin Franklin. North Carolina changed its mind and said the western country still belonged to North Carolina. For a while, two different governments operated and made laws in the Tennessee country. North Carolina claimed to be in charge, and so did Franklin.

Sevier had been elected the first governor of Franklin. The government was dissolved, and he swore allegiance to North Carolina. He was elected to the state senate of North Carolina and worked for the ratification of the new United States Constitution. North Carolina again gave the western lands to the U.S. government. The new state of Tennessee was formed. John Sevier was elected the first governor of the state. The people respected Sevier so much that they elected him to that office three times. In 1811, he was elected as a congressman from Tennessee.

Sevier was a strong supporter of the War of 1812. President James Madison offered him a command in the army, but he turned it down. He died in 1815 while surveying land the United States had bought from the Creek Indians. He was buried beside the Tallapoosa River, but his remains were later moved to Tennessee. His grave is now on the lawn of the Knox County courthouse in Knoxville, Tennessee. Bonnie Kate rests beside him.[6]

Obelisk marking the grave of Tennessee governor John Sevier (1745–1815) on the lawn of the Knox County Courthouse in Knoxville, Tennessee. Photo by Brian Stansberry, 2012 (CC BY 3.0).

Simon Kenton

CHAPTER 26

SIMON KENTON

Man of the Kentucky Forest

BECOMING A WOODSMAN

We all know the name of Daniel Boone, the famous frontiersman and founder of Boonesborough. But many people do not know the name of Simon Kenton. Yet, Boone and Kenton were close friends. Once, Kenton saved Boone's life.

Many men had experiences like Kenton in fighting the Indians and British during the War of Independence. Probably no man was captured as many times as Kenton. Probably no man ever escaped as many times, either. His story is so full of danger and adventure that it is hard to believe some of it is true. Yet it is.

Boone and Kenton were two men that Kentucky needed to become a peaceful, productive state in the new nation. Boone was a blend of hunter and farmer-settler. He was a leader who could hold frontiersmen together as a team. He could keep a young colony together, feed it, and protect it.

Simon Kenton was also a strong, brave man. He could take orders, and he could give orders to others. Usually, his way was to act on his own, to see what needed to be done and do it. People who knew Kenton described him as "a man on his own hook." They meant that he could act with his own judgment. He could figure out a situation and know what to do.

Simon Kenton was captured by the Indians many times, but he always managed to escape. He also avoided death in many battles. God uses people to accomplish His purposes. Perhaps God used Kenton to win battles and save lives so settlers would come to Kentucky, bringing the gospel with them.

Kenton also had the quality of living by the Golden Rule. He spent little time working or fighting for himself. Often it was Kenton who rode or ran through miles of forest, warning settlers of a coming attack.

But Simon Kenton was not so unselfish when he started out in life. In fact, his journeys in the western wilderness started because he acted selfishly.

Growing up on a Virginia farm in Fauquier County, Simon did not like school. In fact, he never learned to read or write more than to sign his name. He also did not care for farm chores. He took every chance to hide from the boring, constant work on the farm. He liked to roam the woods.

Jesus taught His disciples to "do unto others as you would have them do unto you." Simon Kenton spent much of his time and risked his life to save others.

The forest was Simon's school. He learned the ways of the birds and animals. He became familiar with the trees, streams, bushes, and weeds. He also learned to spend time alone without fear. More than all that, he learned to find his own way in new situations. He grew confident in himself. New challenges did not discourage him.

Simon joined a group of hunters. They built a canoe and set off down the Monongahela River toward the Ohio River. But two of the men changed their minds about the trip. The group broke up near the Provence settlement. It was near what is now Pittsburg, Pennsylvania.

After staying in the Provence settlement for a few months, Simon met two new friends. One was a young man named George Strader. The other was an old frontiersman named John Yeager. Simon and George listened with excitement to the old hunter's stories. He told of a land called Kain-tuck-ee. As a boy, Yeager had been captured by Indians and had lived with them for years. He learned their languages and went on long hunting trips with them. He knew their ways and customs. He had seen wonderful hunting grounds.

He wanted to take a trip back. It was just a few days down the Ohio, he said. A man could hunt endless herds of buffalo, deer, and elk. He could come back with his canoe full of skins and sell them for a fortune. Before long, Simon and George were ready to leave for Kain-tuck-ee.

The three were on their way. Simon and George would do the hunting and trapping. John Yeager would do the cooking and dress the skins. In a few months, they would paddle up the Ohio with a load of skins that would make them all rich. It sounded easy.

And it was easy for a while. John's "few days" turned into weeks, but they stopped and visited a few settlements and camps. In the camps, old John made them welcome with his knowledge of the Indian languages and ways. They played and danced with the younger tribe members. All the time, they were learning more of the ways of the wilderness. It would serve John Sevier well in the years to come.

> Life was not easy for Simon Kenton as a young man. He often slept on the ground, went hungry when hunting was poor, and lived for weeks with danger all around. As hard as these experiences were, they prepared him with the strength and skills he needed to be a useful man in the future. God often uses hard times to make us more useful to Him and to other people.

They did not get all the way to Kentucky. Old John had forgotten the landmarks, and they ended up stopping on the Elk River in what is now West Virginia. They built a lean-to cabin with one side open. They stored their bedding and equipment. The pile of hides began growing.

Day by day, the weeks went by and Simon Kenton learned more in the great school of the wilderness. His senses became even sharper. His aim became more accurate. His instincts began to tell him the secrets of the forest that eyes and ears miss.

One night, they came to the little camp on the Elk River. Simon and George were sitting by the fire while old John roasted a turkey over the flames. The three saw some Indians appear out of the twilight with their rifles aiming at the cabin. The two boys ran around the cabin, fleeing for their lives into the dark woods. Old John could not move so quickly. He was shot down.

The two boys met in the woods and traveled toward the Ohio. They had been barefoot when the Indians attacked, and now their feet were torn to pieces by rocks and thorns. They had to crawl the last two days of their trek. Finally, they found a cabin and were given food and rest. They had nearly starved to death.

Trappers

Capture and Escape

But Simon Kenton had become a man in the wilderness. He went on more hunting trips. When Angus McDonald was sent west of the Allegheny Mountains to help defend the settlements from Indian attacks in 1774, Simon got his first military experience. He also met George Rogers Clark. The two men fought in many battles together in the years to come. Simon and another man were asked to raise a group of frontiersmen, which they did. These recruits fought under Clark.

When Lord Dunmore started a war with the Indians later that year, Simon was called on as a scout. His knowledge of the forests made him a wonderful help to the militia. The war was over by the end of the year, but Simon had increased his skills.

He spent the next few years hunting and trapping skins, guiding travelers, and hunting food for settlers. He had several run-ins with Indians. But for the most part, the Indians had been quiet since Lord Dunmore's War in 1774.

In 1776, everything changed. The War of Independence was going strong. The British were doing everything they could to turn the Indians against the settlers.

Early in 1777, George Rogers Clark received a commission as general in the Kentucky militia. He appointed his officers. He chose Simon Kenton as a scout. No man could sneak through the forest better.

Simon spied on Fort Kaskaskia for Clark, helping him win there. Later, he went to Boonesborough to help Daniel Boone defend the fort against the attack by Blackfish and his Shawnees. Before the Shawnee force reached the fort, Boone got tired of waiting.

He asked Kenton to join him on a scout through the country. He wanted to try to recover some horses stolen from Boonesborough. They encountered a small force of Indians and drove them off in a fight. Their secrecy was gone. Boone decided to go back to Boonesborough. But Kenton could not bring himself to give up without at least getting some horses back. He stayed in the woods. A few days later, Kenton appeared once again in Boonesborough. He was leading four horses.

Before the Blackfish attack, Kenton was sent to spy on the Shawnee town of Chillicothe. With two other men, he snuck up on the village and spent hours watching. Most of

Fort Boonesborough, artist and date unknown (PD-Art).

the warriors were on their way to attack Boonesborough, but danger was in the air. There was a pen full of good horses, and Kenton wanted to take as many as he could.

That night, the three men selected several nice horses and led them out of the fence. But they were heard, and the village was alarmed. They rode off through the woods, each man leading two or three horses. They knew they would not be followed until daybreak, and they did their best to make the most of their head start.

An Indian Camp

They were stopped at the river. It was high from recent rains, and the horses would not cross. The men let their horses go and split up to avoid capture.

Many of the Indians were angry at losing their captive, but the chiefs agreed to the British request, and Kenton went to Detroit.

Decisiveness is the ability to make wise, deliberate decisions. Simon Kenton had this quality.

The British treated Kenton kindly. He tried to answer their questions in ways that would not give them true information. They came to like him and allowed him freedom to walk about. He even did odd jobs in the village and saved his money to buy things he needed to escape. Finally, he bought guns, powder, and bullets from a friendly British man. He also got food and extra moccasins. Then, with two other men, he left the fort just after dark one evening.

He heard that most escaped captives were caught because they headed straight south through Indian land to get into American territory. He and his friends went straight west for many miles before turning south. They traveled for 14 days before they felt they were safe. When they finally reached the falls of the Ohio River and safety, they had not seen one Indian in the entire trip.

As soon as Kenton reached the Ohio, he went looking for General George Rogers Clark. In a daring and terrible winter campaign, Clark had just recaptured British forts at Kaskaskia and Vincennes. He wanted to also take the much larger British force at Detroit. After having spent several months at Detroit, Kenton was convinced that it would fall if Clark attacked it with a large force.

RUNNING THE GAUNTLET

Kenton was not fortunate enough to escape. He fired his rifle at some Indians, but it failed to go off. He ran to escape, but he met two Indians. He was captured and tied up.

The Shawnees killed one of Kenton's companions, a man named Montgomery.

They had recently lost a famous captive, Daniel Boone. Their brothers were fighting Boone at Boonesborough. They had another famous frontiersman. He was known to be strong and brave.

But that had to wait until he could be taken to a village and a crowd could gather for the show. For the night, he was tied up in such a way that caused the most pain.

When the group returned to Chilicothe with their captive, there was great celebration. Men, women, and children crowded around to see the captive and congratulate the warriors. Kenton was tied to a pole with his hands above his head at the edge of the village. The few rags he still wore were torn off him. For three or four hours the Indians danced around him, using every trick they knew to torment him without killing him.

The next morning, his captors marched him into the village to the slow beat of a drum. Soon he saw what awaited him. Two lines of people stood facing each other in front of the council house. Each man, woman, and boy held a club or whip. He was going to have to run the gauntlet.

In running the gauntlet, the victim had to run between two lines of people who tried to strike him with a weapon as he passed. If he did not make it to the end of the gauntlet, he was forced to run it again.

A signal was given, and the first blow was struck. Despite his many wounds, Kenton ran. He doubled and dodged, feeling the blows upon his bruised, bleeding back as he ran.

He was too badly hurt to run the gauntlet again that day. The Indians gave him food and water. They also gave him his tattered clothing back.

Then a messenger came from Detroit. The commander there wanted to borrow their captive. Kenton had knowledge of the American forces in Kentucky, and General Hamilton wanted to question him.[1]

But Clark was still at Vincennes. Kenton sent a messenger to him with the information he had learned at Detroit. Clark was not able to collect enough men. Both Virginia and Kentucky had their hands full with fighting Indians and British. Neither could spare men to help. Detroit had to be left to the redcoats.

When he got word that Clark would not be able to attack Detroit, Kenton headed back to Kentucky. He spent the autumn around Boonesborough and the winter at Lexington because Lexington was the newest and weakest fort in Kentucky. It was there that Kenton was needed most.

REDCOATS IN KENTUCKY

When summer came, the British came with it. The redcoat Captain Henry Bird came south with his Indian allies. Bird intended to attack Clark at Louisville. When his Indian friends learned that Bird had two cannons, they asked him to attack Ruddell's and Martin's stations instead. These wilderness stations were simple log forts. They were not built to repel cannon balls.

It only took one shot from the cannon to convince Ruddell's fort to surrender. Three hundred Kentuckians became prisoners. Martin's fort also fell quickly, and another 50 were captured. Captain Bird found himself in trouble because of his success. He had 350 extra mouths to feed. He had taken the horses to carry his prisoners, but he had killed all the cattle. His army was running out of meat for both soldiers and prisoners. There were more Kentucky forts that would fall easily to his big guns. But it was hard to move with so many prisoners.

Bird decided to go back north and leave Kentucky to dispose of his prisoners. He convinced the Indians with him to go home. Meanwhile, the people of Kentucky sent a message to George Rogers Clark. They asked him to help them. Clark moved from Vincennes down to Fort Jefferson on the Mississippi. He was fighting to defend it from another force of British and Indians.

Clark answered Kentucky's call. He left another officer in command of Fort Jefferson and headed for Harrodsburg in Kentucky.

Simon Kenton and another man scouted for Clark. They followed the trail of the redcoats and Indians. They found where they had built a blockhouse, a single building that served as a fort, but left it empty. At this point the two scouts left the chase and returned to Harrodsburg. But not before they snuck up on

His army was running out of meat for both soldiers and prisoners. There were more Kentucky forts that would fall easily to his big guns. But it was hard to move with so many prisoners.

Bird's camp at night and stole his cannon. George Rogers Clark took that cannon on his summer campaign.

Meeting with Clark in Harrodsburg, Kenton agreed to help find volunteers. For the first time, he was made an officer. He was given command of his own company of men. By late July, an army of 1,000 men was raised and equipped.

On August 2, the army reached Blackfish's old town of Chillicothe, but the town was deserted and burned. A deserter from Clark's company had warned the Shawnees that Clark was on his way. The Indians had fled, burning everything they could not carry. The army camped there that night.

The Indians knew Simon Kenton as "The man whose gun is never empty." He was known for his skill at running and reloading his flintlock at the same time. He heroically risked his life to save many people of Kentucky, including his lifelong friend Daniel Boone and also George Rogers Clark.

The next day, the army approached an Indian encampment called Piqua Town. Here was a solid fort built by the British. Hundreds of Indians had gathered there to fight the Americans. The battle lasted all day, but the Shawnees lost.

In November, George Rogers Clark led the last major offensive of the Revolutionary War in the west. With Simon Kenton and Daniel Boone as guides, he led 1,000 men against several Shawnee towns. On the November 10, they attacked and burned the towns. All the food and supplies that the army could not use were also burned.

This was the last time Simon Kenton served under General Clark. Their work for independence was done, and America was free. Both men would have their share of fighting in the Indian wars to come, but they would not fight together.

Kentucky militia under George Rogers Clark destroyed the large Shawnee town of Piqua. Today, the site is part of the George Rogers Clark Park. Photo by Nyttend, 2009 (PD-US).

In the fall of 1783, Simon took a journey that he had been planning for a long time. He went back to Fauquier County, Virginia. His plan was to let his family know he was alive and tell them about the wonderful land of Kentucky. He wanted to bring them back with him.

After some months of preparation, Simon gathered a group that included almost his whole family. His elderly father died just before reaching Kentucky. By covered wagon on land and by flatboat on the rivers, the party of 41 people reached the land and built a settlement.

Simon Kenton lived to be a very old man. He married twice and had 11 children. Eventually, he moved across the river to Ohio. Late in his life, he made a trip to Missouri to see his old friend, Daniel Boone.

Boulder honoring Simon Kenton and Isaac Zane at the eastern end of Water Street (County Road 5) in Zanesfield, Ohio. Photo by Nyttend, 2010 (PD-US).

Patrick Henry addressing the Virginia Assembly.

CHAPTER 27

PATRICK HENRY

The Man Who Defended America with Pen and Tongue

WHAT SHALL WE DO WITH PATRICK?

What shall we do with Patrick?

That was the question in the minds of John Henry and his wife, Sarah. John had taught his son Latin and mathematics. The boy attended school for a bit, too, but he did not do well as a student. It was plain that Patrick was smart. But most of his school work was just too boring for an energetic boy like him.

If you wanted to find Patrick on a day when he was free from the work of the farm, it was best to look on the riverbank. There he might be found, a fishing pole in his hand and a lazy, dreamy look on his suntanned face. If it was winter and hunting season, Patrick would most likely be slipping quietly through the woods with his rifle, looking for a rabbit or a deer.

If the fish weren't biting or the day was rainy and unpleasant, Patrick could usually be found reading his Bible or some book about history. He also loved to spend hours playing his violin. It was clear that Patrick Henry was a bright boy, but he had an active mind that did not do its best work when confined to a desk.

Patrick's parents wanted to help him get a start as a man in business. But what business was he suited for? Nobody wanted to pay him for hunting, fishing, reading his Bible, or playing violin. What profession should he seek?

Patrick Henry

Patrick Henry has been called "The Firebrand of the Revolution." A firebrand is a burning stick. Long ago, there were no matches. Often people would light a big fire with a burning stick from a small fire. Patrick Henry's speeches were like a torch that kindled the desire for freedom and justice in America.

At 15, Patrick's father had him keeping a store. Patrick wanted to please his father, but store keeping wasn't interesting. It was more fun to talk politics with the men who came into the store or take an afternoon off to go fishing. The store was given up.

When he was 18, Patrick married Sarah Shelton. His parents and hers helped the young couple start farming on a 300-acre Virginia farm. Patrick didn't do well at farming, either. The land was worn out from raising tobacco. Besides, Patrick just wasn't cut out to be a farmer.

He tried running a store again but failed. Was there no business in the world where Patrick Henry could succeed?

Young Patrick Finds His Calling

Patrick got some law books and began reading them. The books were not exciting reading like the history books he had read as a boy. But Patrick had a strong sense of justice. He liked how the law was written to protect the rights of people. He decided to become a lawyer.

Patrick had found his calling. He loved to talk about law, justice, and politics. After studying for several months, he got his license to work as a lawyer.

> Patrick Henry understood how important it is for young people to read the Bible. No doubt he gained wisdom from his study of God's Word.

After taking some time to get established, Patrick began to be quite busy as a lawyer. People would bring their cases to him for help because he was a good talker, and he wanted to help people get justice. Still, he was certainly not famous.

His time was coming. The name of Patrick Henry would soon be known all over Virginia. It happened because of the Parson's Case.

To understand the case, you have to remember that this was before the War of Independence. In those days, people in America were still English subjects. England had a national church called the Anglican Church. It belonged to the English government, and the preachers were paid by the government. In Virginia, parsons were paid not in cash, but in tobacco, which they could sell for cash. Remember, this was long before people knew that using tobacco causes cancer.

One year, there was a drought, and the tobacco did not grow well. There was much less tobacco for sale, so people were willing to pay more for it than they had been paying. To keep paying parsons in tobacco would mean that they were being paid much more than before. Virginia passed a law that said parsons could be paid in cash instead of tobacco. That way, they would be still earning what they had earned before.

But King George vetoed the law. He said parsons must be paid in tobacco just as before. When the parsons heard this, one of them went to court to force Virginia to give him more money. He said the people of Virginia must give him as much as he would have earned if he had been receiving tobacco for pay during the time before the king vetoed the law.

Most lawyers did not want to take the case for Virginia. Who would want to argue against the preachers and the king in court? Patrick Henry was willing.

Henry said the king did not have the right to veto laws made by the Virginia lawmakers. He said it was the act of a tyrant who did not want people to be able to govern themselves. He said the people should not be forced to not pay the parson the large amount of money he was asking for.

Patrick Henry was nervous when he started speaking in court that day. His own father was the judge! He had never argued a case in front of his father before. John Henry remembered his son's many failures. What if Patrick said the wrong thing on this very important day?

But soon he forgot his fear. He spoke so boldly and so clearly that it was hard not to agree with him. As he marched ahead through his speech, his words became more moving and his gestures more natural. The people began to listen with serious looks on their faces. They leaned forward in their seats, spellbound by the logic of his argument and the charm of his speech. The parsons got angry and started to leave the courtroom.

Henry argued that a king who would veto a good law of the people to make his parson friends rich was not a just ruler and should not be obeyed. The jury listened carefully to every word he said. When they left the room and later came back to tell their decision, they only awarded the parson one penny. Patrick Henry's speech had triumphed over the king's tyranny! Now many people began to see that King George was not always right about the law.

When the verdict was announced, the courtroom went wild. Judge John Henry sat with tears running down his cheeks. People crowded around Patrick to shake his hand and praise him. They lifted him to their shoulders and carried him around, shouting in glee. Patrick Henry was no longer just a young country lawyer. He was a hero of the people.[2]

Tobacco farm in morning.

O God, thou hast taught me from my youth: and hitherto have I declared thy wondrous works.

Psalm 71:17

Sound the Alarm!

Many people know about the battles of Lexington and Concord on April 19, 1775. Concord was where the patriots had stored gunpowder and cannons in case there was a war with England. The British marched all night to capture the war supplies, but they did not get them. The patriots had been warned in advance, and they moved most of their material to other hiding places.

The next day, far to the south in Virginia, another raid took place. In the town of Williamsburg, the capitol of the colony, there was a big building with eight sides. It was called a magazine. It was a building to store guns and gunpowder in case of attack.

But the British governor of Virginia, Lord Dunmore, had other ideas. He thought about how easily that ammunition could be used by the "rebels." If there was fighting between the British and the colonists, he didn't want the Virginians to have the gunpowder.

So he sent an order out to the British ship, the *Magdalen*, where it was anchored in the James River. In the middle of the night, there was a quiet splashing of oars, and Captain Harry Collins, with some of his British marines, appeared out of the darkness on the shore near Williamsburg. They marched straight to the magazine and took 15 big barrels of gunpowder. Working quickly and quietly, the marines loaded the barrels onto Lord Dunmore's wagon. A cover was thrown over them and the wagon drove away.

The clank of metal wagon tires on cobblestones woke a neighbor and suddenly shouts rang from house to house.[3]

"It's the magazine!"

"They're taking the powder!"

"Sound the alarm!"

Lanterns began to glow. Muskets were snatched from their hooks above fireplaces. Boots clattered in the street. But they were too late. The marines and the wagon had disappeared in the darkness.

The word spread quickly. At daybreak, men began to gather in Williamsburg to see what could be done. The colony was coming to life as news of the theft reached patriot homesteads and plantations. When Patrick got the word, he was delighted.

"This is just what we needed!" he told his friends. "The good governor has just pushed hundreds of uncertain patriots over the edge. The people won't stand for having their gunpowder stolen. This is the beginning!"[4]

220

He sent out a message to his militiamen. "Meet me at New Castle on the second of May on business of the highest importance to American Liberty."[5]

When they met at New Castle on the Pamunkey River, Patrick climbed up on a stump and made one of his inspiring speeches. "Now, if ever we must strike for freedom!"[6] The men roared back at him.

The Hanover County militia marched toward Williamsburg. Some of their Tory neighbors turned out to beg Captain Henry not to start a fight. No one wanted to see their region turned into a battlefield. He did not waver. He sat on his horse and led his men onward. As they marched, other patriots joined them. Soon they were 5,000 strong.

Lord Dunmore heard about the approaching militia while they were still miles away. He hurried his family aboard a British warship. He ordered out the marines. He had cannons placed on the green. But when he heard that Patrick Henry was leading the militia, his heart went cold. That rebel would not stop or change his mind.

From the road toward Williamsburg, a horse and rider appeared in a cloud of dust. The man galloped directly up to the militia leader. "Mr. Patrick Henry, sir?"

"That is my name."

"Well, Captain Henry, I have a message for you from the governor. He sends you this 330 pounds in payment for the gunpowder he removed from the magazine for reasons of public safety."[7]

Patrick sat up straighter in his saddle and smiled. His men crowded around to see what he would do. Smiling, he took the money and signed a receipt. As the messenger turned his horse and rode away, Patrick turned to face his men. There were shouts and laughter as the word spread through the troop. All the men were cheering their leader.

Lord Dunmore saw it differently. He declared Patrick Henry an outlaw. Patrick was more popular than ever. His place in patriot leadership was certain.[8]

Patrick Henry, by George Bagby Matthews, c.1891 (PD-US).

For thou art my hope, O Lord GOD: thou art my trust from my youth.

Psalm 71:5

It can not be emphasized too strongly or too often that this great nation was founded, not by religionists, but by Christians; not on religions but on the gospel of Jesus Christ! For this very reason, peoples of other faiths have been afforded asylum, prosperity, and freedom of worship here.

Patrick Henry

A Leader of Virginia

The next year, young Henry was elected to the Virginia House of Burgesses. He went to the Virginia capitol at Williamsburg to help make laws for the colony. While there, he made a speech against the Stamp Act that made him even more famous.

The Stamp Act was a move by King George to try to get money from the American colonies. He said that England had spent a lot of money to protect the colonies during the French and Indian War. The colonists shouldn't mind paying some taxes to help pay the government's debt. Besides, he had sent soldiers to the colonies to protect them from the Indians.

The colonists didn't see it that way. They said England fought the French to protect its business and trade in North America rather than to protect Americans. After all, the colonies had also spent money and sent many of their men to fight the French. They also said the British armies stationed in America weren't there for protection, but to make the Americans pay the king's taxes. Most of all, they believed the king did not have the right to make them pay taxes at all. They had elected representatives, like Patrick Henry in Virginia, to set their taxes.

Many people in England agreed with the colonists. They knew the king and Parliament had a constitution that limited what they could do. King George was stubborn.

Up and down the American colonies, leaders spoke and wrote against the Stamp Act. In the Virginia House of Burgesses, many men thought the king was wrong. But many did not have the courage to say so in public. That did not stop Patrick Henry.

Patrick was a new member. He was not expected to be a leader in the assembly. But he tore a blank page out of a law book and wrote five resolutions. They said that only Virginia had a right to tax Virginians and that anybody who said otherwise was an enemy of the colony. Then he made a speech that backed up his resolutions and brought assembly members to their feet. Some held their breath as they heard the speaker. He finished by saying that King George was being a tyrant.

Others were shouting that this was treason, and he stated that if it was treason, then they should make the most of it.[9]

Henry's resolutions were passed. They made him famous not only in Virginia, but also throughout the colonies as nearly every newspaper in America printed them. Americans became even more determined not to pay the taxes. Finally, the king and Parliament gave up and repealed the tax. The colonies rejoiced.

The king was slow to learn his lessons. The next year, he and Parliament passed a tax on tea sold in the colonies. The colonists refused to buy the tea. You have heard of the famous Boston Tea Party, when colonists dressed as Indians threw a cargo of tea into Boston Harbor. The people of New York and Philadelphia sent the tea ships back home with their cargoes still aboard. In Maryland, the Sons of Liberty burned a ship full of tea at Annapolis.

King George was red hot with anger. He passed laws to punish Boston. He sent more soldiers to make the people obey his unjust laws.

George III of the United Kingdom, by Allan Ramsay, 1762 (PD-Art).

PATRICK HENRY GOES TO CONGRESS

In 1774 the colonies decided to hold an assembly in Philadelphia and have representatives from each colony come to decide together what to do. It was called the First Continental Congress. Patrick Henry was one of the men sent by Virginia. There he made friends with other great men. He met Sam Adams, one of the fiercest opponents of the illegal taxes, along with Benjamin Franklin, the great statesman.

One day, Henry made a speech urging all the colonies to act together to protect themselves from the king's tyranny. He declared, "The distinctions between Virginians and Pennsylvanians, New Yorkers, and New Englanders are no more. I am not a Virginian, but an American."[10]

As he talked with men from other colonies and heard how the British soldiers were treating the people at Boston, he came to see that there must soon be a war. He went home to Virginia and urged the people to prepare for a struggle. The king's governor drove the Burgesses out of the capitol at Williamsburg, so they assembled in St. John's Church in Richmond.

Patrick Henry again submitted resolutions. He urged Virginia to prepare for war. Many people were afraid. They knew that 13 colonies with no organized army or navy would have a hard time fighting a nation like England.

When his turn came to speak, Henry's face was pale and his voice trembled until his expression sounded through the old church and the audience forgot what the other speakers had said. They sat on the edge of their seats and listened to every word as Patrick Henry delivered one of the most famous

Wherewithal shall a young man cleanse his way? by taking heed thereto according to thy word.

Psalm 119:9

—— 66 ——

The Constitution is not an instrument for the government to restrain the people, it is an instrument for the people to restrain the government.

Patrick Henry

—— 99 ——

John Murray, 4th Earl of Dunmore, by Joshua Reynolds, 1765 (PD-Art).

speeches in American history. At the end of the speech, he said:

> We must fight! I repeat it, Sir, we must fight! An appeal to arms and the God of Hosts is all that is left to us. They tell us, Sir, that we are weak; unable to cope with so formidable an adversary. But when shall we be stronger? Will it be the next week or the next year? Sir, we are not weak, if we make a proper use of the means which the God of Nature hath placed in our power. There is no retreat but in submission and slavery. Our chains are forged! Their clanking may be heard on the plains of Boston! The war is inevitable, and let it come! I repeat it, Sir, let it come! The war is actually begun! The next gale that sweeps from the north will bring to our ears the clash of resounding arms. Our brothers are already in the field! Why stand we here idle! Is life so dear, or peace so sweet, as to be purchased at the price of chains and slavery? Forbid it, Almighty God! I know not what course others may take; but as for me, give me liberty, or give me death.[11]

Henry's speech carried the other Burgesses and most Virginians with him into preparation for war. When Lord Dunmore, the king's royal governor over Virginia, took barrels of gunpowder from the Williamsburg powder house, Henry fought him. Henry said the gunpowder belonged to Virginia, not England. He led the Hanover County militia to Williamsburg to demand payment for the gunpowder. The money was given to him.

Governor Dunmore left Williamsburg and took his family to refuge aboard a British ship. It was the end of British government in Virginia.

Virginians set up their own state government. On June 28, 1776, Patrick Henry was voted the first governor of the free commonwealth of Virginia.

Virginia prepared for war. Some of Henry's militiamen had printed "Liberty or Death" on their hunting shirts. General Washington saw the slogan when they went to Boston to join his army.

From this time on, Patrick Henry was actively involved in the struggle for American independence. Virginia sent him to the Continental Congress. He served as an officer in the army. Not only was he elected Virginia's first state governor, he was elected to that office again and again.

—— 66 ——

There is a just God who presides over the destinies of nations, and who will raise up friends to fight our battles for us. The battle, sir, is not to the strong alone; it is to the vigilant, the active, the brave.[12]

Patrick Henry

—— 99 ——

After winning independence, the 13 new states struggled to find a plan to unite into one nation. When the Constitution was written, Patrick Henry was against it at first. He was afraid it gave too much power to the federal government and not enough power to each state to govern its own affairs. He was one of the main men to support the addition of a Bill of Rights to make sure that every man's rights would be respected. When the Constitution was established, he supported his friend George Washington for president of the new nation.

Patrick Henry declined Washington's offer to become the first Secretary of State, a high position in the government. Later, he refused President John Adams' invitation to serve as an ambassador to France. Henry retired to his estate, Red Hill, in Charlotte County, and his health was no longer strong enough for public service.

Patrick Henry spent the final years of his life at Red Hill, receiving visitors, playing violin, and enjoying his family. He left behind him the testimony of an honest, humble Christian and a reputation as a man God used to establish freedom in America.

Patrick Henry during his famous speech, "Give me liberty, or give me death!", Virginia House of Burgesses.

"

Religion I have disposed of all my property to my family. There is one thing more I wish I could give to them, and that is the Christian religion. If they had that and I had not given them one cent, they would be rich. If they have not that, and I had given them the world, they would be poor.

Patrick Henry

"

Samuel Adams

CHAPTER 28

SAMUEL ADAMS

Father of the Revolution

A POLITICIAN, NOT A BUSINESSMAN

While Patrick Henry was setting the hearts of Americans on fire with his speeches, far to the north was another man doing the same thing with written words. Samuel Adams, a cousin of John Adams, was stirring up opposition to the illegal acts of King George and the Parliament.

Born in Massachusetts in 1722, Samuel loved reading books more than outdoor play and rambling. He graduated from Harvard College when he was only 18. His parents hoped he would become a preacher, but he wanted to become a lawyer. His mother talked him into trying another type of work. Samuel started a business, but it failed. Like Patrick Henry, he wasn't cut out to be a businessman. Next, he went into business with his father. That failed too. Finally, Samuel decided politics was the job for him.

Portrait of Samuel Adams, by John Singleton Copley, c.1772 (PD-Art).

While he was in college, Samuel enjoyed debating. There was much talk in those days of obeying or resisting the king. Samuel joined the debating clubs and argued for hours with his friends. He wrote articles for newspapers, saying people had a right to disobey the king when the king broke the law with his commands. That kind of writing could him in trouble. Samuel always took a stand for what he believed was right.

Samuel made a speech to a group of people in Boston. He said the king's illegal taxes could make the people into slaves. The king had been trying to tax the businesses in America. Samuel said if he could do that, he could tax the land and other property, too.

When the Declaration of Independence was written in 1776, it listed 27 wrong things the king had done against the American colonies. Taxation without representation was just one of those things. He had also closed their courts and canceled out their laws. He had forced Americans to let soldiers live in their homes. He had kept them from trading with other countries. Still, many colonists wanted to remain British citizens. The patriot leaders tried to make peace with the king and Parliament, but King George told the colonies he would treat them as a conquered nation. There was nothing left to do but fight.

If you have the power to remove one regiment, you have power to remove both. — Sam Adams

The people of Boston were reading of the Patrick Henry speeches. The king's Stamp Act had the entire country angry. Samuel took up his pen and wrote articles against the king and the act.

Boston elected Samuel Adams to represent the city in the Massachusetts Assembly. He spoke against the Stamp Act in the assembly. He didn't stop there. He talked to people in the shops and on the streets to tell them what he thought about it. Many people began to think he was right.

When some citizens formed the Sons of Liberty to oppose the act, Samuel Adams was among the leaders. They destroyed the stamps as soon as they arrived. He talked with the store owners of the town. He got them to promise not to buy any goods from England until the tax was taken off. When this happened, merchants in England began to suffer. They had been selling goods to the colonies, and this conflict hurt their business. They asked the king and Parliament to stop the Stamp Act, also.

Finally, the act was stopped. But the king still wanted money from the colonies, so he made another law called the Tea Act. This act put a tax on tea. Most of the colonists drank tea, so this was a good way to raise money. The king said it was a small tax, and the colonists should not mind paying it. Samuel Adams knew that if Americans agreed to pay the tax, the king would place other taxes on them. He and others said they would not allow British ships to bring tea into Boston. The merchants promised to stop buying British goods. The people of Boston began to make their own tea out of the leaves of raspberry and other plants.

Samuel wrote a famous piece called the "Circular Letter," which urged all the colonies to refuse to pay the tax on tea. King George saw a copy of the letter and became angry. That didn't stop Samuel. He kept writing. The people kept reading his articles.

The king sent soldiers to Boston to force the people to pay his tea tax. The people did not like to have soldiers watching them. There were arguments between Bostonians and the soldiers. One evening in 1770, there was a fight in the street. The soldiers killed three men and wounded eight others. Crowds of angry people filled the streets, drawn by the sound of shouting and the ringing of fire bells. The next day, the people crowded into Faneuil Hall, a big public building. They shouted that the soldiers had to leave Boston. Another crowd, gathered in the Old South Church, said the same thing.

With some other leaders, Samuel Adams went to see the governor. Before the king's governor and the general, Samuel Adams and his friends stood strong. The governor offered to send half the soldiers away. Adams said all had to go. Samuel Adams was not a man to back down.

After this meeting, the people looked even more to Samuel as a leader. When the king dropped the price of tea so people would not mind paying the tax, the people agreed with Samuel Adams in saying that they were not protesting the price of the tea. What they didn't like was the king trying to tax the colonists. They would not buy the tea.

When ships came carrying the cheaper tea, Samuel sent a group of men with guns to the harbor to keep the sailors from bringing the tea off the ships. Then there were meetings of the citizens in Old South Church to discuss what else could be done. One of these meetings was held on December 16, 1773. Hundreds of people had come into Boston that day for the meeting. They found the stores and shops closed. People were out in the streets, talking excitedly. At 10 a.m., the people crowded again into the Old South Church. They voted that the tea must never be landed. They told the owner of the ships to ask the governor to let him take his ships out of Boston Harbor.

The last Beatitude in Matthew 5 is "Blessed are those who have been persecuted for righteousness' sake." Samuel Adams was this kind of a man. He knew he could get in trouble with the king, yet he kept writing and speaking the truth.

In the afternoon, the crowd grew bigger. Several men made speeches. Samuel Adams was one of them. One speech asked "how tea would mix with salt water." The meeting went on into the evening. The ship owner came back and said the governor would not allow him to take away his ships. Samuel Adams shouted, "This meeting can do nothing to save the country!"

CONFLICT AHEAD

At that moment, the crowd rose and started leaving the church. Outside was a group men dressed as Mohawk Indians. They were heading down the street toward the harbor. The crowd followed to see the excitement. At the wharf, the group went aboard the ships. They brought up the boxes of tea and broke them open with their hatchets. They threw the tea over the rail into the salty, cold water of Boston Harbor.

That night, Samuel Adams sent riders to carry the news to the other towns of Massachusetts. The next day, Paul Revere mounted his horse and carried saddlebags full of letters to the leaders of the other colonies. He rode all the way to New York, then on to Philadelphia. He was met on the way with joy from

Faneuil Hall, artist unkown, 1830 (PD-US).

the people. He told the story of the tea party, and the happy people met him with cheers, bonfires, and cannon shots. He was the guest of honor at dinner after dinner. Thousands of people gathered in New York and Philadelphia. They promised to stand with the citizens of Boston.

Their help was needed. The king and Parliament passed the Boston Port Bill, which closed Boston Harbor. No ships could sail in or out of the harbor to do business in Boston. That made it hard for the people of Boston to get food, for much of their food came on ships. Another law said there could be no more town meetings. Other laws made things hard as well. The king sent many soldiers to see that the laws were obeyed.[2]

The next year, 1774, it was agreed that all the colonies should send their best men to meet in Philadelphia. This meeting was the first Continental Congress. The reason for the meeting was to talk about how the colonies could work together to protect their rights as Englishmen. The Massachusetts legislature chose Samuel Adams, his cousin, John Adams, and two other men to go for Massachusetts. But Samuel wasn't sure. How could he go? He was a poor man and had no fancy clothes to wear among the rich merchants and planters he would meet there.

At mealtime one day the Adams family had a visitor. He was a tailor in town. Later they were visited by a hat maker and a shoemaker. These men all took measurements of Mr. Adams. A few days later, a trunk appeared at the door. In it were a suit of nice clothes, two pairs of shoes, silver shoe buckles, a three-cornered hat, a gold-headed cane, a handsome red cloak, and gold knee buckles. Samuel's neighbors respected and liked their leader so much that they had paid for a new outfit for him to wear to the Congress!

The king tried to get Adams to stop writing articles against the Crown. He sent messengers to offer him gold and high-paying jobs working for the king. But though Adams was very poor, there was not enough gold in England to make him stop doing what he believed was right. He kept on writing articles and making speeches. And he went to Congress.

The two Adams cousins and their two fellow delegates travelled in a four-horse carriage right past the king's soldiers. In the larger towns people met them and escorted their carriage along. Bells rang, cannons boomed, banquets were given in their honor. All the talk was of Congress. What would happen there? How would it change life in America?

Carpenters' Hall, built c.1770, (PD-US).

Praying for Freedom

The Continental Congress met for the first time on September 5, 1774, in Philadelphia. Thomas Cushing of Massachusetts made a motion that they should open with a public prayer. Two representatives opposed the idea. They believed in prayer, but they felt the representatives would have disagreements because they came from different kinds of churches. Some were Quakers, some were Anabaptists, some were Congregationalists, some were Presbyterians, and some were Episcopalians.

Samuel Adams stood and said he could hear a prayer from any man of piety and virtue, who was at the same time a friend of the country. He had heard there was such a man in Philadelphia, the Reverend Jacob Duché. The motion passed. Peyton Randolph, the President of Congress, called on Reverend Duché and asked him to come the following morning to lead in prayer.

The act of Samuel Adams in suggesting Reverend Duché was important in uniting the hearts of the representatives. Adams was a Congregationalist, and Duché was an Episcopalian. Those two denominations were not friendly to each other. For a Congregationalist to show such respect to an Episcopalian minister was a move that encouraged the other representatives to put aside their differences and work together.

The next day, Reverend Duché came to pray. Congress had just heard a report that Boston had been hit by British cannon. There was a serious mood in the meeting. Many of the delegates had relatives in Boston. As Congress assembled that morning, the men of the southern colonies met the northern men with warmer handshakes and greetings than the day before.

Reverend Duché first read a written prayer that was very appropriate for the occasion. Then he read the Episcopalian devotional for the day, which included Psalm 35: "Plead my cause, O LORD, with them that strive with me: fight against them that fight against me…"

The First Prayer in Congress, September 7, 1774 by Jacob Duché in Carpenters Hall, Philadelphia, by T.H. Matheson, 1848 (PD-US).

After that, Duché launched into heartfelt prayer without reading any notes. Every delegate's heart was filled as Duché's words flew toward heaven. There was more prayer and more Bible reading. The entire opening devotional lasted for three hours. In a letter John Adams wrote to Abigail telling her of the event, he said they all received confirmation that God would give them courage and direction in the course they had undertaken. God would work in their behalf, and it proved to be so.[3]

It means war!"

The group spent nearly a week in New York. When they reached Philadelphia crowds of people on foot, on horseback, and in carriages turned out to welcome them to the city of William Penn. Everyone wanted to see the man who had refused the king's gold. Here was Samuel Adams, the man who had planned the Tea Party, demanded that the king remove his soldiers, and penned the famous Circular Letter.

The Congress met in Carpenter's Hall. Here, Samuel Adams made some friends for life. He was introduced to George Washington, a rich Virginia planter and a hero of the French and Indian War. Also from Virginia were Richard Henry Lee and the great orator, Patrick Henry. Another southerner was Christopher Gadsden, who was called "the Samuel Adams of South Carolina."

Soon Paul Revere came galloping into Philadelphia. There was big news—the patriots of Boston were in danger of being attacked by British troops! The Congress agreed that if Boston was attacked, all the other colonies had the duty to help with the city's defense. It looked as if war was just over the horizon.

As soon as Congress ended, Adams hurried back to Massachusetts. In each town he helped organize companies of "minutemen" ready to fight at a minute's notice. The following spring, a rumor went around that the British were planning on marching to the town of Concord to seize gunpowder and provisions stored there in case the minutemen had to fight. They also hoped to capture John Hancock and Samuel Adams, who were staying in the home of a friend in nearby Lexington. The men were to be sent to England to be tried for treason. Paul Revere and his ring of spies in Boston agreed to watch the British soldiers and spread the word if they left their barracks and headed for Concord.

Like nearly all the Founding Fathers, Samuel Adams was a sincere Christian. In his Last Will and Testament, he wrote: "I .... Rely on the merits of Jesus Christ for a pardon for all of my sins."
— December 29, 1790

On the evening of April 18, 1775, signal lanterns high in the church belfry told the messengers that the British regulars were out and crossing the Charles River on their way to Concord. Paul Revere and William Dawes mounted their horses and galloped out of Boston. On the road they met Dr. Prescott, who helped them spread the word. As the people of Middlesex County were awakened and began to prepare for an attack, some of them mounted horses and rode north and south to spread the alarm. Church bells rang and cannons boomed to spread the news and awaken the countryside. Stopping his horse outside the Clarke house in Lexington, Revere shouted to awaken Adams and Hancock from their sleep. Minutemen guarding the house told Revere not to make so much noise. "You'll soon have noise enough," he replied. "The regulars are coming!" After meeting with Adams and Hancock briefly, he galloped on toward Concord.

THE WAR BEGINS

The British soldiers reached Lexington at daybreak. About 70 patriots stood to defend their homes against nearly ten times as many trained soldiers. The British commander ordered the Minutemen to disperse. It looked as though the soldiers intended to pass on to Concord without attacking Lexington, so the patriots began to walk away. They could slip through the woods and follow the redcoats to see if the patriots at Concord would need their help. Then someone fired a shot. No one knows whether it was a patriot or a solder. But suddenly everybody was shooting, and soon seven patriots lay dead on the ground of Lexington green. The British marched on.

Paul Revere was captured by a British patrol before he could give the warning to Concord. But Dr. Prescott escaped by jumping his horse over a stone wall. Soon more riders were out and Minutemen began coming from all directions to stop the redcoats. When the British reached Concord, they found that the patriots had already moved most of their ammunition and supplies. They destroyed as much as they could find, then were met at the bridge by a group of determined colonists. The aim of the patriots was sure. Many were the deer and wild turkeys those rifles had brought down, and they worked just as well on redcoats.

The British began to retreat toward Boston. Soon they were running for their lives as rifles boomed from behind trees and stone walls along the way. It seemed the patriots just kept coming and coming. And so they did. As the word spread through the country, men left their plows and shovels and picked up their rifles and powder horns.

Near Lexington the gasping British soldiers met other redcoats coming to their aid. But this still was not enough to resist the angry Minutemen. Nearly 300 British fell before they reached the safety of Boston that evening.

Even after this first great battle, many Americans wanted to make peace with England and remain loyal to the British king. Three months later, the second Continental Congress would send the Olive Branch Petition to King George. But that proud, selfish man would reject their offer of peace. The War of Independence had begun!

Statue of Samuel Adams in Boston.

Paul Revere
Gives the Alarm
to the Countryside

CHAPTER 29

PAUL REVERE

The Battle of Lexington and Concord

TROUBLE GROWS IN BOSTON

After the Boston Tea Party, things got worse and worse for the patriots in Massachusetts. To punish the people for daring to disobey their royal master, the English rulers closed the port of Boston to all trade. They also made General Gage the new military governor.

One of the first things Gage did was to dismiss the Colonial Assembly. This meant the people could no longer make their own laws and would have to obey the king. The colonists considered themselves free, and they were upset about this. They organized a new governing body called the Provincial Congress. John Hancock was its president, and Samuel Adams was its leading spirit. The Congress began to prepare for war. It called for an army of 20,000 men to be ready at a minute's notice to march to any point of danger in Massachusetts. They were called minutemen.

General Gage had command of 3,000 redcoats in Boston. He had received orders to capture John Hancock and Samuel Adams so they could be hanged as traitors. His spies had told him the two patriots were staying in the home of a friend in Lexington, a few miles from Boston. They also said the patriots had stored weapons and gunpowder at Concord, near Lexington. Gage had

Portrait of Paul Revere, by John Singleton Copley, 1768 (PD-Art).

Dr. Joseph Warren was one of Boston's leading physicians. He was highly respected by the citizens of the town. He was also a leader in spying on the British troops in Boston. After sending Paul Revere and William Dawes on the famous ride to Lexington and Concord, he fought in the Battle of Bunker Hill. He was one of the last of the patriots to leave the hill when they ran out of powder. He was struck in the head and killed by a British bullet as he fled. His body was buried nearby. When his family had his body dug up nearly a year later, it was identified by Paul Revere. Revere had made a false tooth for Dr. Warren, and this was the clue Revere needed to tell the Warren family that they had the right body.[1]

A view of the town of Boston in New England and British ships of war landing their troops, 1768, by Paul Revere (PD-Art).

a plan to send troops to arrest the two leaders, then to push on and destroy the supplies at Concord.

He was careful to act quietly, but the watchful minutemen spied on him and learned of his plans. Gage's attack failed, and one of the reasons it failed was the work of a patriot named Paul Revere. Revere's midnight ride has become one of the most famous events in American history.[2]

Paul Revere was born in Boston in 1735. He followed his father's trade of silversmith, making things of silver and sometimes gold. He also learned the trade of copperplate engraving. He produced many prints of famous events in history. He also made plates used in printing Massachusetts' paper money.

Revere had taken part in the Boston Tea Party, and in 1774 he joined about 30 other men in forming a party to spy on the British and learn their plans. Always vigilant, these men took news of suspicious movements of the British to patriot leaders such as Samuel Adams, John Hancock, or Dr. Joseph Warren.

> Ever since sin came into the world, there have been people who wanted to take away the freedom of others. We must always be careful and willing to defend freedom and justice.

On the evening of April 18, 1775, Revere's group reported to Dr. Warren that they had seen unusual movements of British soldiers and boats. They suspected General Gage was about to carry out his plan to capture the patriot leaders in Lexington and the military supplies at Concord.

America's Most Famous Ride

Warren called for Paul Revere and William Dawes. He dispatched them on horseback to Lexington and Concord to alarm the patriots along the way. They had to be careful, for there were British soldiers all over the countryside. They couldn't be caught before they completed their mission, so he sent them out by different roads, hoping at least one of them would make it through.

Soon Dawes was riding across Boston Neck. Paul Revere went home and prepared for a long ride through the night. He sent a friend to hang signal lanterns in the tower of the Old North Church to tell which route the British would take in starting their march to Lexington. "One if by land and two if by sea" was the code. This would let the patriots in Charlestown know what the British were doing. Revere rowed a small boat across the river, right under the noses of the men aboard the British ships lying at anchor.

Boston Massacre, between British soldiers and citizens of Boston on March 5, 1770, by Paul Revere, 1770 (PD-US).

Once on the other side, he borrowed a horse. As he galloped toward Lexington, he stopped at every patriot home and woke the families. "The regulars are coming out!" he shouted. As he rode, bonfires began to glow from the tops of hills. Somewhere a trumpet sounded its alarm. Drums began to beat. Village church bells began to ring. Other men mounted their horses and rode to alarm other minutemen to prepare for battle.

Revere's horse was suddenly startled by two English officers who sprang from the darkness and tried to capture him. He took a side path and escaped them in the dark. He reached Lexington and the house of Reverend Jonas Clarke, where Adams and Hancock were staying. As he rode up shouting, eight minutemen who were guarding the leaders told him not to make so much noise because people were asleep inside.

"Noise! You'll have noise enough before long! The regulars are coming out!"[3] he swept from his horse and strode into the house. Adams, Hancock, and Revere discussed what to. Dawes arrived, and soon he and Revere were on their way

The Midnight Ride of Paul Revere, artist unknown, c.1942 (PD-US).

again. Along the way, they were joined by Dr. Prescott, who offered to help them spread the word.

About halfway from Lexington to Concord, they ran into British officers on horseback. The redcoats shouted at them to stop. Prescott was able to jump his horse over a wall and escape, but Revere and Dawes were both captured. Prescott made it to Concord and gave the warning that brought men with muskets from their homes and farms by the hundreds.[4]

In the meantime, Lieutenant-Colonel Smith led 800 British soldiers to Lexington. Before they had gone far, they heard the church bells, signal guns, and drumbeats. They saw the glow of signal fires. Then they knew the patriots were alarmed and ready to fight.

Smith knew he was in for a battle and that he might be too late to capture Adams and Hancock. He sent a rider back to Boston to ask for more soldiers. He ordered Major Pitcairn to go ahead with a light infantry, hoping they could get to Lexington faster than the whole army could with all its equipment. He hoped they would get there before Adams and Hancock could get away.

Colonel Smith had a good reason to be concerned. Thousands of patriots who were ready to fight and die for their freedom were hearing the alarm signals. Men stumbled from their beds and snatched their muskets. They checked their powder horns and shot pouches, then slung them over their shoulders while bidding their wives and children good-bye. Off they tramped toward meeting places they arranged in advance.

> **"**
>
> *Out started six officers, seized my bridle, put their pistols to my breast, ordered me to dismount, which I did. One of them, who appeared to have the command there, and much of a gentleman, asked me where I came from; I told him. He asked what time I left. I told him, he seemed surprised, said "Sir, may I crave your name?" I answered "My name is Revere."[5]*
>
> Paul Revere
>
> **"**

The Death of General Warren at the Battle of Bunker's Hill, June 17, 1775, by John Trumbull, 1786 (PD-Art).

FIRST BLOOD FOR INDEPENDENCE

The sun was just coming up when Major Pitcairn marched into Lexington. Fewer than 100 minutemen were formed up to meet him. Knowing he had ten times as many men as the patriots, Pitcairn ordered the patriots to leave. "Disperse, ye rebels!"[6] he shouted. The minutemen saw they were outnumbered, so they began to move away. They intended to withdraw until more patriots could join them and they could attack the British. But then a shot rang out. It might have come from the British side, or it might have been one of the minutemen. Suddenly, all the guns were blazing, and several patriots were killed or wounded. The rest ran for cover, knowing they would have a chance to fight again later in the day.

> Samuel Adams called it a glorious morning because this battle was the first time a large group of Americans had fought with British soldiers. Adams felt sure that the colonies would fight a war for their freedom.

Adams and Hancock were not at Reverend Clarke's house when Pitcairn arrived. Hours before, the officers who had captured Revere and Dawes had been marching with them back toward Lexington. They also had some other patriot prisoners with them. As they marched, the British leader heard a gunshot near Lexington. He asked Revere what the shot meant. Revere told him it meant that the people were awake and spreading the word to prepare to fight. The officer let his prisoners go. He kept Revere's horse, but Dawes rode away to warn more patriots.

Revere walked back to Lexington to join Adams and Hancock. He helped them carry their belongings as they retreated to a hiding place in nearby Woburn. All three men lived to see America free from English rule. On their way to Woburn, they heard guns firing behind them. It was the Battle of Lexington. The sound stirred the patriotic soul of Adams. He said, "Oh, what a glorious morning is this!"[7]

The first blow for liberty, by A.H. Ritchie, date unknown (PD-Art).

From Lexington, Major Pitcairn hurried on to Concord. It was around 7a.m. when he arrived. Dr. Prescott had alarmed the town hours before Pitcairn arrived.

> One British officer was amazed at how many minutemen appeared along the escape route back to Boston. "They seemed to have dropped from the clouds,"[8] he said.

People had been busy moving and hiding the military supplies, so Pitcairn's men found little to destroy. They set fire to the courthouse, spiked a few cannons, cut down the Liberty Pole, and dumped out some barrels of flour. While they worked, 200 of them stood guard at the town bridge. Minutemen from were gathering on the other side of the river.

When the patriot force grew to around 400 men, they advanced on the bridge. Guns on both sides boomed, and several men on each side went down. The British retreated from the bridge, and the patriots came swarming over. The English leaders knew the patriot force was growing too fast to be driven back. They headed back toward Lexington.

THE REDCOATS' RETREAT

The fight was just beginning. The patriots had a great advantage over the red-coated soldiers who were trained to stand up and shoot across open fields. The Americans knew how to slip from tree to tree in the woods and take cover behind walls in the fields. When the British charged them, they ran back into the woods and appeared again farther down the road toward Boston. Much of the road ran through wooded country where the patriots shot the British soldiers without ever being seen.

The British troops were tired and hungry. They marched nearly 20 miles to get from Boston to Concord. Now they were trying to get back to safety and rest. Muskets kept booming from the woods, and redcoat after redcoat went down. Soon they were running in terror.

When the redcoats got back to Lexington, their reinforcements had arrived. Twelve hundred fresh troops led by Lord Percy saved the entire force from capture. The exhausted British soldiers rushed to get behind the lines of new troops and fell to the ground, weak from weariness and terror.

Hugh Percy, 2nd Duke of Northumberland, artist and date unknown (PD-Art).

They could not rest long. The patriot force was growing. They kept up the same kind of running attack all through the afternoon. Redcoat after redcoat threw up his arms and fell while his comrades fired at enemies they could seldom see. The patriots kept coming. One British officer later said, "They seemed to have dropped from the clouds."[9] Mile after mile, the redcoats fled in terror. At last, they got close enough to Boston that the British ships in the harbor could shell the minutemen chasing them. The patriots backed off.

The Battle of Bunker Hill, June 17, 1775, lithograph by Nathaniel Currier after painting by J, Trumbull.

General Gates failed. Hancock and Adams escaped. The Americans moved most of the guns and powder out of Concord before his soldiers arrived. The British army lost over 300 soldiers. There were fewer than 100 patriots killed. It was a glorious day for the patriots. They learned they were strong. They had defeated a British army! Many Americans were encouraged. More men joined the patriot militia. Within a few days, 16,000 Americans surrounded Boston.

Two months later, the British charged the Americans in the Battle of Bunker Hill. The patriots drove them back twice. Then they ran out of gunpowder. They had to retreat. Again, they killed many more British soldiers. Finally, General Washington arrived to take charge. After months of siege, the British had to leave Boston.

Paul Revere served in the American army and then went back to his business. He was not a hero in any great battles, but he is still remembered as a great patriot for his work in helping America become a free country. He was an old man of 83 when he died in the city he had helped free from the British.[10]

Paul Revere by Gilbert Stuart, 1813 (PD-Art).

This is one of the most famous poems in America. It was written by Henry Wadsworth Longfellow.

PAUL REVERE'S RIDE

LISTEN, my children, and you shall hear
Of the midnight ride of Paul Revere,
On the eighteenth of April, in Seventy-five;
Hardly a man is now alive
Who remembers that famous day and year.
He said to his friend, 'If the British march
By land or sea from the town to-night,
Hang a lantern aloft in the belfry arch
Of the North Church tower as a signal light,—
One, if by land, and two, if by sea;
And I on the opposite shore will be,
Ready to ride and spread the alarm
Through every Middlesex village and farm,
For the country folk to be up and to arm.'

Then he said, 'Good-night!' and with muffled oar
Silently rowed to the Charlestown shore,
Just as the moon rose over the bay,
Where swinging wide at her moorings lay
The Somerset, British man-of-war;
A phantom ship, with each mast and spar
Across the moon like a prison bar,
And a huge black hulk, that was magnified
By its own reflection in the tide.

Meanwhile, his friend, through alley and street,
Wanders and watches with eager ears,
Till in the silence around him he hears
The muster of men at the barrack door,
The sound of arms, and the tramp of feet,
And the measured tread of the grenadiers,
Marching down to their boats on the shore.

Image from *Paul Revere, the Torch Bearer of the Revolution*, 1916 (PD-US).

Then he climbed the tower of the Old North Church,
By the wooden stairs, with stealthy tread,
To the belfry-chamber overhead,
And startled the pigeons from their perch
On the sombre rafters, that round him made
Masses and moving shapes of shade,—
By the trembling ladder, steep and tall,
To the highest window in the wall,
Where he paused to listen and look down
A moment on the roofs of the town,
And the moonlight flowing over all.

Beneath, in the churchyard, lay the dead,
In their night-encampment on the hill,
Wrapped in silence so deep and still
That he could hear, like a sentinel's tread,
The watchful night-wind, as it went
Creeping along from tent to tent,
And seeming to whisper, 'All is well!'
A moment only he feels the spell
Of the place and the hour, and the secret dread
Of the lonely belfry and the dead;
For suddenly all his thoughts are bent
On a shadowy something far away,
Where the river widens to meet the bay,—
A line of black that bends and floats
On the rising tide, like a bridge of boats.

Meanwhile, impatient to mount and ride,
Booted and spurred, with a heavy stride
On the opposite shore walked Paul Revere.
Now he patted his horse's side,
Now gazed at the landscape far and near,
Then, impetuous, stamped the earth,
And turned and tightened his saddle-girth;
But mostly he watched with eager search
The belfry-tower of the Old North Church,

Image from *Paul Revere, the Torch Bearer of the Revolution*, 1916 (PD-US).

As it rose above the graves on the hill,
Lonely and spectral and sombre and still.
And lo! as he looks, on the belfry's height
A glimmer, and then a gleam of light!
He springs to the saddle, the bridle he turns,
But lingers and gazes, till full on his sight
A second lamp in the belfry burns!

A hurry of hoofs in a village street,
A shape in the moonlight, a bulk in the dark,
And beneath, from the pebbles, in passing, a spark
Struck out by a steed flying fearless and fleet;
That was all! And yet, through the gloom and the light,
The fate of a nation was riding that night;
And the spark struck out by that steed, in his flight,
Kindled the land into flame with its heat.

He has left the village and mounted the steep,
And beneath him, tranquil and broad and deep,
Is the Mystic, meeting the ocean tides;
And under the alders that skirt its edge,
Now soft on the sand, now loud on the ledge,
Is heard the tramp of his steed as he rides.

Image from *Paul Revere, the Torch Bearer of the Revolution,* 1916 (PD-US).

It was twelve by the village clock,
When he crossed the bridge into Medford town.
He heard the crowing of the cock,
And the barking of the farmer's dog,
And felt the damp of the river fog,
That rises after the sun goes down.

It was one by the village clock,
When he galloped into Lexington.
He saw the gilded weathercock
Swim in the moonlight as he passed,
And the meeting-house windows, blank and bare,
Gaze at him with a spectral glare,

As if they already stood aghast
At the bloody work they would look upon.

It was two by the village clock,
When he came to the bridge in Concord town.
He heard the bleating of the flock,
And the twitter of birds among the trees,
And felt the breath of the morning breeze
Blowing over the meadows brown.
And one was safe and asleep in his bed.
Who at the bridge would be first to fall,
Who that day would be lying dead,
Pierced by a British musket-ball.

You know the rest. In the books you have read,
How the British Regulars fired and fled,—
How the farmers gave them ball for ball,
From behind each fence and farm-yard wall,
Chasing the red-coats down the lane,
Then crossing the fields to emerge again
Under the trees at the turn of the road,
And only pausing to fire and load.

So through the night rode Paul Revere;
And so through the night went his cry of alarm
To every Middlesex village and farm,—
A cry of defiance and not of fear,
A voice in the darkness, a knock at the door
And a word that shall echo forevermore!
For, borne on the night-wind of the Past,
Through all our history, to the last,
In the hour of darkness and peril and need,
The people will waken and listen to hear
The hurrying hoof-beats of that steed,
And the midnight message of Paul Revere.

Bronze Statue of Paul Revere in the historic North End,
Boston, sculpted by Cyrus Dallin.

Thomas Jefferson

CHAPTER 30

THOMAS JEFFERSON

Patriot Genius

THE MAKING OF A STATESMAN

Thomas Jefferson was America's third president. But that was only a part of all that he did for America.

Jefferson was born in 1743 near Charlottesville, Virginia. His family lived on a plantation of almost 2,000 acres. His father was a man of strength and energy. He also had a good education. Young Thomas was strong and active like his father. He loved the outdoors. He enjoyed hunting for deer, turkeys, and other game in the wooded mountains around his home. He also loved paddling his boat in the river or taking a swim on a warm day. One of the things he loved most was riding horses.

Like his father, Thomas was a good horseman, and he liked horses that were well-suited for riding. He was a daring rider, galloping through the woods and across the fields.

Thomas also loved books. He became one of the most educated men in America. He was interested in many different subjects, and he read about them all. He started going to school when he was only five years old. After school, he read other books. But he still found time for play and outdoor sports.

Thomas started college at Williamsburg, Virginia, when he was 17. Williamsburg was the state capitol, even though it was a small city of only about 1,000 people. Still, it held the capitol and the College of William and Mary. It was a town of social activity. Many rich and educated people came to Williamsburg often. Thomas met many interesting friends there.

Thomas Jefferson and Patrick Henry had a great influence on each other. We should all be careful to choose friends who will encourage us to do right and be our best. We should also be careful to be a good influence on others.

College of William & Mary , Wren building with Italianate towers, artist unknown, c. 1859, (PD-US).

When the state lawmakers met (they were called the House of Burgesses), Thomas saw many important people come to Williamsburg. They were not all members of the House of Burgesses, but also people who came to talk about business and politics with them. Planters came to town in fancy carriages drawn by beautiful horses that Thomas loved to watch. Wives and daughters came to see friends whom they only saw once a year. Some of them attended the governor's reception.

During his college years, Thomas became friends with many leading men of the Virginia colony. In fact, he made friends of all kinds. He was known as a man of intelligence, good manners, and cheerfulness. People liked to be around him.

He also met some men who would be important leaders in the future. One of them was a young law clerk named Patrick Henry. Henry was studying in a lawyer's office to become a lawyer himself. He was a pleasant, fun-loving young man who loved to tell stories and play the violin. Jefferson played the violin also, and the two friends spent many happy hours playing music and talking together.

At this time, Thomas Jefferson was described as being six feet and two inches tall, slim, with sandy hair, freckles, hazel-gray eyes, and large feet and hands. Unlike the relaxed, stooping Henry, he stood tall and straight as an arrow. He was an example of healthy young manhood.

After graduation from college, Jefferson stayed in Williamsburg to study law with a famous Virginia lawyer. His friend, Patrick Henry had been elected to the House of Burgesses, so the two young men still got together from time to time. Henry would often stay in Jefferson's home when he was in town for meeting of the Burgesses.

When Henry made his fiery speech to the Burgesses about the evils of the Stamp Act, Thomas Jefferson stood in the doorway and listened. No one admired Patrick Henry's speech more than Thomas did. He was excited about his friend's way of making words come alive and making his hearers feel their power. Thomas was not a gifted speaker. But in a few years, he would show what a great writer he was when he took his pen in hand and wrote the great Declaration of Independence.

Chamber of the House of Burgesses in the Capitol at Williamsburg, Virginia, photo by Frances Benjamin Johnston (PD-US).

It was not long before Jefferson's neighbors elected him to a seat in the House as well. He quickly became a leading voice in opposing the king's tax on tea. This made the king's governor angry, so he broke up the meeting and told the lawmakers to go home. Before they went, some of the members signed a paper that called on Virginians to stop buying goods from England.

When he was 29 years old, Jefferson married a young widow named Martha Skelton. After a wedding celebration that lasted several days, Thomas put his bride into a carriage drawn by four horses and began the 100-mile drive to his mansion near Charlottesville called Monticello. The house is still standing today on top of a high hill. Its name means, "Little Mountain" in Italian.

When the bride first saw her new home, it was late at night, and she and her husband were hungry and tired from their trip. All the servants had gone to their rooms to sleep. But the young couple built a fire and prepared some food. It was a strange beginning, but they lived for many years in their beautiful hilltop home.

Thomas Jefferson's father died when Thomas was a boy, leaving him an estate of 5,000 acres of land. Now his wife made him even wealthier because she had been given 40,000 acres upon her father's death. Together, they made Monticello more beautiful than ever as Thomas loved improving his land and growing new varieties of plants and trees.

Portrait of Thomas Jefferson while in London, by Mather Brown, 1786 (PD-Art).

Monticello, photo by Martin Falbisoner, 2013 (CC BY-SA 3.0).

The Battle of Lexington, April 19, 1775.

Great events were taking place up and down the American colonies, and a faithful leader like Jefferson could not stay at home for years at a time. Soon he was back, meeting with the Burgesses about what Virginia should do as the colonies moved toward war with England. The year after his wedding, the news came that patriots in Boston had dumped British tea in the harbor to protest the tea tax. Then the king closed Boston harbor hoping to starve the people into obeying him. Next, the colonies sent men to the first Continental Congress in Philadelphia to try to get all the colonies working together to resist the wrong acts of the king. The Virginia leaders formed a Committee of Correspondence to keep in touch with the other colonies.

Jefferson's Masterpiece—the Declaration of Independence

The sound of gunfire broke the peace in Lexington and Concord in Massachusetts. On the morning of April 19, 1775, hundreds of patriots left their farms and shops to help Lexington and Concord drive the Redcoats out of their villages and back to their barracks in Boston. An American army began to form, and the Continental Congress asked George Washington to lead it. While he was on the way to Boston to take charge, he heard about the battle of Bunker Hill, where the patriots had stood through three charges of the king's soldiers, retreating only when they ran out of gunpowder.

Even after the fight at Lexington and Concord, America tried to make peace with the king. They sent him a letter called the Olive Branch Petition, trying to restore friendship between the king and his colonies. But the king would not listen. It looked as if a real war had begun.

That government is best which governs the least, because its people discipline themselves.

Thomas Jefferson

Richard Henry Lee made a stirring speech to Congress urging a declaration of independence from England. He closed with these ringing words:

"Why then sir, why do we longer delay? Why still deliberate? Let this happy day give birth to an American Republic. Let her arise not to devastate and to conquer but to reestablish the reign of peace and law…to prepare an asylum where the unhappy may find solace, and the persecuted repost. If we are not this day wanting in our duty, the names of the American Legislators of 1776 will be placed by posterity at the side of all of those whose memory has been and ever will be dear to virtuous men and good citizens."[1]

Thomas Jefferson, Roger Sherman, Benjamin Franklin, Robert Livingston, and John Adams, 1776. All signers of the Decloration of Independence.

The next summer, the Continental Congress met in Philadelphia. Thomas Jefferson was sent to the meeting by Virginia, along with Richard Henry Lee and Benjamin Harrison. Richard Henry Lee made a motion declaring that the 13 colonies no longer belonged to Great Britain. The representatives voted on the motion, and it passed. Now someone had to write a paper telling the other colonists and the rest of the world why Americans had chosen to be free.

Five men were chosen to work on the paper. It was to be called the Declaration of Independence. Benjamin Franklin, the oldest representative, was chosen to be on the committee because of his wisdom. He was from Pennsylvania. The Congress also asked John Adams of Massachusetts, Roger Sherman of Connecticut, Robert Livingston of New York, and Thomas Jefferson of

There were 27 reasons listed in the Declaration that told the world why the colonies were separating from England. The king had broken up the colonial governments, he had forced Americans to house British soldiers in their homes, he had allowed his navy to kidnap American sailors to serve on his ships, and he had encouraged the Indian tribes to make war. These are just a few of the reasons that the Declaration listed.

Portrait of Thomas Jefferson hanging in West Point, by Thomas Sully, 1821 (PD-Art).

—— " ——

"... all men are created equal, and are endowed by their Creator with certain unalienable rights..."

Thomas Jefferson
in the Declaration of Independence

—— " ——

Did you know that when he was president, Thomas Jefferson called for the Bible to be the primary textbook used in Washington, DC, schools?

Virginia. When the five men talked it over, Thomas Jefferson was asked to do the writing. He was as brilliant with his pen as Patrick Henry was with his tongue.

Jefferson had a big job to do. The Declaration had to be well written so no one could misunderstand the meaning. It had to give the reasons the colonies were no longer owned by the king. It had to say exactly why they were setting up a new government. Many people in America were still not sure they should break away from England. Also, America had friends in the English government who had defended the colonies in Parliament. Everyone had to understand what the Americans were doing and why they were doing it. The document needed to unite as many of the colonists as possible to fight together for independence.

The Declaration of Independence was presented to the Continental Congress and debated among the members. Some changes were made, then the paper was adopted by Congress on July 4, 1776. Copies were made and sent by to all the colonies and the commanders of the Continental Army. Americans celebrated with parades, bonfires, fireworks, and music. The Declaration was received in different places on different days because some colonies were far from Philadelphia, so our first Independence Day celebrations did not all take place on the Fourth of July.

A LEADER OF AMERICA

Now that Virginia was no longer an English colony, she would need a new set of laws made by the people rather than by the king. Jefferson returned to his home state to help form the first state government of Virginia. The first governor was his friend Patrick Henry. After Henry left the office, Jefferson was elected governor in his place. America was still at war with England at that time, so Governor Jefferson had a big job as he guided the new state and did all he could to help America win independence.

After the war was over and America was free, the government sent Jefferson across the ocean as minister to France. His wife had died as a young woman, but he took his two daughters with him. He loved his family and the servants who worked for him at his plantation home. He was always kind to his slaves and hoped that slavery would be against the law in America and everyone could be free one day.

After being in France five years, Jefferson came home. A crowd of his slaves, delighted to hear he was coming, walked several miles down the road to meet him. They offered to unhitch the horses from his carriage and pull it up the steep road to Monticello themselves. The horses stayed in harness, but when the carriage arrived home, the master of the house was lifted in the arms of his loving servants and carried into the house with shouts of joy.

Again, his country called him. George Washington, the new president, asked Jefferson to work for him as Secretary of State. It was a hard job. There were many disagreements between Jefferson and Alexander Hamilton, the Secretary of the Treasury. Jefferson wanted to keep the national government small and weak so that it could never take away the freedom of its people and the states. Hamilton believed the government needed to be stronger so it could protect its people from foreign enemies and keep the states from fighting among themselves. Finally, Jefferson grew so tired of the conflict that he quit his job and went home.

The practice of morality being necessary for the well being of society, He [God] has taken care to impress its precepts so indelibly on our hearts that they shall not be effaced by the subtleties of our brain. We all agree in the obligation of the moral principles of Jesus and nowhere will they be found delivered in greater purity than in His discourses.

Thomas Jefferson

THE FAITH OF THOMAS JEFFERSON

Many people today believe Jefferson was hostile to the Christian faith. Nothing could be farther from the truth. As president of the United States, he attended Christian church services regularly. He gave his own money to many different church and missions causes. Today you might see a book called the Jefferson Bible. That is not what Jefferson called it. He actually did this twice. The first time he gave it to be used in the evangelization of the Kaskaskia Indians. He said the words of Christ were the purest form of religion the world had ever seen.

Later on in life, he again extracted the words of Jesus from a Bible. What he had done was select some of his favorite sayings of Jesus.

He called his devotional book *The Life and Morals of Jesus of Nazareth.* He never intended it to be called a Bible. Jefferson himself declared, "I am a real Christian, that is to say, a disciple of the doctrines of Jesus."[2]

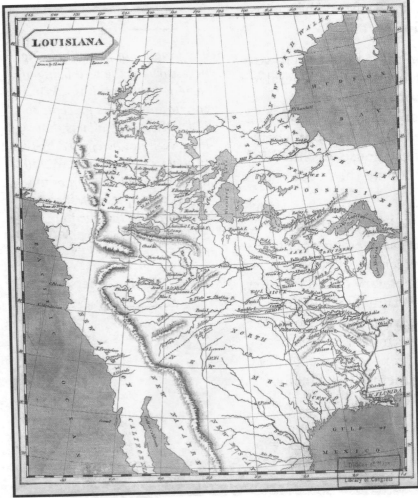

1804 map of "Louisiana" (PD-US).

A bigger job was coming to Thomas Jefferson. In 1800, the people elected him president of the United States. Many people loved him because he was a friend to the poor as well as the rich. He said the new government should be plain and simple, not like the kingdoms of Europe where the rich were close friends of the king and the poor people were not treated fairly. He dressed plainly and was careful not to act as if he thought he was better than others because of his high position.

People also liked Jefferson as president because he was careful with the country's money. He cut the number of people who worked for the government and reduced the size of the army and the navy. He spent as little money as he could to run the government.

One of the biggest decisions Jefferson made as president was the Louisiana Purchase. Thanks to George Rogers Clark and his band of frontier fighters, England had been forced to give up all the land east of the Mississippi River. This made America a much larger country.

In 1800, France took from Spain all the land between the Mississippi River and the Rocky Mountains. Spain had been refusing to let the United States use the Mississippi River to get to the ocean. Americans wondered if Napoleon, the leader of France, would do the same. America needed to ship goods down the river and into the ocean to trade with other countries.

Thomas Jefferson Memorial at Missouri History Museum in St. Louis, Missouri, USA.

President Jefferson wanted to buy New Orleans from France. New Orleans is a big city near where the Mississippi flows into the ocean. He also wanted a strip of land on the east side of the river. This would give American ships the freedom to use the Mississippi River.

It was the right time to act. Napoleon was about to go to war against England, and he needed money for ships, guns, and other things for war. He wanted to sell America much more land than Jefferson asked for. He offered all of Louisiana for $15 million. America bought 530 million acres for less than three cents per acre!

The state of Louisiana today is only a small part of what was called Louisiana then. The Louisiana Purchase gave America the land that is now several states. It made the new country more than twice as big as it had been before.

Napoleon Bonaparte, by D.J. Pound, 1860.

In 1804, Jefferson was elected to serve as president once again. After his second term was over, he did the same thing Washington had done: he refused to run for a third term. Instead, he went home to Monticello. He spent his last years doing the things he loved to do and greeting the many visitors who came to see him. He was such a wise man that many people came long distances to ask his advice. He was called "The Sage of Monticello."

Determine never to be idle ... It is wonderful how much may be done if we are always doing.[3]

Thomas Jefferson

It was fitting that Thomas Jefferson died on the Fourth of July. It had been exactly 50 years since he had signed the Declaration of Independence. On the same day, his old friend John Adams died in Quincy, Massachusetts. Together, they had seen the new nation grow and prosper for the first half century of its life.[4]

Jefferson Memorial at night.

William Moultrie

CHAPTER 31

COLONEL WILLIAM MOULTRIE

Defender of Charleston

WARSHIPS IN THE HARBOR

It was 1775 in Virginia. There had been trouble between the English colonial governor, Lord Dunmore, and the colonists. Finally, so many people were upset at Lord Dunmore that he left and took refuge on a British war ship in Norfolk Harbor. But he wasn't finished feuding with the Americans. On New Year's Day, 1776, he ordered the ships in the harbor to fire their cannons at Norfolk, the largest city in Virginia. It was destroyed.

Lord Dunmore had done many terrible things to the Virginia colonists, but this was the worst! News of the attack traveled from Maine to Georgia.

Early in the fall of 1775, the British government had planned to strike against the colonies in the south. North Carolina was the first to be punished. This is because it had been the first American colony to declare that it would be free from British rule. To carry out the threat, Sir Henry Clinton sailed from Boston with 2,000 British soldiers.

There were minutemen in Carolina, just as there were in Massachusetts. Just as in the attack on Lexington and Concord, farmers left their fields and

General William Moultrie, engraving by unspecified artist, from painting by Alonzo Chappel, date unknown (PD-US).

Palmetto trees, unlike other trees, are made of spongy material. The walls of the fort were constructed of palmetto logs. The victory was attributed mainly to the logs absorbing the impact of the British cannon balls. The Palmetto tree has since become a symbol of liberty in South Carolina.

Portrait of Admiral Sir Peter Parker, by Lemuel Francis Abbott, c.1799 (PD-Art).

shopkeepers left their shops to rally against the redcoats. In ten days, there were 10,000 American patriots ready to fight. When Clinton arrived, he decided to stay on his ship. He waited for more ships to come from England and help him.

This fleet was under the command of Sir Peter Parker. The English ships had a hard trip. His sailors had trouble with strong winds, and the ships were tossed about by storms. It took nearly three months for them to join Clinton at the Cape Fear River. By that time it was the first day of May, 1776.

Sir Clinton and Sir Parker could not agree on what action to take. Clinton had a great respect for the minutemen of the Old North state, as North Carolina was called. They were strong, hard-working men who knew how to fight. He wanted to attack from the Chesapeake. But the royal governor of South Carolina, Lord Campbell, wanted to attack Charleston, South Carolina, first. He assured the others that if they could take Charleston, the settlers of South Carolina who were still loyal to the king would rise up and help the redcoats defeat the patriots. After some arguing, Campbell won out. Charleston would be attacked.

Meanwhile, the people of South Carolina knew war clouds were gathering. They were not surprised when white sails appeared over the horizon and Parker's fleet appeared in front of Charleston. There were over 50 ships! Some of them were war ships, and some carried supplies. Things looked dark for the city, but the people had fought before, and they were not afraid to fight again. The British had brought war to their city. Now they would give them war in return.

The patriots had weeks to prepare for defense. It was now the end of May, and they were ready. They tore down city buildings to make room for cannons to fire. Seven hundred wagons had been taken from the Tories and used to help build fortress walls. People gave lead from their homes to melt into bullets. Fireboats were made ready to run into the British ships and burn them if they got too close. Sixty-five hundred militiamen marched from all over South Carolina and nearby colonies to defend the city.

They believed they could defend themselves better if they built another fort at the end of Sullivan's Island, near Charleston. This fort would stand next to the channel the British ships would use to get near the city. Colonel William Moultrie was ordered to build a square fort on the island, large enough to hold 1,000 men. Colonel Moultrie was known to be a good fighter.

Hundreds of men began cutting down palmetto trees for logs. The logs were hauled to the southern end of the island. Here they were stacked on top of each other and bolted together. They made two walls a few feet apart. Then they filled the space between the logs with sand. They had a strong, thick wall to protect them from bullets and cannon balls. If a ball broke a log, it would just sink into the soft sand and stop. At least, that is what the patriots hoped would happen. They named it Fort Sullivan.

It was hard working in the South Carolina sun, but they kept working to build platforms to place cannons. The platforms were six feet high, and they rested on brick columns. The men could fire between the columns at the enemy. The rear of the fort and the eastern side were not as strong because they faced away from the way the British would come. The patriots had 31 cannons, not nearly as many as were on the British. Not all of them could be pointed toward the ships at one time.

Invasion fleet assembling in lower New York Harbor off the coast of Staten Island, 1776, in preparation for the Battle of Long Island, 1876 (PD-US).

On the day of the battle, the patriots realized they had a problem. Of the 450 men in the fort, only about 30 of them knew how to fire a cannon! But most of the men were good with rifles, so they were able to help the gunners aim the cannons.

One day in early June, General Charles Lee, who had been sent down to take charge of the forces in Charleston, went over to the island to look around. He was a soldier who had fought for the British for years. Now he was in the American army. Looking over the defenses of the fort, he saw that it was a roughly-built, unfinished structure. He said to Moultrie that the ships would anchor off in the channel, and make the fort like a slaughter pen.[1]

Lee was no hero. In fact, he would later be thrown out of the American army. He went back to the city and told Governor Rutledge that the best thing to do would be to abandon the fort. But the governor had faith in Colonel Moultrie. He asked Moultrie if he thought he could defend the fort.[2]

Moultrie was a man of few words, but he meant what he said. He told the governor that he thought he could.[3]

"General Lee wishes you to give up the fort," Governor Rutledge said. "But you are not to do it without an order from me, and I will sooner cut off my right hand than write one."

Many military officers looking over the situation at Charleston would have thought the British would win the city easily. The redcoats planned to land on Long Island, then wade across the shallow water that separated it from Sullivan's Island. Next, the cannon from the ships were to silence the cannon

The colonel never seemed to think about retreating. Years later, he wrote, "I was never uneasy because I never thought the enemy could force me to retire."[4] His confidence served him well.

in the fort. Finally, the soldiers were to storm the position and wipe out the defenders. This would leave the channel clear for the ships to capture the city.

Sir Peter Parker thought he would do something similar. But Parker was slow to move and too confident. He waited over three weeks before attacking. That gave the colonists more time to prepare their defenses. They did not waste any time.

Friday, June 28, was bright and sunny. It was a beautiful day, though a hot one. Early in the day, Colonel Moultrie paid a visit to Colonel Thompson on the north end of the island. Thompson had command of a little fort full of American sharpshooters. It was their job to prevent Clinton's troops from getting across the shallow bay.

As the two men watched, the British war ships began to spread their topsails and raise their anchors. One by one, the great ships began to move. The wind filled the canvases, and they sailed up the harbor. Moultrie put spurs to his horse and galloped back to the log fort. He had shouted that they should beat the long roll, and Captain Marion and Colonel Motte passed the order along.

The Fleet Out on the Waves

Another man might have been discouraged at the smallness of the fort and the greatness of the enemy force. A friend of Moultrie's visited him one day before the battle. This man was the captain of a privateer, a ship that was paid to take attack British merchant vessels and take them as prizes. He understood fighting from a ship. The two men stood on the palmetto walls and looked over the little fort and the great fleet out on the waves.

A privateer wanted to know what Colonel Moultrie thought of it.[5] Moultrie replied that the Americans would beat the invaders.

A friend, pointing out to the British ships, said that when they came alongside the fort that it would be knocked down in less than 30 minutes.[6]

The steadfast patriot replied calmly that they would fight behind the ruins and prevent the men from landing.

The drums beat rapidly, and the men ran to their posts. It was an important moment for both Moultrie and his fort. Just then, a blue flag with the crescent of South Carolina was raised to the top of a pole.

Just a year before, the people of Boston had crowded the rooftops to watch the minutemen fight the British in the Battle of Bunker Hill. Now it was the people of Charleston, far to the south, who covered the roofs and church bell towers all day. They watched anxiously as the little fort battled the might of the British navy.

Sir Peter Parker's fleet was powerful. He was ready for the battle, and his confidence was strong. Two of his ships carried 50 guns each. Four of them carried 28 each. The tide was coming in, and the wind was just right to send the ships sweeping into place. Inside the fort, Colonel William Moultrie was excited. All around him, the loyal men of South Carolina were eager to fight for their homes and their families.

Charles Lee Esq'r. - major general of the Continental-Army in America, Johann Michael Probst, c.1809 (PD-US).

The British ships were within range. "Fire!" shouted Moultrie, and the heavy guns of the fort began to roar.

A mile from the fort, a bomb ship cast its anchor. This ship had mortars instead of cannons. A mortar is a large gun that fires shells to go over fort walls and explode inside the fort. The men in the fort saw a puff of smoke far away, then the boom of a mortar. A big shell sailed upward and came down with a boom inside the fort. It buried itself in the sand, and the explosion hurt no one. Clouds of sand flew into the air, but no harm was done.

Four of the largest war ships moved into range. They dropped anchors at both ends so they would keep their broadsides facing the fort. They could shoot at the fort with many of their guns. The smaller ships lined up behind them. When all was in place, there were 150 shooting at the fort.

From the beginning of the battle, the British were frustrated. The bomb ship sent 50 shells into the fort, but they all buried themselves deep in the soft sand. The hot metal fragments were stopped as soon as the shells blew apart.

> Colonel Moultrie exposed himself to danger in going around the fort to encourage his men to do their best. The power of encouragement is a very great power. Let's all try to be more encouraging to others who need it.

In the middle of the day, Parker ordered three ships to take a position southwest of the fort. From there, they could rake the gun platforms inside the fort with thousands of bullets. But God had other plans. Two of the ships ran into each other, and all three became stuck in shallow water.[8]

Sir Peter was still trying to pound the fort walls to pieces. Ball after ball was sent flying across the water, only to sink into the sand or bounce off a log wall. Only one of the American cannons had been silenced after hours of steady bombardment. The ground trembled beneath the feet of the patriots, but the walls stood.

Meanwhile, Colonel Moultrie and a helper walked from cannon to cannon with a bucket and dipper. They gave each of the tired men a drink of water as they passed.

Sir Peter's flagship was hard hit by the patriot cannon fire. His mainmast was struck nine times, and seven 32-pound balls shattered a mast. The ship had so many holes that it would have sunk if the water had not been smooth and the wind light. The ship's carpenters tried to stop the leaks.[10]

> God had his purposes for America, just as he has for all nations. During the War of Independence, things often happened that seemed unlikely. The fact that 13 colonies were able to win their freedom from the most powerful nation on earth stands as a sign of Providential protection. The Founding Fathers understood this. When Benjamin Rush asked John Adams whether he thought America could win her freedom, Adams replied, "If we trust in God and confess our sins."[9]

The patriots were running out of gunpowder. Moultrie ordered his men to only fire their guns once in every ten minutes. How could they fight on? General Lee sent a runner with a message. He said for Colonel Moultrie to spike his guns and retreat when the powder was gone. But Moultrie was not the kind of man to give up. The quality of endurance is "the inner strength to bear adversity."[11] The patriots in Fort Sullivan certainly needed endurance.

Late in the afternoon, the American fire nearly stopped. The British wondered if they were giving up. They were not. A fresh supply of powder was on its way, and soon the battle would again be red hot.

The powder had been sent from Governor Rutledge, and there was a note with it for Moultrie. It said, "Honor and victory, my good sir, to you and your worthy men with you. Don't make too free with your cannon. Keep cool and do mischief."

> *For you have need of endurance, so that when you have done the will of God, you may receive what was promised*
>
> *—Hebrews 10:36 (NASB)*

There was plenty of "mischief" made on the British ships. The cannon of the fort thundered to life once more. The British fired at the log walls but did little harm. A soldier by the name of McDaniel was mortally wounded by a cannon ball. As he was being carried away, he shouted to the other men, "Fight on, brave boys, and don't let liberty die with this day!"[13]

The crescent flag fell as its pole was sliced apart by a cannon ball. The people of Charleston watching the battle thought the fort had surrendered. Their faces pale, they fought back tears of dismay. Sergeant William Jasper came out from behind a brick pillar. Bravely, he walked the entire length of the fort, not thinking of the bullets and balls zipping around him. He picked up the splintered flagpole. Tearing the flag from it, he tied it to a cannon's ramrod and sank the rod into the sand on top of the wall.

William Moultrie Esq.

It was getting late in the day. The sun sank over the swamps to the west as the scene of the battle grew quiet and dark. The British had given up. The victory belonged to Colonel Moultrie and his brave men. The British ships lay quietly at anchor as the sailors tended to their wounded and dead. They began to sail away in the middle of the night. Lights glimmered softly in the windows of Charleston as people returned to their homes.

The next day was a day of celebration. Hundreds of people came from Charleston to the fort to greet the heroes. Governor Rutledge came with a group of ladies to present a silk banner to the fort. He called for Sergeant Jasper and presented his own sword as a reward to the hero. He also offered to promote Jasper to the rank of lieutenant, but Jasper modestly declined. He preferred to be a sergeant.

It took weeks for the giant British fleet to sail away. It was the first week in August before the last war ship faded from sight in the distance.

In the ten-hour battle, the redcoats had fired nearly 10,000 shells. They had only silenced one patriot gun. The American victory stands as one of the most important ones of the War of Independence. Many southern colonists who had not been sure about the idea of independence now swarmed to the cause of freedom.

The brave Colonel Moultrie was showered with honors for his courage. The fort he defended so bravely was renamed Fort Moultrie in his honor. Throughout the rest of his life, he continued to serve South Carolina and the United States. He was twice elected to be governor of South Carolina.[14]

Grave of William Moultrie, near Fort Moultrie, South Carolina, by J. Williams, 2003 (CC BY 2.5).

The Rescue of
Major Israel Putnam

CHAPTER 32

ISRAEL PUTNAM

Old Put

THE WOLF HUNTER

The battle of Bunker Hill is one of the most famous battles fought in America. It was a hard battle for the Americans. The British had many more men. They had better guns and more gunpowder. The Americans did not have bayonets, which made it hard to fight. Their muskets only held one shot. If the enemy was charging, there was no time to load the gun again. Without bayonets, muskets could only be used as clubs. But the patriots drove back the British twice as they charged up the hill. Only when they ran out of powder did they retreat.

One of the leaders of the Americans that day was Israel Putnam. He was a brave man. As the patriots saw him walking among them, they saw he was not afraid of the British. That gave the patriots more courage, too.

Putnam was called "Old Put." He was known as a strong leader and a brave soldier. His men were willing to follow him because they knew he would fight just as hard as they would. There were many stories told of his bravery and his adventures.

Major General Israel Putnam, by Fabronius, 1864 (PD-US).

Endurance is the strength to suffer problems with strength. This seemed to characterize the life of Israel Putnam. Remember when you face tough situations that God has a bigger purpose than you can see at the time.

Birthplace of Israel Putnam, Danvers, Massachusetts, by Detroit Publishing Co., c.1900, (PD-US).

Israel was born on his father's farm near Danvers, Massachusetts, in 1718. He was the tenth of 11 children. He grew up working hard. He loved the farm, and he would love farming all his life.

Israel did not go to school for long. But he could read, write, and do arithmetic. He was able to learn many things without a schoolteacher. He learned much from nature and living on the farm. He also grew strong and tough. He loved rowdy sports and was always one of the best athletes.

There was not much time for play for a farm boy in those days. Still, Israel and his friends found ways to have fun. One sport was to go "nesting," climbing trees to get abandoned birds' nests. Climbing to the highest branches of a tree one day, Israel got a surprise. The limb he was trying to climb on broke off in his hands. He fell, but his clothes caught on a lower branch and he found himself hanging in the air. He yelled for help from his friends. One of them had brought a gun. Israel commanded him to shoot the branch from which he was hanging. The boy did not want to take a chance of hitting Israel, but was finally convinced. He made a good shot and Israel fell to the ground. He had only a few bruises. The next day, he was back at the same tree and managed to get the nest that he had been seeking the day before.

> Israel understood that hard work and careful saving are the way to wealth. Benjamin Franklin wrote about this in *Poor Richard's Almanac*:
>
> "Plough deep while sluggards sleep, and you shall have corn to sell and to keep."[2]

Once, Israel's father bought a bull from a neighbor's farm. He sent Israel to drive the bull home. But the bull was angry. He chased Israel out of the pasture. Israel came back wearing spurs and somehow got on top of the bull's back. Jabbing the animal with his spurs, Israel made him run until he was so tired that he got stuck in the mud at the end of the field. Israel got the bull out of the mud and drove him home. The bull did not seem to want to fight after that.

A Wolf in the Cave

Storytime with Uncle Rick

Fight for Freedom

One winter day, someone found the tracks of the wolf in the snow. There were three toes missing from one of the tracks. Many farmers brought their dogs and hunted the wolf. Finally, she ran into a narrow cave. The men tried to get their dogs to go into the cave and kill the wolf, but the dogs were afraid. They knew there was not enough room for many of them in the cave. The wolf would be hard to fight. The dogs stood in front of the cave and barked, but they would not go in.

Finally, Israel Putnam spoke up. "We must kill this wolf or many more of our sheep will die. She has already killed 70 of my sheep and goats. I'll go in and shoot her."[3]

Some of his friends tried to make him change his mind. They told him it was too dangerous. Israel knew what had to be done.

He tied a rope to his ankle and told his friends to pull him out when he tugged on the rope. Carrying a torch, he crawled into the cave. The ground was rough and rocky in the cave. The torch was smoky and did not give much light. Israel kept crawling forward until he saw two eyes glowing at him from the darkness. He had found the wolf.

He gave a little tug on the rope and his friends pulled him out. He was scratched and bruised, but he took his musket and crawled back into the cave. There were the eyes, glowing in the faint light of his torch. He heard the wolf give a savage growl.

Boom! Israel's musket fired. In the narrow, rocky cave the blast was so loud that he could not hear for a few minutes afterward. When his friends heard the musket fire, they pulled him out. They were afraid he might have only hurt the wolf. A wounded wolf in a narrow cave would slash a man to pieces.

Israel was very bruised and sore. His shirt had been nearly ripped off him, and the rocks had beaten him from head to foot. He was bleeding from several wounds. But there was no more sound from the cave. Was the wolf dead?

There was only one way to find out. Brave Israel rested for a few minutes and lit another torch. Back into the cave he crawled. This time, he had a dead wolf by the ears when he was pulled into the light.

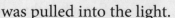

General Israel Putnam.

When Israel was a young man, he married Sarah Pope. They bought a big farm in Connecticut near the town of Brooklyn. The young couple worked hard, and God blessed them. They grew fruits and animals. His farm was known for producing apples, sheep, and goats.

The farmers of the Brooklyn area had a problem. They had hunted down most of the wolves that loved to kill their sheep, but there was still one wolf left. People thought it was the last wolf in Connecticut. It was a she-wolf that would go away for a while and then come back and raise a litter of pups among their farms. She and her pups killed many sheep and goats. The farmers were losing money. Finally, all the pups had been killed. Though the mother had been hunted many times, she was sneaky. No one had been able to shoot her. She once lost three toes in a trap, but she escaped. In one night, the wolf killed 70 sheep and goats.

WITH THE RANGERS

There were more adventures waiting for Israel Putnam. Some of them came in the French and Indian War when Putnam joined the famous Rogers Rangers and became a captain. They were a special group of soldiers trained by Major Robert Rogers to scout the enemy and sometimes fight desperate battles.

Once, Major Rogers, Captain Putnam, and a small group of Rangers ran into a French soldier in the woods. Rogers aimed his gun at the Frenchman, but it failed to fire. The soldier drew a knife to stab Rogers. Captain Putnam was nearby, and he knocked down the Frenchman with the butt of his rifle. The Rangers ran through the woods and escaped the other French soldiers.

One warm evening, Putnam and a soldier named Durkee were scouting near Fort Ticonderoga. They spotted some campfires shining through the trees of the forest. They crept through the woods until they were close enough to see that the fires were surrounded by enemy soldiers. They realized they were right in the middle of the enemy's camp! They turned and ran.

A hail of French bullets followed them. Durkee was wounded, but they managed to escape in the dark. Stopping for a rest, Putnam offered Durkee a drink from his canteen. When he took the canteen off his shoulder, he found that it had been drained by a bullet hole. The two men checked their clothes and their other gear for holes. Putnam found 14 holes in his blanket, which had been rolled up over his shoulder.

Putnam was a skilled woodsman. He knew the ways of the woods and of the Indians. An adventure he had later in the French and Indian War proved this.

Putnam went home for the winter. Returning to his position in Rogers' Rangers, he was stationed at Fort Edward. Sentries had to be stationed all around the fort to prevent Indians from sneaking up on English soldiers. There was one outpost in particular that had lost so many of its sentries that no one would volunteer to stand guard there. One after another, the soldiers stationed in that place had disappeared. No bodies were found.

Because he was an officer, Putnam was not required to stand guard. But he was curious about what happened to the guards. He volunteered to stand watch on the post. His friends warned him that it was dangerous. That did not change Israel Putnam's mind.

He arrived at his assigned post before sunset. He spent a long time just looking around, getting familiar with the area. He tried to memorize every rock, bush, and tree. Even then, his surroundings seemed strange when the sun went down and the moon rose.

General Major Israel Putnam, artist unknown, 1778 (PD-US).

Nothing happened. Midnight came and went. He heard shuffling in the bushes. His ears told him that the noise was not made by an Indian. An Indian would have been much quieter. After listening for a while, he decided that the noise must be made by a hog rooting in the leaves for an acorn or root to eat.

Just to be sure, he issued the challenge: "Who goes there!"[4] When no answer came, he fired his musket at the dark shape in the moonlight. He did not hear a hog's grunt. He heard a man's groan.

He approached the creature. It was black and furry. He pulled on the fur, and a bearskin peeled off of a dead Indian. This disguise had fooled the other sentinels. The Indian had crept near them in his costume, stabbed them, and carried them away. The mystery was solved.

FIGHTS AND A FIRE

General Webb, the English commander, wanted a French prisoner. He hoped to find out from him what the enemy was planning to do. He sent Captain Putnam to do this dangerous job.

"Old Put" took five men with him and set out. He hid his men in tall grass near a trail. A Frenchman and an Indian came along. The Indian was in the lead, so Putnam let him pass. Then, when the Frenchman was right in front of him, he jumped up and ordered the man to surrender. He took off running, leading Putnam on a chase through the woods. Putnam caught the Frenchman by the shoulder. Putnam found that the other man was stronger. He could not hold him. He aimed his musket at the man's chest and pulled the trigger. The gun did not fire. Put discovered that his men had not followed him. It was Putnam's turn to flee.

> A faithful leader never asks his followers to do things he or she would be afraid to do. Israel Putnam was always willing to do the most dangerous things.

The Indian turned to aid his friend. Putnam sprinted down the trail, followed by an angry Frenchman with the Indian close behind.

As the running trio approached the hiding place of Putnam's men, they stood up to fight. The Indian gave a cry of warning to the Frenchman, and they both gave up the chase. They ran off through the forest.

Putnam was enraged at his failure and ashamed of his men. He scolded them and sent them back to camp. He continued the mission and brought in a prisoner by himself.

Old Put's courage was legendary. It became even more widely known after an event in the winter of 1757 nearly cost him his life, along with many other lives.

The barracks at Fort Edward caught fire one night, and soon the building was all ablaze. With horror, the soldiers saw that the fire would soon spread to the powder magazine next to the barracks. If that happened, the entire fort would be blown to bits.

As he always did, Putnam took the place of the most danger. Climbing up a ladder, he ordered the other men to bring him buckets of water. As they did, he threw the water on the

Major Israel Putnam in British Uniform, artist unknown, 1855 (PD-US).

flaming building. He was so near the flames that the mittens burned off his hands. His commander begged him to run for his life. There were 300 barrels of gunpowder in the magazine.

Putnam kept working. The commander gave up and handed Putnam another pair of mittens, soaked in water.

He stood looking up at Putnam. "Well, if we must be blown up we will all go together,"[5] he said.

Finally, the fire died out. There was only a strip of charred timber between the powder and the ashes of the fire. Putnam saved the fort. His arms, face, and legs were blistered. When he pulled off the second pair of mittens, the skin of his hands came off too. He spent a month in the hospital healing from his wounds. Before the winter was over, he was off scouting again. At the head of his company of rangers, he patrolled the forests toward the enemy stronghold of Ticonderoga.

Putnam Saving Fort Edward.

The French and Indians knew about Putnam. He had led his men in many successful fights. They were eager for a chance to get revenge. They were constantly on the watch for their opportunity.

One day, it seemed their chance had come. He and a small group of men were surprised by a large group of Indians on the bank of the Hudson River. The river was between them and the fort, so it seemed there was no escape. They could not cross the river without being shot. Just downstream was a dangerous set of rapids. Putnam did not hesitate. He ordered his men back into their boat and pushed off as the Indians rushed up and crowded on the bank. The braves sent a shower of musket balls after them, but all missed their target. The Indians stood, sure they would see the boat turn over and every man drowned in the rapids.

Putnam calmly steered the boat through the roaring white water and huge boulders. In just a few seconds, his boat was in the smooth water a quarter of a mile downstream. After that time, the Indians looked on him as more than human. They thought that he was under the special protection of the Great Spirit.

Major General Israel Putnam
of Connecticut

CHAPTER 33

ISRAEL PUTNAM

Wolf Fighter Becomes General

A PRISONER IN PERIL

Putnam and Major Rogers had been sent out to locate a war party that had been raiding between Fort Edward and the lakes. As they were marching through the woods, Putnam and his fighters were in front. Suddenly, the air was alive with yells and the booming of muskets. The French fighter Marin had prepared an ambush with his Indian followers. Putnam's walked right into it. Several of them fell in their tracks.

Putnam was surprised but calm. He gave orders to return fire and sent a messenger for more men.

Rather than retreat, he went ahead. He was facing an Indian chief. Putnam pointed his musket at the man and pulled the trigger. The gun failed to fire.

The chief threatened Putnam with a tomahawk. Putnam had no choice but to surrender. He was tied to a tree, and his captor returned to the battle.

This was not a good place to be. Bullets were flying in every direction as Putnam stood bound and helpless. His clothes were pierced with several bullets. For more than an hour, he stood unable to move his arms and legs.

A young Indian playfully threw his tomahawk at his head, trying to see how close he could come without killing him. A French officer pointed his gun at Putnam, but he missed. The Frenchman was so frustrated that he struck his victim a blow on his jaw with the gun that nearly killed him.

A good horse is a man's best friend in times of danger.[1]

Israel Putnam

The spring after Putnam's recovery from his burns, the Rangers were retreating after a battle. They ran into another band of Americans who fired on them, mistaking them for the enemy. Little damage was done before the other company recognized them for friends. Putnam was angry at the mistaken attack, but he kept his sense of humor. He told the leader, "Friends or enemies, you all deserve to be hanged for not killing more, when you had so fair a shot."[2]

Genl. Israel Putnam: the iron son of "76" Effecting his escape from the British dragoons, by Currier & Ives, 1845 (PD-US).

The provincials, the military units raised up to defend their provinces, won the day, but when Miran and his Indians withdrew, they took their prisoners with them. Putnam's captor tied his wrists together and loaded him with a heavy pack. He took his shoes off. Then he left him with another Indian and walked away.

They were not far along the trail before Putnam was in very bad condition. His feet were bruised and gashed. His hands were painfully swollen from his bonds. He was suffering from the blow of the musket blow on his jaw. He would gladly have died by a merciful gunshot. But then the situation got even worse.

The small group of Indians he was with arrived at their meeting place before their comrades. As they milled around him, talking and gesturing, he realized they intended to burn him at the stake. At that moment he was in such terrible pain that he would have been glad to die. But death by an Indian burning meant a long, slow death in unspeakable agony.

Putnam was as brave as any man alive, but he watched in horror as his captors prepared for their fun. They stripped his clothes off, tied him to a tree, and piled dry brush around him. Soon the fuel was blazing. Putnam shifted from side to side, but he could not get away from the heat. His tormentors yelled, laughed, and danced around him. He gave up all hope and tried to think about the better life that awaited him on the other side of death.

Suddenly, a man in a French uniform pushed through the crowd. He kicked the burning branches aside and untied Putnam. It was Marin.

RELEASE AND HOMECOMING

Barely alive, Putnam was marched north to Fort Ticonderoga. He met the commander of the fort, the Marquis de Montcalm. Montcalm sent him to Montreal. At Montreal, he met another American officer, Colonel Peter Schuyler. Schuyler had some influence on the French, and he persuaded them to treat Putnam more kindly.

The capture of some French forts that year had left the British with many prisoners. They were eager to trade the French captives to get their own men back, so Putnam was released.

Phillip Schuyler, engraving (bust) by Hall from painting by John Trumbull, 1792 (PD-US).

With a group of other former prisoners, he began to make his way back home.

In the group was a lady named Mrs. Howe. Her husband had been killed three years. Mrs. Howe and her children had been prisoners ever since. Putnam took the Howes under his wing. He made himself their protector on the long journey. He shared his meals with the family.

What a welcome he received when he finally reached his Connecticut farm! His family had heard of his captivity and had almost given him up for dead. Now at last he was with them again, and it was a great time of rejoicing.

Putnam was not home long before his wife died. Israel and his children worked hard in the fields. The next year, he joined the Congregational Church in Brooklyn.

In 1767, he married the widow Deborah Gardiner. The two were happy together, and Israel's children had a mother once again. The next seven years were happy ones, spent with his wife and children on the farm he loved.

Louis-Joseph de Montcalm

OLD PUT GOES TO WAR AGAIN

Israel Putnam stood firm as a patriot, but he was still friends with some of the British officers he had fought beside in the French and Indian War. In a conversation one day, General Gage boasted to Putnam that 5,000 British soldiers could march across America without any trouble.

The next year, news came of the fight at Concord. Putman was plowing a cornfield when the news reached him. He acted swiftly. Leaving the oxen and the plow in the field, he ran to the house. Without even changing clothes, he mounted his horse and galloped away. He reached Cambridge, Massachusetts, the next morning and before the day was over he reached Concord. When Washington was made commander-in-chief, Putnam was made a brigadier general. He was given command of the troops at Cambridge.

At Bunker Hill, Putnam held his men as the British stormed up the hill. When they had to retreat, he was one of the last to leave the field. The British general Howe was so impressed by Putnam's courage that he asked him to leave the patriots and join the British army as a major-general. Putnam refused. Four days

Ay, if they behaved properly, and paid as they went. But if they showed the least hostility, the American women would knock them over the head with their ladles![3]

Israel Putnam

General Putnam leaving his plow for the defense of his country, artist and date unknown (PD-US).

Battle of Bunker Hill, by E. Percy Moran, 1909 (PD-Art).

later, Washington made him a major-general in the American army.

In 1776, General Washington sent Old Put to New York and then on to Brooklyn Heights. Just two days after he arrived to take charge, he was attacked by 20,000 British soldiers. His force of 5,000 recruits was defeated. Later, he fought in the battles of Harlem Heights, Chatterton Hill, Fort Washington, and Princeton.

While Washington was suffering through the terrible winter of 1777 at Valley Forge, Putnam was suffering with his men at the Hudson highlands. Though he was nearly 60 years old, "Old Put" stayed with his men, enduring the cold and lack of supplies.

Before the winter was over, Putnam lost his job. His small force had lost several battles near New York. The Continental Congress did not trust him, even though he had fought well with the few troops he had. Washington did not want to do so, but he sent General McDougal to replace Putnam.

Putnam was asked to go home to Connecticut and find more men who would join the army. Washington needed more soldiers. At first, few men would join. They had heard that the French king was sending ships and soldiers to help the Americans. They thought this would be enough to defeat the British. But Old Put was a hero to Connecticut, so he was able to persuade them. Soon men were joining just because Old Put had asked them to.

The American army was about to lose one of its most famous heroes. In the winter of 1779, Old Put was posted near Morristown, New Jersey. He went on a short visit home to see his family. When he returned, he stayed with Colonel Wadsworth at Harford, Connecticut. He suffered a stroke and was partly paralyzed. The war was over for Old Put.

He returned to his farm and his family. There he spent the rest of his life, surrounded by the friends and neighbors of his youth. He lived another 11 years. He was able to walk, ride, and visit his friends. Two years before he died, a friend began to write Old Put's biography. It is still read today. It is the first biography written in America about an American.[4]

TEN TIMES AS MANY REDCOATS

That winter, Putnam had a narrow escape. He was visiting an army outpost near Horseneck, Connecticut, to inspect the defenses there. While shaving one morning, he saw in the mirror that redcoats were coming over a hill toward the camp. Old Put did not even take time to wipe the soap from his face. He grabbed his sword, ran out of the house, and leaped on his horse. Shouting encouragement to his men, he galloped toward the hilltop where they were forming to meet the British. He arranged them so the redcoats could not surround them and directed the firing of their cannons and rifles. Soon he saw that his troop could not hold out. There were ten times as many redcoats as Americans.

Putnam ordered his men to retreat and form up on another hill that would be easier to defend. He put spurs to his mount and sped away toward Stamford to bring a troop of militia to help. Several dragoons saw him and went racing after him. Bullets whistled past his head. Steel horseshoes struck sparks from stones.

Coming to the top of a hill by a meeting house, Putnam saw that the other side was a steep, rocky slope. It was too dangerous to ride a horse down. Old Put was brave, and his men needed help. He put spurs to his mount and went clattering down. Close behind him, the British dragoons pulled their panting horses to a sudden stop. Only a crazy man would try to ride down that slope, they thought. They were angry to see their enemy escape. They fired their guns at him as he galloped away. One bullet went through Old Put's cap. He just laughed and shouted back at the British over his shoulder and rode on.

About half a mile from the hill, Putnam approached a farmhouse. The mother inside heard the hoof beats of his racing horse. Afraid that her children might be trampled, she rushed to the door

and called them to come in. Just then, the general galloped up. His hat had blown off and his hair was blowing about his face. Old Put was flying for his life, but he took time to warn the woman.

He shouted for them to get their children inside because the British were upon them.[5]

It only took seconds to deliver the warning. He continued toward Stamford.

When he returned with reinforcements, the British had destroyed the Horseneck salt works and damaged several patriot homes. Putnam followed the invaders even though he was still outnumbered. He was scooping up stragglers from the redcoats. He captured nearly 40 prisoners.

Putnam's escape at Horseneck, by Johnson & Miles, 1877 (PD-US).

277

George Whitefield

CHAPTER 34

THE BLACK ROBE REGIMENT

Ministers of Freedom

GEORGE WHITEFIELD — THE GREAT AWAKENER

Every American needs to learn about the Constitution. The Constitution is the document that explains what America is and how our nation works. It is the foundation of our government. It tells what our rights as citizens are.

After the Constitution was accepted by all the states in 1789, some of the states wanted the Constitution to be even clearer about what the rights of Americans. So, the new government made some changes in it. Changes to the Constitution are called amendments. The first ten amendments ever made were all voted on and passed at the same time. These ten amendments are called the Bill of Rights.

Rev. George Whitefield, by John Russell, 1770 (PD-US).

The First Amendment deals with several different issues. The first of those issues is the freedom of religion. The amendment says Congress may not make a law about establishing a religion. In other words, America cannot require its citizens to belong to any religion, as some countries do. It also says Congress cannot keep people from the "free exercise" of their religion.

Why was the freedom of religion the first freedom mentioned in the Bill of Rights? It is because the freedom to worship God is the most important freedom of all.

The Pilgrims left England because they had not been allowed to worship in the way they believed the Bible taught. The king wanted everyone to worship the way he told them. When the Pilgrims formed their own churches and chose their own preachers, the king got angry. He locked Christians up in prison

Amendment I

Congress shall make no law respecting an establishment of religion, or prohibiting the free exercise thereof; or abridging the freedom of speech, or of the press; or the right of the people peaceably to assemble, and to petition the government for a redress of grievances.

Bunyan in prison, by William Cathcart, 1881 (PD-US).

for going to these churches. He locked preachers in jail if they preached without a license from the government.

John Bunyan, who wrote the famous book *Pilgrim's Progress*, was such a preacher. He believed God calls preachers to preach and that they do not need permission from any man, even the king. He spent many years in jail for preaching without a license.

The king of England was the head of the Anglican Church (also called the Church of England). It was the official church of the nation of England. When the Founding Fathers wrote the Constitution, they did not want a national church. They had seen how wrong it was in England. Americans had grown up in the New World, far from the control of the national church. Many of the colonists were still Anglican, but there were also Baptists, Presbyterians, Quakers, and others.

Most of these people formed their own churches in their own towns. The churches did not have to obey a national church. They were led by ministers who were voted on by the church members. The church members made their own rules for the church. This was an important influence in the birth of self-government in America.

There were many churches in America because there were many Christians. When people believe the Bible, they know God wants them to join together in churches to worship, serve, and spread the gospel. The reason there were so many churches and Christians in the American colonies during the War of Independence was something called the Great Awakening.

The Great Awakening was a spiritual revival that swept over the American colonies in the years before the War of Independence. Founding Fathers such as Patrick Henry and Benjamin Franklin wrote about the influence of that revival.

Patrick Henry is known as the great orator of independence. How did he learn to speak so powerfully and with such beautiful expression? Perhaps part of the answer lies in his boyhood. His mother attended the Presbyterian church where the famous Reverend Samuel Davies preached. Davies had been used by God to give the gospel to thousands of people. Many of them

Not forsaking the assembling of ourselves together, as the manner of some is; but exhorting one another: and so much the more, as ye see the day approaching.

—Hebrews 10:25

had become Christians. Reverend Davies was a gifted speaker. Patrick's mother took him to church regularly. Patrick loved the sermons. He listened carefully. He would recite portions of them at his mother's request. As a man, he said Reverend Davies had "the most pronounced influence"[1] on him. He said Davies was the greatest orator he had ever heard.

Samuel Davies, artist and date unknown (PD-Art).

GEORGE WHITEFIELD COMES TO AMERICA

Now we will let Benjamin Franklin introduce us to a Great Awakening preacher who was even more famous than Davies. This is the Reverend George Whitefield (pronounced Whitfield), a traveling preacher from England. He carried the gospel all the way from Georgia to Maine. Franklin was a printer, and Whitefield hired him to print some of his sermons. The two men became close friends. Franklin admired Whitefield. He was impressed with the results of his friend's ministry when he preached in Philadelphia. He described it in his autobiography.

He told how Whitefield came to town on a preaching tour in 1739. At first, he was permitted to preach in the local churches. But the local ministers turned against him. Some of them were jealous of the big crowds he drew and the love the people had for him. After that, he had to preach in the fields, which he had done many times before. Multitudes of people came to hear his sermons, and they were from many different churches. Franklin was amazed at Whitefield's influence. He noticed that the people admired and respected him, even though he preached against their sins.

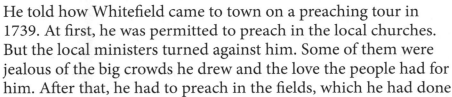

Franklin wrote, "It was wonderful to see the Change soon made in the Manners [behavior] of our Inhabitants; from being thoughtless or indifferent about Religion, it seem'd as if all the World were growing Religious; so that one could not walk thro' the Town in an Evening without Hearing Psalms sung in different Families of every Street."[2]

Franklin said there should be a building large enough for Whitefield to use in ministering to the thousands of people who came to hear him. A fund was started to collect money for the purpose. Because so many people loved Whitefield and wanted him to be able to share the gospel freely, the money was very quickly raised. A building was started and, as Franklin said, "the Work was carried on with such Spirit as to be finished in a much shorter time than could have been expected. Both House and Ground were vested in Trustees, expressly for the Use of any Preacher of any religious Persuasion who might desire to say something to the People of Philadelphia, the Design [purpose] in

(PD-US)

George Whitefield

building not being to accommodate any particular Sect, but the Inhabitants in general…"[3]

Whitefield's first concern was salvation. He was also concerned about the needs of the poor. In Georgia, he had seen hundreds of dirty and starving orphans. His heart longed to make a home for them and teach them about Jesus. He wanted to give them food and clothing and to take care of them when they were sick. This work was expensive, and he often told his listeners about it so they could give to the orphans.

Franklin told Whitefield he should build the orphanage in Philadelphia and bring the orphans there. After all, it was hard to get good building materials and skilled tradesmen in the wilderness colony of Georgia. It would be cheaper to transport the children to Philadelphia. Whitefield believed Georgia was where God wanted the building. He would not change his mind. Franklin decided he would not give any money to the project.

But even the Franklin could not resist the power in Whitefield's preaching. Ben attended another sermon soon after talking with Whitefield about the orphanage. He realized the preacher was about to end his sermon with a collection for the orphans. He had money with him. In his pocket were some copper coins, some silver dollars, and some Spanish gold money. He determined that no matter what Whitefield said, he was not going to give a cent.

But as the preaching went on, his determination began to soften. He decided he could give the copper. Then "another stroke of his oratory made me ashamed of that, and determined me to give the silver; and he finished so admirably that I emptied my pocket … gold and all."[4]

Persuasiveness means to skillfully handle truth to lead others in a right path. Whitefield certainly was used by God to lead others to turn from their sin and live for the Lord.

Franklin wasn't the only person whose heart was touched by the preaching. A friend of his was there that day who also did not intend to give. In fact, that man had left all his money at home so that he could not change his mind when Whitefield spoke. But as the sermon moved toward its end, he grew uneasy. He wanted desperately to give. He was so upset that he turned to another man and begged for a loan to put in the collection. But it seemed he had asked the only man there who could resist Whitefield. He answered in his mild tone, "At any other time, Friend Hopkinson, I would lend to thee freely; but not now; for thee seems to be out of thy right senses."[5]

Before the preaching house could be built, Franklin often went to hear Whitefield preach in the fields and streets. The young preacher was gifted with a booming voice, which he had made even stronger through practice. Listening to him one day in Philadelphia, Franklin wondered how many people could stand close enough to hear him. He began to walk backward until he could no longer hear the preaching clearly. Then he paced off a circle at the same distance from the preacher. Later he figured the problem out mathematically. He estimated Whitefield could preach to 30,000 people and be clearly heard.

God gifted Whitefield in many ways. He had a deep faith in God and the Bible. He had a bright mind. His voice, besides being loud and clear, was also pleasant. Sarah Edwards, the wife of famous preacher Jonathan Edwards, called his voice "sweet." Franklin said it was "like a beautiful piece of music."[6] David Garrick, a famous English actor, said he would give a large amount of money to be able to say "oh" like Whitefield did.

But it was not just natural talent that brought out the crowds. The power of God was with Whitefield. People came by the thousands and received the new birth. As he preached, the Holy Spirit would come down in amazing ways. People would be sobbing for their sins or shouting with joy after they felt God's forgiveness. As Franklin wrote, whole communities would be changed.

When God sends his power through a humble preacher, there will be enemies. Many preachers would not allow Whitefield to preach in their pulpits. He did not have a church of his own, and that seemed strange to them. He did strange things such as preaching to slum people. He worked with people of many denominations. He did not seem to realize that he was a minister of the Church of England. Most of all, they were jealous of him. The people of the community loved him far more than they loved the stuffy preachers of the king's church.

Whitefield, Davies, and the other preachers of the Great Awakening had a strong influence on the people of the colonies and the men who would lead them in fighting for freedom. Without their preaching, there might never have been a War of Independence. They were as much a part of America's birth as the soldiers and statesmen who fought the war and built the new nation. These were the ones King George called "The Black Robe Regiment."

When they worked with people from many different churches, it showed that the king's church could not tell men what they must believe.

When they taught that all authority comes from God, people began to understand that the king did not have the right to disobey the law and mistreat the colonies.

Storytime with Uncle Rick

Fight for Freedom

Once, Whitefield arrived in a city and ran into one of those preachers. The man looked at him with an angry face. "I am sorry to see you here," he growled. Whitefield replied calmly, "So is the devil."

Franklin had seen the same thing in Philadelphia. He had written articles against this in his newspaper. One day, he had a discussion with a local preacher.

"You talk about being called to the work of the ministry," he said. "If ability and great power in the pulpit are evidence of being called of God, then Whitefield must have had a louder call than any of you."

"But he is very peculiar in his methods, and harsh in his treatment of sinners," replied the minister.

"But if we sinners do not object, why should you saints? We have heard him say nothing but the truth yet," Franklin protested.

"All that may be true," continued the minister, "but so much excitement is not healthy for the spiritual growth of the people."

"When did you, or anyone else, ever see so great moral and spiritual improvement of the people," asked Franklin, "as we have seen since Whitefield has been preaching here? The whole population appears to be thinking about religion."

"It is just excitement!" exclaimed the minister; "and when Whitefield is gone, the excitement will be gone. The last state of the people will be worse than the first."[7]

But the minister was wrong. Whitefield and the other preachers of the Great Awakening had a lasting influence on the colonies. They preached that all men are sinners who need a Savior. People began to see that all men are created equal.

RICHARD ALLEN — PATRIOT PREACHER

Richard Allen was not a soldier but a preacher. He was born a slave in 1760. As a boy, he was sold to Benjamin Chew, a Delaware farmer. Young Richard heard the Methodist preachers of his day. He became a Christian.

Mr. Chew was impressed with the godly life Richard lived. He allowed Richard to hold worship services in the Chew home. Mr. Chew himself became a Christian in one of these services. Later, he arranged for Richard to become free.

> The number of people who turned out to honor Richard Allen at his funeral shows the power of influence. Richard had ministered to sick people when he was in danger of catching the deadly disease himself. People admired him for that. They also respected him for his honest life and powerful preaching. We should try to have a godly influence on those around us.

Richard traveled a lot to preach. He preached in eastern Pennsylvania and neighboring states. He used every chance he got to preach to all people. He knew all people need Jesus.

Richard Allen also ministered to the physical needs of people. When the yellow fever swept through Philadelphia in 1793, nearly all the doctors left the city to save their own lives. But Richard Allen did not flee. Instead, he worked beside Dr. Benjamin Rush, who was a member of the Continental Congress and a signer of the Declaration of Independence. All through that dangerous time, the two men worked endless hours to help the sick people.

Richard Allen, from the frontispiece of *History of the African Methodist Episcopal Church*, by Daniel A. Payne, 1891 (PD-US).

Allen's heroic service during this terrible time is one of the noblest examples of service to others. He urged others to help their fellow man as well.[8]

Richard Allen died in 1831. It was said that the crowd that gathered to honor him "exceeded anything of the kind ever before witnessed in the country." Richard Allen was known as "a man of deep piety, the strictest integrity, and indomitable perseverance; and his moral influence was unbounded."

> Allen's faith was evident in his works. He openly gave thanks to God for the chance to serve Him and man. He said:
>
> "I believe it is my greatest honor and happiness to be Thy disciple; how miserable and blind are those that live without God in the world, who despise the light of Thy holy faith. Make me to part with all the enjoyments of life; nay, even life itself, rather than forfeit this jewel of great price."[9]

BIBLIOGRAPHY

Bakeless, John and Katherine. *Spies of the Revolution*, New York: Scholastic Book Services, 1962.

Barton, David. *America's Godly Heritage*. Aledo TX: Wallbuilders Press, 2004.

Barton, David. *Benjamin Rush: Signer of the Declaration of Independence*. Aledo, TX: Wallbuilders Press, 1999.

Barton, David. *Original Intent: The Courts, The Constitution, and Religion*. Aledo, TX: Wallbuilders Press, 2005.

Barton, David. *Setting the Record Straight: American History in Black and White*. Aledo, TX: Wallbuilders Press, 2004.

Barton, David. *The Bulletproof George Washington*. Aledo, TX: Wallbuilders Press, 1990.

Blaisdell, Albert F. and Ball, Francis K. *Hero Stories from American History for Elementary Schools*. New York: Ginn and Co, 1903.

Boyer, Marilyn and Grace Tumas. *Portraits of Integrity*. Rustburg, VA: Learning Parent, 2012.

Boyer, Marilyn: *For You They Signed*. Green Forest, AR: Master Books, 2009.

Brooks, Elbridge. *The True Story of Benjamin Franklin: The American Statesman*. Boston: Lothrop, Lee and Shepard Co, 1898.

Brooks, Elbridge. *The True Story of George Washington: Called the Father of His Country*. Boston: Lothrop Publishing Co, 1895.

Campion, Nardi Reeder. *Patrick Henry: Firebrand of the Revolution*. Boston: Little, Brown and Co, 1961.

Cheripko, Jan. *Caesar Rodney's Ride: The Story of an American Patriot*. Honesdale, PA: Boyds Mill Press, 2004.

DeMorgan, John. *Marion and His Men or the Swamp Fox of Carolina*. Philadelphia: David McKay, Publisher, 1892.

Fradin, Dennis. *The Signers: The 56 Stories Behind the Declaration of the Independence*. New York: Walker Publishers, 2004.

Gordy, Wilbur F. *American Leaders and Heroes: A Preliminary Text-book in United States History*.New York: Charles Scribner's Sons, 1904.

Mace, William H. *A Beginner's History*, New York: Rand McNally and Co., 1909.

Mace, William H. *A Primary History: Stories of Heroism*. New York: Rand McNally and Co, 1909.

McPherson, Stephanie. *Liberty or Death: A Story about Patrick Henry*. Minneapolis, MN: Carolrhoda Books, 2003.

Meyer, Edith Patterson. *Petticoat Patriots of the American Revolution*. New York: Vanguard Press, 1976.

Montgomery, D.H. *The Beginner's American History*. New York: Ginn and Co, 1892.

Palmer, Kate Salley. *Francis Marion and the Legend of the Swamp Fox*. Central, SC: Warbranch Press, 2005.

Watson, Henry C. *Noble Deeds of Our Fathers as told by Soldiers of the Revolution*. Boston: Lee and Shepard Publishers, 1888.

White, Henry Alexander. *Beginner's History of the United States: Stories of the Men Who Made our Country*. New York: American Book Company, 1911.

ENDNOTES

Chapter 1 – George Washington - Growing in Greatness

1. Albert F. Blaisdell and Francis K. Ball, *Hero Stories from American History* (Boston: Ginn and Company, 1903), 68.

2. Ibid., 64

3. William Mace, *A Beginner's History* (New York: Rand, McNally & Company, 1921), 117.

4. George Washington to John Sullivan, 6 July 1777, *The Writings of George Washington*, ed. John C. Fitzpatrick, vol. 8 (Washington: Government Printing Office, 1933), 359.

5. Henry White, *Beginner's History of the United States: Stories of the Men Who Made our Country* (New York: American Book Company), 97–98.

6. Mace, *A Beginner's History*, 119–121.

7. White, *Beginner's History of the United States*, 101–102.

8. Paul Royster, ed., "The Journal of Major George Washington (1754)," University of Nebraska-Lincoln, accessed June 29, 2015, http://digitalcommons.unl.edu/cgi/viewcontent.cgi?article=1033&context=etas.

9. White, *Beginners History of the United States*, 102-103.

10. Royster, "The Journal of Major George Washington," 1754.

11. White, *Beginners History of the United States*, 104–105.

12. Mace, *A Beginner's History*, 124.

13. Ibid., 123–126.

14. White, *Beginners History of the United States*, 104–105.

15. George Washington to Robert Dinwiddie, 29 May 1754. Founders Online, National Archives, http://founders.archives.gov/documents/Washington/02-01-02-0054.

16. Joseph Banvard, *Tragic Scenes in the History of Maryland and The Old French War* (Boston: Gould and Lincoln, 1856), 153.

17. Ibid., 154.

Chapter 2 – George Washington - God's Man for America

1. "The George Washington Papers at the Library of Congress, 1741–1799," The Library of Congress, accessed June 25, 2015, http://memory.loc.gov/cgi-bin/query/P?mgw:2:./temp/~ammem_AzdT::.

2. "Martha Washington Quotes," BrainyQuote, accessed June 25, 2015, http://www.brainyquote.com/quotes/quotes/m/marthawash160612.html.

3. William Mace, *A Beginner's History*, (New York: Rand, McNally & Company, 1921), 127.

4. Ibid., 128.

5. William Mace, *A Primary History: Stories of Heroism* (Chicago: Rand McNally, & Company, 1909), 173.

6. Mace, *A Beginner's History*, 129–130.

7. Mace, *A Beginner's History*, 131.

8. Ibid., 131–132.

9. "Battle of Long Island," George Washington's Mount Vernon, accessed June 25, 2015, http://www.mount-vernon.org/research-collections/digital-encyclopedia/article/battle-of-long-island/.

10. Wilbur Gordy, *American Leaders and Heroes* (New York: Charles Scribner's Sons, 1901), 206.

11. Albert F. Blaisdell and Francis K. Ball, *Hero Stories from American History* (Boston: Ginn and Company, 1903), 51–61.

12. Walker P. Whitman, *A Christian History of the American Republic: A Textbook for Secondary Schools* (Boston: Green Leaf Press, 1948), 42.

13. Mace, *A Beginner's History*, 134.

14. Gordy, *American Leaders and Heroes*, 199–203.

15. Mace, *A Beginner's History*, 138.

16. Whitman, *A Christian History of the American Republic*, 42.

17. Mace, *A Beginner's History*, 138–145.

18. "The Man Who Would Not be King," Cato Institute, accessed June 25, 2015, http://www.cato.org/publications/commentary/man-who-would-not-be-king.

Chapter 3 – Benjamin Franklin -The Making of the Man

1. Wilbur Gordy, *American Leaders and Heroes* (New York: Charles Scribner's Sons, 1901), 178–179.

2. William Mace, *A Beginner's History*, (New York: Rand, McNally & Company, 1921), 147–149.

3. Gordy, *American Leaders and Heroes*, 175–177.

4. Mace, *A Beginner's History*, 148.

5. Elbridge Brooks, *True story of Benjamin Franklin: The American Statesman* (Boston: Lothrop, Lee, Shepard, and Co, 1898).

6. D.H. Montgomery, *The Beginner's American History* (NY: Ginn and Co, 1892), 92–93.

7. Gordy, *American Leaders and Heroes*, 176–177.

8. Henry White, *Beginner's History of the United States: Stories of the Men Who Made our Country*, (New York: American Book Company), 97–98.

9. Benjamin Franklin, "Plan for Attaining Moral Perfection," in *Autobiography of Benjamin Franklin*, ed. Frank Woodworth Pine (New York: Henry Holt and Company, 1916), https://www.gutenberg.org/files/20203/20203-h/20203-h.htm.

10. Montgomery, *The Beginner's American History*, 97–99.

11. Mace, *A Beginner's History*, 148–149.

12. Benjamin Franklin, *Poor Richard's Almanack* (Waterloo, IA: U.S.C. Publishing Co., 1914), 32, https://books.google.com/books?id=o6lJAAAAIAAJ&pg=PP1#v=onepage&q&f=false.

13. Mace, *A Beginner's History*, 148–149.

14. Dennis Fradin, *The Signers: The 56 Stories Behind the Declaration of the Independence* (New York: Walker Publishers , 2004).

15. Gordy, *American Leaders and Heroes*, 177–179.

16. Mace, *A Beginner's History*, 150.

17. Gordy, *American Leaders and Heroes*, 180–182.

18. Mace, *A Beginner's History*, 150.

19. Franklin, *Poor Richard's Almanack*, 57.

20. Brooks, *The True Story of Benjamin Franklin*.

Chapter 4 – Benjamin Franklin -The Great Statesman

1. Franklin, Benjamin, and Leonard Woods Labaree. *The Papers of Benjamin Franklin*. (New Haven: Yale University Press, 1959), 469.

2. Daniel Dorchester, *Christianity in the United States from the First Settlements to the Present Time* (New York: Hunt and Eaton, 1890), 264–265.

3. William Mace, *A Beginner's History* (New York: Rand, McNally & Company, 1921), 151–153.

4. Ibid.

5. Marilyn Boyer, *For You They Signed* (Green Forest, AR: Master Books, 2009), 163.

6. Mace, *A Beginner's History*, 152–154.

7. William Jennings Bryan, ed., *The World's Famous Orations*, vol. 3, Great Britain 710-1777 (1906; New York: bartleby.com, 2006), http://www.bartleby.com/268/3/24.html.

8. Henry White, *Beginner's History of the United States: Stories of the Men Who Made our Country* (New York: American Book Company), 153.

9. Henry Gilpin, ed., *The Papers of James Madison*, vol. 2 (New York: J. & H.G. Langley, 1841), 984–986.

10. Elbridge Brooks, *True story of Benjamin Franklin: The American Statesman* (Boston: Lothrop, Lee, Shepard, and Co, 1898), 244–47.

11. Charles A. Goodrich, *Lives of the Signers to the Declaration of Independence* (New York: Thomas Mather, 1837), 282.

Chapter 5 – Mad Anthony Wayne and the Storming of Stony Point

1. Richard Frothingham, *The Rise of the Republic of the United States* (Boston: Little, Brown, and Co., 1872), 393.

2. Marilyn Boyer, *For You They Signed* (Green Forest, AR: Master Books, 2009), 179.

3. Charles H. Bradford, *Dorchester Heights: Prelude to Independence*, 48-54, http://www.dorchesteratheneum.org/pdf/Dorchester%20Heights.pdf.

4. "Letters of the Reverend William Gordon, Historian of the American Revolution, 1770–1799," in Mass. Hist. Soc. *Proceedings*.

5. Albert F. Blaisdell and Francis K. Ball, *Hero Stories from American History*, (Boston: Ginn and Company, 1903), 77–82.

6. John Wingate Thornton, *The Pulpit of the American Revolution or The political sermons of the period of 1776* (Boston: Lothrop, 1876), https://archive.org/details/thepulpit00thoruoft.

7. Blaisdell and Ball, *Hero Stories*, 80.

8. Ibid., 81.

9. Ibid., 86.

10. Ibid.

11. Ibid., 88.

12. Ibid.

13. Ibid., 77–89.

Chapter 6 – Caesar Rodney - The Midnight Ride

1. George H. Ryden, ed., *Letters to and from Caesar Rodney, 1756-1784* (Delaware: Historical Society of Delaware, 1933).

2. Jan Cheripko, *Caesar Rodney's Ride: The Story of an American Patriot* (Honesdale, PA: Boyds Mill Press, 2004), 25.

3. William Balch, *Garfield's Words: Suggestive Passages from the Public and Private Writings of James Abram Garfield* (Boston: Houghton, Mifflin, and Company, 1881), 114.

4. Charles A. Goodrich, *Lives of the Signers to the Declaration of Independence* (New York: Thomas Mather, 1837), 230–231.

5. Marilyn Boyer, *For You They Signed* (Green Forest, AR: Master Books, 2009), 231–232.

6. "George Washington Quotes," Goodreads, accessed June 26, 2015, http://www.goodreads.com/quotes/30819-human-happiness-and-moral-duty-are-inseparably-connected.

7. David C. Whitney, *Founders of Freedom in America: Lives of the Men who Signed the Declaration of Independence and so Helped to establish the United States of America* (Chicago: Ferguson Publishing, 1964), 190.

8. Cheripko, *Caesar Rodney's Ride*, 30–31.

9. Lyman Henry Butterfield, ed., *Letters of Benjamin Rush*, vol. 1 (London: Oxford University Press, 1951), 534.

10. Cheripko, *Caesar Rodney's Ride*, 31.

11. Ibid., 34.

12. John Sanderson, *Sanderson's Biography of the Signers of the Declaration of Independence*, Robert T. Conrad, ed., vol. 8 (Philadelphia: Thomas, Cowperthwait, and Co. , 1847), 119–122.

13. "Caesar Rodney," The Society of the Descendants of the Signers of the Declaration of Independence, accessed June 26, 2015, http://www.dsdi1776.com/signers-by-state/caesar-rodney/.

14. Merle Sinclair and Annabel Douglas MacArthur, *They Signed for Us* (New York: Duell, Sloan and Pearce, 1957), 10.

15. Sanderson, *Biography*, 119–122.

16. "Sybil Ludington," Historic Patterson, New York, accessed June 26, 2015, http://www.historicpatterson.org/Exhibits/ExhSybilLudington.php.

17. "Caesar Rodney's Ride," Wikisource, accessed June 26, 2015, https://en.wikisource.org/wiki/Caesar_Rodney's_Ride.

Chapter 7 – Benjamin Rush - The Good Doctor

1. Benjamin Rush, *Essays: Literary, Moral, and Philosophical* (Philadelphia: Thomas and William Bradford, 1806), 112.

2. David Barton, *Benjamin Rush: Signer of the Declaration of Independence* (Aledo, TX: WallBuilders, 2008), 9–12.

3. Rush, *Essays*, 57–73.

4. Barton, *Benjamin Rush*, 12–13.

5. Lyman Henry Butterfield, ed., *Letters of Benjamin Rush*, vol. 1 (London: Oxford University Press, 1951), 83.

6. "Benjamin Rush," Colonial Hall, accessed June 26, 2015, http://colonialhall.com/rush/rush.php.

7. Barton, *Benjamin Rush*, 93.

8. Butterfield, *Letters*, 86–89.

9. Barton, *Benjamin Rush*, 81–84.

10. Rush, *Essays*, 93.

11. L. Carroll Judson, *The Sages and Heroes of the American Revolution* (Philadelphia: Moss & Brother, 1854), 314–315.

12. Ibid.

Chapter 8 – African-American Patriots – Forging the Way for Freedom

1. David Barton, "A Black Patriot: Wentworth Cheswell," WallBuilders, las modified February 2009, http://www.wallbuilders.com/libissuesarticles.asp?id=20990.

2. William C. Nell, *The Colored Patriots of the American Revolution, With Sketches of Several Distinguished Colored Persons: To Which is Added a Brief Survey of the Conditions and Prospects of Colored Americans* (Boston: Robert F. Wallcut, 1855), 120–121.

3. "James Armistead," Biography.com, accessed June 26, 2015, http://www.biography.com/people/james-armistead-537566.

4. Phillis Wheatley, "Aboard the Angelic Train," *Lapham's Quarterly*, accessed June 26, 2015, http://www.laphamsquarterly.org/religion/aboard-angelic-train.

5. G. Herbert Renfro, ed., *Life and Works of Phillis Wheatley* (Washington, D.C.: A. Jenkins, 1916).

6. "Phillis Wheatley," George Washington's Mount Vernon, accessed June 26, 2015, http://www.mountvernon.org/research-collections/digital-encyclopedia/article/phillis-wheatley/.

Chapter 9 – Daniel Morgan - From Teamster to Major General

1. Henry White, *Beginner's History of the United States: Stories of the Men Who Made our Country* (New York: American Book Company), 152.

2. Albert F. Blaisdell and Francis K. Ball, *Hero Stories from American History* (Boston: Ginn and Company, 1903), 106–107.

3. Ibid., 109.

4. Ibid., 109–112.

5. James Frassett, "Daniel Morgan: The Early Years," Sons of the American Revolution: Sons of Liberty Chapter, last updated 2000, http://www.revolutionarywararchives.org/morganearlyyears.html.

6. Blaisdell and Ball, *Hero Stories*, 112–113.

7. Ibid.

8. Ibid.

9. Ibid., 111–112.

Chapter 10 – Dan Morgan - Sharpshooter

1. Albert F. Blaisdell and Francis K. Ball, *Hero Stories from American History* (Boston: Ginn and Company, 1903), 114.

2. Ibid.

3. Ibid., 117.

4. Ibid.

5. Ibid., 118.

6. Ibid.

7. John Buchanan, *The Road to Guilford Courthouse: The American Revolution in the Carolinas* (Hoboken: Wiley, 1999), 316.

8. Sir George Otto Trevelyan, *George the Third and Charles Fox: The Concluding Part of The American Revolution* (New York and elsewhere: Longmans, Green and Co, 1914).

9. Blaisdell and Ball, *Hero Stories*, 114–122.

10. William Mace, *A Beginner's History* (New York: Rand, McNally & Company, 1921), 187–188.

11. Ibid., 187.

Chapter 11 – Daniel Boone - Hunter and Pioneer of Kentucky

1. Daniel Boone, "Daniel Boone Settles Kentucky," The National Center for Public Policy Research, accessed June 26, 2015, http://www.nationalcenter.org/BooneKentucky.html.

2. Wilbur Gordy, *American Leaders and Heroes* (New York: Charles Scribner's Sons, 1901), 224–225.

3. Ibid., 225–226.

4. Theodore Roosevelt, *The Winning of the West* (New York: G.P. Putnam's Sons, 1896).

5. "Daniel Boone Quotes," Brainy Quote, accessed June 26, 2015, http://www.brainyquote.com/quotes/quotes/d/danielboon142243.html.

6. Mace, *A Beginner's History*, 203–206.

7. Gordy, American Leaders and Heroes, 229–230.

8. William Mace, *A Beginner's History* (New York: Rand, McNally & Company, 1921), 206–208.

9. John Faragher, *Daniel Boone: The Life and Legend of an American Pioneer* (New York: Holt, 1993), 86.

10. Henry White, *Beginner's History of the United States: Stories of the Men Who Made our Country*, (New York: American Book Company, 1916), 146–147.

Chapter 12 – Daniel Boone - Captured by Indians

1. William Mace, *A Beginner's History* (New York: Rand, McNally & Company, 1921), 207–209.

2. D.H. Montgomery, *The Beginner's American History* (NY: Ginn and Co, 1892), 136–139.

3. Mace, *A Beginner's History*, 207–209.

4. "Daniel Boone History," Public Bookshelf, accessed June 26, 2015, http://www.publicbookshelf.com/public_html/The_Great_Republic_By_the_Master_Historians_Vol_II/danielboo_ih.html.

5. "Boone, Daniel," Ohio History Central, accessed June 26, 2015, http://www.ohiohistorycentral.org/w/Boone,_Daniel.

Chapter 13 – Francis Marion - The Swamp Fox

1. John De Morgan, *The Patriot: Marion and His Men, or the Swamp Fox of Carolina* (Larry Harrison, 2000).

2. Ibid.

3. W. Gilmore Simms, *The Life of Francis Marion* (New York: George F. Cooledge and Brother, 1844).

4. William Mace, *A Beginner's History* (New York: Rand, McNally & Company, 1921), 191.

5. Ibid., 189–191.

6. U.S. Library of Congress, *An Album of American Battle Art*, 1755-1918 (Washington, D.C.: Government Printing Office, 1947; reprint, New York: Da Capo, 1972).

7. Mace, *A Beginner's History*, 192.

Chapter 14 – Francis Marion - The Tables Turn in South Carolina

1. William Mace, *A Beginner's History*, (New York: Rand, McNally & Company, 1921), 190–191.

2. Wilbur Gordy, *American Leaders and Heroes* (New York: Charles Scribner's Sons, 1901), 217–218.

3. Mace, *A Beginner's History*, 190.

4. Henry White, *Beginner's History of the United States: Stories of the Men Who Made our Country*, (New York: American Book Company, 1916), 156–160.

5. Mace, *A Beginner's History*, 189.

6. Thomas Francis Donnelly, *A Primary History of the United States for Intermediate Classes* (New York: A.S. Barnes and Company, 1885), 112.

7. U.S. Library of Congress, *An Album of American Battle Art, 1755-1918* (Washington, D.C.: Government Printing Office, 1947; reprint, New York: Da Capo, 1972).

8. "Fort Motte Battle Site — Fort Motte, South Carolina," South Carolina's Information Highway, accessed June 29, 2015, http://www.sciway.net/sc-photos/calhoun-county/fort-motte-battle-site.html.

Chapter 15 – Colonel Isaac Shelby - The Battle of Kings Mountain

1. Albert F. Blaisdell and Francis K. Ball, *Hero Stories from American History* (Boston: Ginn and Company, 1903), 92–94.

2. Ibid., 97.

3. Ibid., 97.

4. Ibid., 95–100.

5. "Fort Motte Battle Site."

Chapter 16 – George Rogers Clark - The Hero of Vincennes

1. William Henry Perrin, J. H. Battle, and G. C. Kniffin, *Kentucky: A History of the State, Embracing a Concise Account of the Origin* (Louisville: F.A. Battey and Company, 1887), 37.

2. "Virginia-Kentucky Border," Virginia Places, accessed June 29, 2015, http://www.virginiaplaces.org/boundaries/kyboundary.html.

3. Ibid., 220.

4. William Mace, *A Beginner's History*, (New York: Rand, McNally & Company, 1921), 219.

5. Ibid., 221.

6. Ibid., 218–223.

7. Marilyn Boyer and Grace Tumas, *Portraits of Integrity* (Rustburg, VA: Learning Parent, 2012), 28.

8. D.H. Montgomery, *The Beginner's American History*, (NY: Ginn and Co., 1892), 148–149.

9. Mace, *A Beginner's History*, 224.

10. "National Register of Historic Places Program: George Rogers Clark National Historical Park, Knox County, Indiana," National Parks Service, accessed June 29, 2015, http://www.nps.gov/nr/feature/parkweek/2012/George_Rogers_Clark.htm.

Chapter 17 – James Robertson - Tennessee Pioneer

1. "Poor Richard's Almanack," Wikiquote, accessed June 29, 2015, https://en.wikiquote.org/wiki/Poor_Richard's_Almanack.

2. "Special Message to the Congress: The President's First Economic Report," Harry S. Truman Library and Museum, accessed June 29, 2015, http://trumanlibrary.org/publicpapers/viewpapers.php?pid=2043.

3. D.H. Montgomery, *The Beginner's American History* (New York: Ginn and Co., 1892), 140–142.

4. Ibid.

5. Ibid., 140–143.

Chapter 18 – John Hancock - Dedicated Patriot

1. Dennis Fradin, *The Signers: The 56 Stories Behind the Signers of the Declaration of Independence* (New York: Walker Childrens, 2003).

2. Wilbur Gordy, *American Leaders and Heroes* (New York: Charles Scribner's Sons, 1901), 156–161.

3. James Spear Loring, *The Hundred Boston Orators Appointed by the Municipal Authorities and Other Public Bodies* (Boston: John P. Jewett and Company, 1852), 77.

4. William Mace, *A Beginner's History* (New York: Rand, McNally & Company, 1921), 174–176.

5. John Hancock Life Insurance Company, *John Hancock: Great American Patriot* (Boston: John Hancock Life Insurance Company, n.d.), 9-11, http://www.johnhancock.com/resources/pdf/JohnHancockGreatAmerican-Patriot.pdf.

6. "Proclamation — Thanksgiving Day — 1791, Massachusetts," WallBuilders, accessed June 29, 2015, http://www.wallbuilders.com/libissuesarticles.asp?id=18294.

7. "USS John Hancock (DD 981)," Navy Site, accessed June 29, 2015, http://www.navysite.de/dd/dd981.htm.

Chapter 19 – John Hart - Honest Patriot

1. Marilyn Boyer, *For You They Signed* (Green Forest, AR: Master Books, 2009), 124–125.

2. William S. Stryker, ed., *Documents Relating to the Revolutionary History of New Jersey*, vol. 1 (Trenton: The John L. Murphy Publishing Co., 1901), 213.

3. "John Hart," The Society of the Descendants of the Signers of the Declaration of Independence, last updated December 11, 2011, http://www.dsdi1776.com/signers-by-state/john-hart/.

4. Boyer, *For You They Signed*, 124–125.

5. John Sanderson, *Sanderson's Biography of the Signers of the Declaration of Independence*, Robert T. Conrad, ed., vol. 8 (Philadelphia: Thomas, Cowperthwait, and Co. , 1847), 300–307.

6. Boyer, *For You They Signed*, 124–125.

Chapter 20 – Lydia Darragh - Petticoat Patriot

1. "Lydia Darragh: Quaker, Pacifist, and American Spy," Revolutionary-War.net, accessed June 29, 2015, http://www.revolutionary-war.net/lydia-darragh.html.

2. Henry C. Watson, *Noble Deeds of Our Fathers* (Boston: Lee and Shepherd, 1888), 36–40.

3. John and Katherine Bakeless, *Spies of the Revolution* (Philadelphia: J.B. Lippincott Company, 1962), 172–186.

4. Ibid., 173–186.

5. Marilyn Boyer and Grace Tumas, *Portraits of Integrity* (Rustburg, VA: Learning Parent, 2012), 10.

6. City Historical Society of Philadelphia, Publications [or Publication] of the City History Society of Philadelphia, vol. 1 (Philadelphia: The Society, 1917), 391.

7. Ibid.

8. Bakeless, *Spies of the Revolution*, 172–186.

Chapter 21 – Two Patriot Women - Standing Up to Tyranny

1. ""Nancy Morgan Hart," Simpson History, accessed June 29, 2015, http://simpsonhistory.com/notes/benjaminhart.html.

2. Ibid.

3. Edith Patterson Meyer, *Petticoat Patriots of the American Revolution* (New York: The Vanguard Press, 1976), 128–130.

4. Ibid.

5. Ibid.

6. Ibid., 156–163.

7. Ibid.

8. "Object of the Month: Deborah Sampson, Soldier in Disguise," Massachusetts Historical Society, last updated March 2005, http://www.masshist.org/object-of-the-month/objects/deborah-sampson-soldier-in-disguise-2005-03-01.

Chapter 22 – Nathan Hale - Patriot Spy

1. "Hale, Nathan," Our Campaigns, last updated November 19, 2007, http://www.ourcampaigns.com/CandidateDetail.html?CandidateID=168039.

2. Albert F. Blaisdell and Francis K. Ball, *Hero Stories from American History* (Boston: Ginn and Company, 1903), 53.

3. Alexander Rose, *Washington's Spies: The Story of America's First Spy Ring* (New York: Bantam, 2014).

4. Ibid., 60.

5. Ibid., 52–61.

6. Ibid., 59–60.

Chapter 23 – Richard Caswell - The Father of North Carolina

1. "Battle of Moore's Creek Bridge," Wikipedia, last updated April 20, 2015, https://en.wikipedia.org/wiki/Battle_of_Moore%27s_Creek_Bridge.

2. Henry Alexander White, *Beginner's History of the United States: Stories of the Men Who Made our Country* (N Y: American Book Company, 1911), 121–127.

3. "Richard Caswell," North Carolina History Project, accessed June 29, 2015, http://www.northcarolinahistory.org/encyclopedia/476/entry/.

4. White, *Beginner's History*, 121–127.

Chapter 24 – Nathanael Greene - The Fighting Quaker

1. William H. Mace, *A Beginner's History* (New York: Rand McNally and Co., 1909), 182–184.

2. Albert F. Blaisdell and Francis K. Ball, *Hero Stories from American History* (New York: Ginn and Co, 1903), 214.

3. Ibid.

4. Ibid, 215.

5. Ibid., 217.

6. Ibid.

7. Ibid.

8. Ibid.

Chapter 25 – John Sevier - Nolichucky Jack

1. William H. Mace, *A Beginner's History* (New York: Rand McNally and Co., 1909), 211.

2. Ibid., 217–218.

3. Ibid., 211–212.

4. Gordon T. Belt, "Sarah Hawkins Sevier: Tennessee's 'forgotten heroine,'" The Posterity Project, last updated March 4, 2013, http://posterityproject.blogspot.com/2013/03/sarah-hawkins-sevier-forgotten-heroine.html.

5. "To George Washington from John Sevier, 25 December 1798," Founders Online, National Archives, accessed June 29, 2015, http://founders.archives.gov/documents/Washington/06-03-02-0195.

6. "John Sevier Grave and Monument," knoxvilletennessee.com, http://www.knoxvilletennessee.com/john-sevier-monument.html.

Chapter 26 – Simon Kenton - Man of the Kentucky Forest

1. Edna Kenton, *Simon Kenton: His Life and Period 1755-1836* (North Stratford: Ayer Publishing, 1985).

Chapter 27 – Patrick Henry - The Man who Defended America with Pen and Tongue

1. "Patrick Henry Quotes," Brainy Quote, accessed June 29, 2015, http://www.brainyquote.com/quotes/quotes/p/patrickhen383739.html.

2. William H. Mace, *A Beginner's History* (New York: Rand McNally and Co., 1909), 161–163.

3. Nardi Reeder Campion, *Patrick Henry: Firebrand of the Revolution* (Boston: Little, Brown, and Co., 1961), 177–190.

4. Ibid.

5. Ibid.

6. Ibid.

7. Ibid.

8. Ibid.

9. Albert F. Blaisdell and Francis K Ball, *Hero Stories from American History* (New York: Ginn and Co, 1903), 152–154.

10. Mace, A Beginner's History, 163.

11. Ibid., 164–165.

12. William Wirt, *The Life of Patrick Henry* (New York: M'Elrath and Bangs, 1831).

Chapter 28 – Sam Adams - Father of the Revolution

1. "Samuel Adams, The Liberties of Our Country Are Worth Defending," The Federalist Papers Project, accessed June 29, 2015, http://www.thefederalistpapers.org/founders/samuel-adams/samuel-adams-the-liberties-of-our-country-are-worth-defending.

2. William H. Mace, *A Beginner's History* (New York: Rand McNally and Co., 1909), 167–170.

3. "Letter from John Adams to Abigail Adams, 16 September 1774," Massachusetts Historical Society, accessed June 29, 2015, http://www.masshist.org/digital-adams/archive/doc?id=L17740916ja.

Chapter 29 – Paul Revere - The Battle of Lexington and Concord

1. "Doctor Joseph Warren," National Park Service, accessed June 29, 2015, Boston National Park Service http://www.nps.gov/bost/learn/historyculture/warren.htm.

2. Albert F Blaisdell, and Francis K. Ball, *Hero Stories from American History* (New York: Ginn and Co, 1903), 166.

3. Blaisdell and Ball, *Hero Stories*, 168–169.

4. Ibid.

5. "Paul Revere's Account of His Midnight Ride to Lexington," America's Homepage, accessed June 29, 2015, http://ahp.gatech.edu/midnight_ride_1775.html.

6. Wilbur F. Gordy, *American Leaders and Heroes* (New York: Charles Scribner's Sons, 1904), 169.

7. Ibid., 170.

8. Ibid, 173.

9. Ibid.

10. Ibid., 169–1734.

Chapter 30 – Thomas Jefferson - Patriot Genius

1. "Richard Henry Lee," The James Madison Research Library and Information Center, accessed June 29, 2015, http://www.madisonbrigade.com/rh_lee.htm.

2. "The Letters of Thomas Jefferson 1743-1826," American History from Revolution to Reconstruction and Beyond, accessed June 29, 2015, http://www.let.rug.nl/usa/presidents/thomas-jefferson/letters-of-thomas-jefferson/jefl239.php.

3. "From Thomas Jefferson to Martha Jefferson, 5 May 1787," Founders Online, National Archives, accessed June 29, 2015, http://founders.archives.gov/documents/Jefferson/01-11-02-0327.

4. William H. Mace, *A Beginner's History* (New York: Rand McNally and Co., 1909), 238.

Chapter 31 – Colonel William Moultrie - Defender of Charleston

1. Albert F. Blaisdell and Francis K. Ball, *Hero Stories from American History* (New York: Ginn and Co, 1903), 39.

2. Ibid., 36–49.

3. Ibid., 40.

4. Ibid., 40.

5. Ibid., 40.

6. Ibid., 41.

7. Ibid., 42.

8. Henry Alexander White, *Beginner's History of the United States: Stories of the Men Who Made our Country* (New York: American Book Company, 1911), 130–132.

9. Kelly Gneiting, "A Reverse of the '5,000 Year Leap' Brings Back the John Adams's of America," Independent American Party, last updated March 13, 2014, http://www.independentamericanparty.org/2014/03/a-reverse-of-the-5000-year-leap-beckons-the-john-adamss-of-america-by-kelly-gneiting/.

10. Ibid.

11. Marilyn Boyer and Grace Tumas, *Portraits of Integrity* (Rustburg, VA: Learning Parent, 2012), 98.

12. Blaisdell and Ball, *Hero Stories*, 46–47.

13. Ibid., 47.

14. Ibid., 46–49.

Chapter 32 – Israel Putnam - Old Put

1. William Farrand Livingston, *Israel Putnam: Pioneer, Ranger, and Major-General, 1718-1790* (New York: G.P. Putnam's Sons, 1901), 227.

2. "Poor Richard's Almanack," Internet Archive, accessed June 29, 2015, https://archive.org/stream/poorrichardsalma00franrich/poorrichardsalma00franrich_djvu.txt.

3. George C. Hill, *General Israel Putnam* (Cranberry, NJ: Scholars Book Shelf, 1865).

4. Livingston, *Israel Putnam*, 45.

5. Frederick Ober, *"Old Put" the Patriot* (New York: D. Appleton and Co., 1904), 78.

Chapter 33 – Israel Putnam - Wolf Fighter Becomes General

1. "Israel Putnam Quotes," AZ Quotes, accessed June 29, 2015, http://www.azquotes.com/author/20080-Israel_Putnam

2. Frederick Ober, *"Old Put" the Patriot* (New York: D. Appleton and Co., 1904), 84.

3. "Israel Putnam," The Connecticut Society of the Sons of the American Revolution, accessed June 29, 2015, http://www.connecticutsar.org/patriots/putnam_israel.htm.

4. *Life of Israel Putnam* by David Humphreys, 1788.

5. William Farrand Livingston, *Israel Putnam: Pioneer, Ranger, and Major-General, 1718-1790* (New York: G.P. Putnam's Sons, 1901), http://archive.org/stream/israelputnampion00liviiala/israelputnampion00liviiala_djvu.txt.

Chapter 34 – The Black Robe Regiment – Ministers of Freedom

1. Nardi Reeder Campion, *Patrick Henry: Firebrand of the Revolution* (Boston: Little, Brown and Co., 1961).

2. Benjamin Franklin, *The Autobiography of Benjamin Franklin* (New York: Houghton-Mifflin, 1923).

3. Ibid.

4. Ibid.

5. Benjamin Franklin, *The Selected Works of Benjamin Franklin*, E. Sargent, ed., (Boston: Phillips, Sampson, & Co., 1855), 204.

6. Benjamin Franklin, *Autobiography*.

7. Franklin, *Autobiography*.

8. See comment box above

9. Richard Allen, *The Life, Experience, and Gospel Labors of the Rt. Rev. Richard Allen* (Philadelphia: F. Ford and M.A. Ripley, 1880), 30.